Questioning the Utopian Springs of Market Economy

Revisiting the magnetic poles of Karl Polanyi and Friedrich Hayek on the utopian springs of political economy, this book seeks to provide a compass for questioning the market economy of the twenty-first century.

For Polanyi, in *The Great Transformation*, the utopian springs of the dogma of liberalism existed within the extension of the market mechanism to the 'fictitious commodities' of land, labour, and money. There was nothing natural about *laissez-faire*. The progress of the utopia of a self-regulating market was backed by the state and checked by a double movement, which attempted to subordinate the laws of the market to the substance of human society through principles of self-protection, legislative intervention, and regulation. For Hayek, in *The Road to Serfdom*, the utopia of freedom was threatened by the abandonment of individualism and classical liberalism. The tyranny of government interventionism led to the loss of freedom, the creation of an oppressive society, and the despotism of dictatorship that led to the serfdom of the individual. Economic planning in the form of socialism and fascism had commonalities that stifled individual freedom. Against the power of the state, the guiding principle of the policy of freedom for the individual was advocated. Taking these different aspects of market economy as its point of departure, this book promises to deliver a set of essays by leading commentators on twenty-first-century political economy debates relevant to the present conjuncture of neoliberalism.

The chapters in this book were originally published in a special issue of the journal *Globalizations*.

Damien Cahill is Associate Professor of Political Economy at the University of Sydney, Australia. His publications include *Neoliberalism* (with Martijn Konings, 2017) and *The End of Laissez-Faire? On the Durability of Embedded Neoliberalism* (2014).

Martijn Konings is Professor of Political Economy and Social Theory at the University of Sydney, Australia. His publications include *The Development of American Finance* (2011), *The Emotional Logic of Capitalism* (2015), *Neoliberalism* (with Damien Cahill, 2017), and *Capital and Time: For a New Critique of Neoliberal Reason* (2018).

Adam David Morton is Professor of Political Economy at the University of Sydney, Australia. He is the author of *Unravelling Gramsci: Hegemony and Passive Revolution in the Global Political Economy* (2007), *Revolution and State in Modern Mexico: The Political Economy of Uneven Development* (2011), which was the recipient of the 2012 Book Prize of the British International Studies Association (BISA) International Political Economy Group (IPEG), and *Global Capitalism, Global War, Global Crisis* (with Andreas Bieler, 2018).

Rethinking Globalizations

Edited by Barry K. Gills, University of Helsinki, Finland and Kevin Gray, University of Sussex, UK.

This series is designed to break new ground in the literature on globalization and its academic and popular understanding. Rather than perpetuating or simply reacting to the economic understanding of globalization, this series seeks to capture the term and broaden its meaning to encompass a wide range of issues and disciplines and convey a sense of alternative possibilities for the future.

The Role of Religion in Struggles for Global Justice
Faith in Justice
Edited by Peter J. Smith, Katharina Glaab, Claudia Baumgart-Ochse and Elizabeth Smythe

Vivir Bien as an Alternative to Neoliberal Globalization
Can Indigenous Terminologies Decolonize the State?
Eija Ranta

Feminist Global Political Economies of the Everyday
Edited by Juanita Elias and Adrienne Roberts

The Politics of Destination in the 2030 Sustainable Development Goals
Leaving No-one Behind?
Edited by Clive Gabay and Suzan Ilcan

BRICS and MICs
Implications for Global Agrarian Transformation
Edited by Ben Cousins, Saturnino M. Borras Jr., Sergio Sauer and Jingzhong Ye

Migration, Civil Society and Global Governance
Edited by Carl-Ulrik Schierup, Branka Likic-Brboric, Raúl Delgado Wise and Gülay Toksöz

Questioning the Utopian Springs of Market Economy
Damien Cahill, Martijn Konings, and Adam David Morton

For more information about this series, please visit:
www.routledge.com/Rethinking-Globalizations/book-series/RG

Questioning the Utopian Springs of Market Economy

Edited by
Damien Cahill, Martijn Konings,
and Adam David Morton

LONDON AND NEW YORK

First published 2021
by Routledge
2 Park Square, Milton Park, Abingdon, Oxon OX14 4RN

and by Routledge
52 Vanderbilt Avenue, New York, NY 10017

Routledge is an imprint of the Taylor & Francis Group, an informa business

Chapters 1–2 and 4–11 © 2021 Taylor & Francis
Chapter 3 © 2018 Gareth Dale. Originally published as Open Access.

With the exception of Chapter 3, no part of this book may be reprinted or reproduced or utilised in any form or by any electronic, mechanical, or other means, now known or hereafter invented, including photocopying and recording, or in any information storage or retrieval system, without permission in writing from the publishers. For details on the rights for Chapter 3, please see the chapter's Open Access footnote.

Trademark notice: Product or corporate names may be trademarks or registered trademarks, and are used only for identification and explanation without intent to infringe.

British Library Cataloguing in Publication Data
A catalogue record for this book is available from the British Library

ISBN 13: 978-0-367-54626-7

Typeset in Minion Pro
by Newgen Publishing UK

Publisher's Note
The publisher accepts responsibility for any inconsistencies that may have arisen during the conversion of this book from journal articles to book chapters, namely the inclusion of journal terminology.

Disclaimer
Every effort has been made to contact copyright holders for their permission to reprint material in this book. The publishers would be grateful to hear from any copyright holder who is not here acknowledged and will undertake to rectify any errors or omissions in future editions of this book.

Contents

Citation Information		vii
Notes on Contributors		ix

Introduction: Questioning the utopian springs of market economy   1
Damien Cahill, Martijn Konings and Adam David Morton

1   Polanyi vs Hayek?   8
    Philip Mirowski

2   Polanyi's two transformations revisited: a 'bottom up' perspective   25
    Sandra Halperin

3   'Our world was made by nature': constructions of spontaneous order   38
    Gareth Dale

4   Market/society: mapping conceptions of power, ideology and subjectivity
    in Polanyi, Hayek, Foucault, Lukács   55
    Nicola Short

5   The great trasformismo: Antonio Gramsci and Karl Polanyi on the rise of Fascism   70
    Adam David Morton

6   Polanyi, Hayek and embedded neoliberalism   91
    Damien Cahill

7   Karl Polanyi as a spatial theorist   109
    Philip Roberts

8   Against exceptionalism: the legitimacy of the neoliberal age   121
    Martijn Konings

9   Neoliberalism as a real utopia? Karl Polanyi and the theoretical
    practice of F. A. Hayek   134
    João Rodrigues

10	Hayek and the *Methodenstreit* at the LSE *Jeremy Shearmur*	147
11	Reading Polanyi in Erbil: understanding socio-political factors in the development of Iraqi Kurdistan *Robert Smith*	159
	Index	172

Citation Information

The chapters in this book were originally published in *Globalizations*, volume 15, issue 7 (December 2018). When citing this material, please use the original page numbering for each article, as follows:

Introduction
Questioning the utopian springs of market economy
Damien Cahill, Martijn Konings and Adam David Morton
Globalizations, volume 15, issue 7 (December 2018), pp. 887–893

Chapter 1
Polanyi vs Hayek?
Philip Mirowski
Globalizations, volume 15, issue 7 (December 2018), pp. 894–910

Chapter 2
Polanyi's two transformations revisited: a 'bottom up' perspective
Sandra Halperin
Globalizations, volume 15, issue 7 (December 2018), pp. 911–923

Chapter 3
'Our world was made by nature': constructions of spontaneous order
Gareth Dale
Globalizations, volume 15, issue 7 (December 2018), pp. 924–940

Chapter 4
Market/society: mapping conceptions of power, ideology and subjectivity in Polanyi, Hayek, Foucault, Lukács
Nicola Short
Globalizations, volume 15, issue 7 (December 2018), pp. 941–955

Chapter 5
The great trasformismo
Adam David Morton
Globalizations, volume 15, issue 7 (December 2018) pp. 956–976

Chapter 6

Polanyi, Hayek and embedded neoliberalism
Damien Cahill
Globalizations, volume 15, issue 7 (December 2018), pp. 977–994

Chapter 7

Karl Polanyi as a spatial theorist
Philip Roberts
Globalizations, volume 15, issue 7 (December 2018), pp. 995–1006

Chapter 8

Against exceptionalism: the legitimacy of the neoliberal age
Martijn Konings
Globalizations, volume 15, issue 7 (December 2018), pp. 1007–1019

Chapter 9

Neoliberalism as a real utopia? Karl Polanyi and the theoretical practice of F. A. Hayek
João Rodrigues
Globalizations, volume 15, issue 7 (December 2018), pp. 1020–1032

Chapter 10

Hayek and the Methodenstreit *at the LSE*
Jeremy Shearmur
Globalizations, volume 15, issue 7 (December 2018), pp. 1033–1044

Chapter 11

Reading Polanyi in Erbil: understanding socio-political factors in the development of Iraqi Kurdistan
Robert Smith
Globalizations, volume 15, issue 7 (December 2018), pp. 1045–1057

For any permission-related enquiries please visit:
www.tandfonline.com/page/help/permissions

Notes on Contributors

Damien Cahill is Associate Professor of Political Economy at the University of Sydney, Australia.

Gareth Dale teaches politics at Brunel University London, UK.

Sandra Halperin is Professor of International Relations and Director of the Centre for Islamic and West Asian Studies at Royal Holloway, University of London, UK.

Martijn Konings is Professor of Political Economy and Social Theory at the University of Sydney, Australia.

Philip Mirowski is Carl Koch Professor of Economics and the History and Philosophy of Science at the University of Notre Dame, IN, USA.

Adam David Morton is Professor of Political Economy in the Department of Political Economy at the University of Sydney, Australia.

Philip Roberts is Associate Lecturer in Development Politics at the University of York, UK.

João Rodrigues is Assistant Professor of Economics in the Faculty of Economics and a researcher in the Centre for Social Studies, both at the University of Coimbra, Portugal.

Jeremy Shearmur is Emeritus Fellow at the Australian National University, Canberra, Australia.

Nicola Short is Associate Professor of Political Economy in the Department of Politics, York University, Toronto, Canada.

Robert Smith is Lecturer in International Relations at Coventry University, UK.

INTRODUCTION

Questioning the utopian springs of market economy

Damien Cahill, Martijn Konings and Adam David Morton

This volume brings together papers that were initially presented, or otherwise have their origins, in an international conference 'Questioning the Utopian Springs of Market Economy', held at the University of Sydney (15–16 August 2014). The occasion was to coincide with the fiftieth anniversary of the publication of two seminal political economy texts, namely Karl Polanyi's *The Great Transformation* and Friedrich Hayek's *The Road to Serfdom* that were both published in 1944. The conference was organized around three keynote plenaries – delivered by Philip Mirowski, Sandra Halperin and Gareth Dale – of which revised versions appear in this issue. There were also a number of parallel paper sessions over the course of two days. The idea of pairing the two books as the topic of a conference was experimental but the energy that pervaded the conference convinced us of the intellectual significance and political usefulness of considering these interventions side by side and this is what led us to continue the project after the conference by curating this special issue. We would like to thank everyone who was involved in the conference for contributing to the project.

In many ways, both Karl Polanyi's *The Great Transformation* and Friedrich Hayek's *The Road to Serfdom* could not be more antithetical, indeed antagonistic. The purpose of this journal special issue is to revisit these magnetic poles of political economy as a compass for questioning the market economy of the twenty-first century. For Polanyi, the utopian springs of the dogma of liberalism existed within the extension of the market mechanism to the 'fictitious commodities' of land, labour, and money. There was nothing natural about *laissez-faire*. The progress of the utopia of a self-regulating market was backed by the state and checked by a double movement, which attempted to subordinate the laws of the market to the substance of human society through principles of self-protection, legislative intervention, and regulation. For Hayek, the utopia of freedom was threatened by the abandonment of individualism and classical liberalism. The tyranny of government interventionism led to the loss of freedom, the creation of an oppressive society, and the despotism of dictatorship that led to the serfdom of the individual. Economic planning in the form of socialism and fascism had commonalities that stifled individual freedom. Against the power of the state, the guiding principle of the policy of freedom for the individual was advocated.

Hayek's *The Road to Serfdom* was thus a broadside against what he viewed as the 'collectivist' consensus of the time. Both the left and right of politics, Hayek argued, had a misplaced faith in economic planning. In this sense social democracy, communism and fascism were all varieties of a collectivist orientation that subordinated markets and individual liberty to politics. With the end of the Second World War approaching and many turning their minds to the problem of 'winning the peace', Hayek's intervention was designed as a warning against the inevitable drift towards authoritarianism, should the collectivist trend prevail. Polanyi was very much part of that collectivist consensus. In *The Great Transformation*, he attributed the human disaster of two world wars and the

Great Depression to the rise of the self-regulating market. The nineteenth-century commitment by policy-makers to a radical form of *laissez-faire* liberalism eroded the social foundations of the economy and provoked counter-movements – both political and regulatory – that bred nationalism, fascism and war. In contrast to Hayek, Polanyi's alternative vision was for a radical democratization of the capitalist economy.

Each book became classics amidst the heyday of the political movements that they criticized: Hayek's immediately shot to prominence as the social-democratic consensus that would shape the economic reconstruction of Western capitalism was being institutionalized. Polanyi's book, while never quite without a readership, had to wait for several decades to attain significant influence and only became the key point of reference for debate with the rise of neoliberalism from the 1980s onwards.

Yet, despite the fact that Hayek and Polanyi have become iconic figures of the defense and critique of neoliberalism, they are rarely read alongside each other. Typically, the work of each is marshalled in justifications or critiques of precisely the broad concept of neoliberalism. Of course, the idea that there is a certain conceptual incommensurability in their thought is not entirely off the mark and we do not want to detract from the legitimacy of such approaches. Both the conference and this special issue are motivated by the sense that important insights can be gained by staging a more direct confrontation – not primarily as an exercise in intellectual history but for the purpose of calibrating our compass for questioning the market economy of the twenty-first century.

After all, each of these books asks how the economic system should be organized, what the proper role of the state within it is, and how these logics work to organize society as a whole. We have centred this confrontation on what each thinker does to clarify the utopian sources of the capitalist market economy. Polanyi's *The Great Transformation* is framed as a critique of the 'stark utopia' of the 'self-adjusting market' and all this implied (Polanyi 1944/1957, p. 3). Unconstrained free markets were in conflict with human nature and its distinctive needs for community and social organization. Of course, then, for Polanyi the unrestrained 'disembedding' of the market in fact held out the prospect of precisely a *dys*topia. Accordingly, the progress of the self-regulating market needed to be backed by the state and checked by a 'double movement', which attempted to subordinate the laws of the market to the substance of human society through principles of self-protection, legislative intervention, and regulation.

Whereas for Polanyi the problem was that liberal theory and its followers were unable to recognize their utopian image of the free market for the irrational fantasy that it was, Hayek couched his concerns in a somewhat similar language, expressing fears that it was the fantasy of utopian collectivism that would lead humanity down the path of a dystopian totalitarianism. For Hayek, human freedom was threatened by the abandonment of individualism and classical liberalism in favour of a utopian collectivism. *The Road to Serfdom* was Hayek's attempt to dispel the delusion that anything other than civilizational ruin could result from such an attachment:

> That democratic socialism, the great utopia of the last few generations, is not only unachievable, but that to strive for it produces something so utterly different that few of those who now wish it would be prepared to accept the consequences, many will not believe until the connection has been laid bare in all its aspects. (Hayek 1944/2001, p. 32)

That pursuing the utopia of socialism will in practice lead us down the path of a totalitarian dystopian future is of course a common argument for the necessity of capitalism. But nowhere was this case made so uncompromisingly and with such enthusiasm than in Hayek's work and, in particular, in *The Road to Serfdom*. The arguments contained therein saw even minor transgressions of the proper constitutional limits of state power as setting in train a nightmarish concatenation of events that would inevitably lead to a totalitarian state. In other works, Hayek was less paranoid about the dangers of state intervention but his case for capitalism nonetheless retained its vigour. Whereas we might have come to think of Margaret Thatcher's 'there is no alternative' as a despondent admission of defeat and a sheer exhaustion of political inspiration that would be to misinterpret the role that such a dictum has always played in neoliberal thought. Premonitions of a dystopian future have always had their own utopian zeal. This is particularly clear in Hayek's *oeuvre* that, even as it has matured to the point of recognizing different configurations of state and market, could potentially be acceptable and consistent with a broadly capitalist organization of economic life, which would never let go of the idea that any problems in the organization of human life could be addressed by 'more' and 'freer' markets.

Far from the lifeless, utilitarian structure depicted by neoclassical theory, for Hayek the market was always a radically decentralizing and empowering institution, the only viable way to break up coalitions of privilege and concentrations of power. He saw himself as providing the utopian image that he felt liberalism had always lacked, an aspect of politics where they had been outflanked by socialists. Hayek therefore had a paradoxical relation to classic liberalism. On one hand he was seeking to recover its core ideas but, on the other hand, he was keenly aware that this could not simply be a return to past practices. Taking Hayek's work as expressing a logic of neoliberalism brings to light aspects of it that are sometimes overlooked in Polanyian critiques of neoliberalism in general. Neoliberalism is often more complex than critiques of market 'disembedding' suggest: neoliberalism is always 'embedded', always supported in complex ways by specific social interests, ideological impulses and political alliances, and critiques of neoliberalism need to be able to account for this embeddedness (Cahill 2014). Polanyi's thinking beyond the depiction of the rise and fall of the 'satanic mill' – involving the germinal concepts of embeddedness, the double movement, and the fictitious commodities of market economy – can and should be repurposed to this end. This volume ought then to be received as a continuation of the project of *comparative economy*: a 'Polanyi-plus' approach to economic geography, economic and historical sociology, feminist economics, political ecology, political economy and international studies, which entails a creative interdisciplinary border-crossing of methodological explorations that may span capitalist and non-capitalist forms related to spaces of uneven development (Peck 2013, pp. 1562–1563). The essays presented here can and should be read as a continuation of that project.

Philip Mirowski commences that journey by undertaking a wide-ranging comparative assessment of the thought of both Hayek and Polanyi. Problematizing the idea that they can be approached as polar intellectual opposites and paying considerable attention to the political and intellectual context in which their thought developed, he reconstructs some points of contact between their philosophies and demonstrates that there are many ways in which their work can be seen to dialogue, even if often indirectly rather than directly. Considerable insight could be gained if we let go of the idea that they represent little more than the emblematic ideologues of neoliberalism and social democracy.

In her pathbreaking *War and Social Change in Modern Europe*, Sandra Halperin surveys the broad landscape involved in the constitution of the 'disembedding' of capitalism in the nineteenth century, followed by the 're-embedding' of economies in Europe during the post-Second World War Keynesian-Fordist compromise, and then again the 'disembedding' (*viz.* de-nationalizing) of capital in the era of neoliberalization (Halperin 2004). Hence 'the 1950s and 1960s may appear to have been a brief interlude in the disembedded economic expansion that has characterised industrialisation from the start' (Halperin 2016, p. 186). Furthering a 'bottom up' perspective on social change, Halperin here focuses much more on the social struggles that brought about the collapse of state and international structures leading up to the Second World War. An alternative 'double movement' is posited – between dominant classes and a rising 'red tide' of disaffected workers – that better explains the demise of the states-system at this time and the changes that followed.

Gareth Dale analyses the significance of the concept of 'spontaneity' in the work of both Polanyi and Hayek. Hayek contrasted the spontaneous order of the market and freedom with the deliberately planned order of the state and the authoritarian system. Polanyi, on the other hand, placed enormous faith in the spontaneous reaction of society against the dislocation wrought by the 'self-regulating' market. By deploying the concept of spontaneity, Dale argues that each thinker misses some of the power relations at the heart of capitalist society.

Nicola Short examines Polanyi's *The Great Transformation* and Hayek's *The Road to Serfdom* by reading these texts alongside Michel Foucault's *The Birth of Biopolitics* and Georg Luckacs' *History and Class Consciousness*. Foucault's work on neoliberalism has given a major boost to work on neoliberalism in critical social theory and Short enters into these debates by bringing a Lukacsian angle to bear on the themes taken up in such debates. She argues that it permits us to move past unhelpful subjective/material dichotomies in the theorization of neoliberalism.

One of the more explicit extensions of the comparative economy agenda is made in Adam David Morton's contribution. He wants to examine the historical geographies constituting the spaces and places of the political economy of modern capitalism through a focus on fascism in the contributions of both Karl Polanyi and Antonio Gramsci. Uniquely he juxtaposes Polanyi (on economic liberalism and market economy, on the survivals of feudalism, and on history in the gear of fascist social change) with Gramsci (on economic liberalism and the determinate market, on the historical nexus linked to the concept and condition of passive revolution, and on fascism as the 'new' liberalism) to reveal the transformations wrought across the states-system of Europe prior to the crises that engulfed capitalism leading to the rise of fascism in the twentieth century. Here Morton's contribution lies in considering the rise of fascism as a congenital bias for reaction within capitalism, which has a bearing on present circumstances of right-wing populism. Rather than part of a 'great transformation' he thus focuses on the slow and protracted processes of class restoration that shaped the conditions of passive revolution, or a 'Great *Trasformismo*', which marked the consolidation and expansion of capitalist social relations under fascism.

Damien Cahill draws upon Polanyi and Hayek in order to illuminate some of the central dynamics of the neoliberal order. Departing from much Polanyi-inspired scholarship – that tends to view neoliberalism as entailing a 'disembedding' of economic processes from their social support structures – Cahill argues that neoliberal policies have become deeply embedded in institutions, class relations and ideological norms. This realization helps to explain both neoliberalism's apparent durability in the face of crisis and its immanent contradictions. With respect to Hayek, Cahill counterposes his analysis to the tendency to read neoliberalism through a literal interpretation of Hayek's arguments. In contrast, Cahill argues that Hayek's ideas offer a malleable set of explanations about the relationship between states and markets that provide ideological buttressing for the neoliberal order but that should not be taken to be its central driving force. This point resonates with wider arguments elsewhere on the role of canonical neoliberal texts being less about 'free markets' and more about remaking states and households (see Bruff and Starnes 2018).

Recognized in *The Great Transformation* was how the institution of market economy 'developed in leaps and bounds; it engulfed space and time' (Polanyi 1944/1957: 130). Furthermore, Polanyi famously remarked that under an untrammelled extension of market economy:

Nature would be reduced to its elements, neighbourhoods and landscapes defiled, rivers polluted, military safety jeopardised, the power to produce food and raw materials destroyed. (Polanyi 1944/1957, p. 73)

Perhaps for these reasons, James O'Connor (1988/1998, p. 159) has argued that, 'Polanyi's work remains a shining light in a heaven filled with dying stars and black holes of bourgeois naturalism, neo-Malthusianism, Club of Rome technocratism, romantic deep ecologyism, and United Nations one-worldism'. Hyperpole aside, Philip Roberts delivers a close reading of Polanyi to trace how spatialized concepts permeate his analysis. Rather than read space 'in' to Polanyi, however, Roberts' contribution is to trace space 'out' of Polanyi, which adds another level of theoretical rigour and logical consistency to the agenda of comparative economy. It does so by uncovering a vantage point that deals with space, place, scale, fixity, and motion to consider the potential implications of this new geographical reading of Polanyi for the comparative economy.

Martijn Konings revisits the failure of expectations regarding a Polanyian double movement in the wake of the financial crisis of 2007–2008. He argues that this failure has typically been accounted for in 'exceptionalist' terms, which view the persistence of neoliberalism as a result of processes of institutional capture that allow elites to bypass democratic institutions. He argues that such a 'Schmittian' approach underestimates the endogenous sources of legitimacy and resilience that neoliberal governance commands and suggests an understanding of the immanent logic of neoliberalism through a reinterpretation of Hayek's formulation of it.

João Rodrigues brings Hayek and Polanyi into the conversation as a way of making legible the relationship between neoliberal theory and practice. Rodrigues argues that Hayek was well aware of the inherently social and institutional nature of capitalist economic processes and, in this sense, was closer to Polanyi than many scholars have hitherto appreciated. Moreover, Hayek viewed the state as a necessary and active agent in constructing a neoliberal society. Neoliberalism, Rodrigues contends, is thus a 'real utopia' and the distance between theory and practice is therefore far less pronounced than some of its critics have assumed.

In an exploration of intellectual economic history, Jeremy Shearmur delves into the targets of Friedrich Hayek's Inaugural Address at the London School of Economics, 'The Trend of Economic Thinking', from 1933. In embryo in Hayek's 'Inaugural Address', Shearmur argues, is a focus on the key role economics has in showing what we cannot achieve: of showing that some attractive ideals are utopian. In developing this theme, Hayek referred to Ludwig von Mises' arguments about the problems of economic calculation under socialism. Shearmur revisits these contours to offer an exclusive contribution to the overall volume, a resolutely Hayekian focus on the role of structural constraints imposed by a flourishing market economy and how that becomes a more general motif in Hayek's work.

Finally, Robert Smith propels us to consider some of the wider writings by Karl Polanyi on anthropology, economic history and trading empires in order to assist in 'reading Polanyi in Erbil' and, specifically, in relation to the Kurdistan Regional Government. Polanyi forces us to consider the relationships between society, economics and politics, Smith argues. For example, Polanyi's research of the pre-modern economy of Mesopotamia provides a new way of thinking about the development of the economy in Iraqi territory after Saddam. Kurdistan, with its complex interweaving of the personal and political and the public and the private, provides a compelling case study of what Polanyi referred to as instances of *culture contact*, which occur between societies in different geographical regions. Where destruction occurs, 'not economic exploitation, as often assumed, but the disintegration of the cultural environment of the victim is then the cause of the degradation'

(Polanyi 1944/1957, p. 157). Rather than social existence wrought by economic principles, injurious damage is committed to the institutions underpinning societies. Deciphering Kurdistan through Polanyi offers new openings for such analysis beyond the observation that 'normally, the economic order is merely a function of the social order' (Polanyi 1944/1957, p. 71). Recognizing limitations in Polanyi is crucial, argues Smith, but the Austro-Hungarian economic historian also provides a potential basic starting point for analysis into the elemental forces of 'culture contact', which revolutionized the colonial world and the dismal scenes of early capitalism as well as the fragmented 'over-stating' of the post-colonial Arab state in places such as in Iraq (see also Ayubi 1995).

It is for the above reasons that we offer these original contributions to comparative economy to reveal horizons beyond many germinal concepts and thereby hopefully extend heterodox and open-ended conversations across intradisciplinary and interdisciplinary debate in and beyond political economy.

Disclosure statement

No potential conflict of interest was reported by the authors.

ORCID

Adam David Morton http://orcid.org/0000-0003-1003-8101

References

Ayubi, N. N. (1995). *Over-stating the Arab state: Politics and society in the middle east.* London: IB Tauris.
Bruff, I., & Starnes, K. (2018). Framing the neoliberal canon: Resisting the market myth via literary enquiry. *Globalizations.* doi:10.1080/14747731.2018.1502489.
Cahill, D. (2014). *The end of laissez-faire? On the durability of embedded neoliberalism.* Cheltenham: Edward Elgar.
Halperin, S. (2004). *War and social change in modern Europe: The great transformation revisited.* Cambridge: Cambridge University Press.

Halperin, S. (2016). Modernity and the embedding of economic expansion. *European Journal of Social Theory, 19*(2), 172–190.

Hayek, F. A. (1944/2001). *The road to serfdom*. London: Routledge.

O'Connor, J. (1988/1998). The second contradiction of capitalism. In J. O'Connor (Ed.), *Natural causes: Essays in ecological Marxism* (pp. 158–177). New York, NY: Guildford Press.

Peck, J. (2013). For Polanyian economic geographies. *Environment and Planning A, 45*(7), 1545–1568.

Polanyi, K. (1944/1957). *The great transformation: The political and economic origins of our time*. Boston, MA: Beacon Press.

Polanyi vs Hayek?

Philip Mirowski

ABSTRACT

Karl Polanyi and Friedrich Hayek are often portrayed as implacable intellectual opponents but their respective historical trajectories suggest some telling similarities. Here we describe some key similarities in their approach to markets, as a prelude to evaluating the political consequences of relying upon their Austrian conceptions of nature-based and constructivist framing of markets. Perhaps it is time to transcend their dichotomy.

Heroes and villains

Nothing captures the public imagination like a rousing narrative of 'good guys' versus 'bad guys'.[1] This archetype has also informed a certain genre of intellectual history, not to mention the classical sociology of intellectuals. In these types of histories, it became rather common to drape an intellectual biography around the clotheshorse of the 'public intellectual', revealing how the person in question had remained true to their vocation, or in some cases, deviated from the script in otherwise comprehensible ways. The narrative would predictably delight in their heroic facility in charming the public, praise the policies that they had propounded, marvel how they navigated the political shoals, and generally endorse the notion that their notoriety was a consequence of their own personal morality and their dogged intentionality. That intellectuals and their ideas were treated as two aspects of the same coherent individual, the quiddity of the one underwriting the solidity of the other. The standard trope of such histories would be to insist that the person in question was an ever-constant Captain of his own Fate. If there happened to be changes in conception over the course of the life, they would be treated as minor course corrections in a steady trajectory. Rarely would the biographer entertain the notion that the protagonist's role was effectively reconstructed by their environment and their epigones, or that their reception was largely governed by forces beyond the ken of the public intellectual. That would violate the standard archetype of heroic self-determination.

Here I venture to suggest that most of the work done on Karl Polanyi and Friedrich Hayek over the last 70 years conforms to these nineteenth-century tropes of heroic intellectual stalwarts, to the detriment of any possibility of serious comparisons. For two thinkers who had more or less repudiated methodological individualism, their intellectual interpreters seemed to have misplaced the memo.[2] One motive for this isolation is that Polanyi and Hayek have become the intellectual standard-bearers for two opposed political movements, namely, a variant of a sociologically-inclined non-Marxian socialism, in the first instance, and a well-entrenched neoliberalism, in the second. Part of the reason this panned out in the way it did was that both figures cut their teeth on the early Socialist Calculation Controversy in Vienna in the 1920s, an experience that set them down their respective paths in forging the later arguments which would make each famous.[3] The massive hagiographic literature on Hayek openly admits this was the case, although it barely notices Karl Polanyi in Vienna. The hagiographic literature on Polanyi, by contrast, at least acknowledges that the perceived enemy at the outset was early Austrian neoliberals like Ludwig von Mises and Hayek (Dale, 2010; Polanyi-Levitt, 2013, pp. 29–32; 47–50). Evidence includes the fact that Karl Polanyi in 1922 penned one of the earlier responses to Mises' assertion that economic calculation would be impossible under socialism. Indeed, some modern glosses of Neoliberalism from the Left, such as Jamie Peck's *Constructions of Neoliberal Reason* (2010), sets up his own biographical account in his Chapter 2 as a sort of parallel saga of the adventures of Friedrich Hayek and Karl Polanyi, even though there is no evidence that the trajectories of the two figures ever actually intersected.[4] Whatever the camp, their hero is inevitably feted as a Friend of the People, while their opponents, naturally, are Enemies of the same.

It is convenient for the curtain-raiser that *The Great Transformation* and *The Road to Serfdom* both appeared in 1944, thus setting up an irresistible conflict arc over the determination as to whom will triumph in the fullness of time. This dramaturgy has rarely been the handiwork of the main protagonists on either side, although it must be admitted that Hayek pointed the way with his denunciation of intellectuals with whom he disagreed as 'secondhand dealers in ideas' in his 1949 fit of pique:

> The main reason for this state of affairs is probably that, for the exceptionally able man [*sic*] who accepts the present order of society, a multitude of other avenues to influence and power are open, while to the disaffected and dissatisfied an intellectual career is the path to both influence and power.[5]

Later neoliberal followers were quick to take up the gauntlet: 'Polanyi's popularity thus represents the triumph of yearning and romanticism over science in disciplines like sociology. *The Great Transformation* ultimately offers more insight into the nature of the professoriat than it does to societies they study'.[6]

It was left to a rather more pugnacious member of the Neoliberal Thought Collective, a Bronx-born Thomist, Murray Rothbard, to tar Karl Polanyi personally with unsavoury motives:

> I therefore must conclude that this is Polanyi's sole basic complaint against the free society and the free market: they do not permit him, or any of his friends, or anyone else, to use force to coerce someone else into doing what Polanyi or anyone else wants; they do not permit force and violence; they do not permit dictation; they do not permit theft; they do not permit exploitation. I must conclude that the type of world that Polanyi would force us back into, is precisely the world of coercion, dictation, and exploitation. And all this in the name of "humanity"? Truly, Polanyi, like his fellow thinkers, is the "humanitarian with the guillotine …
>
> In fact, it is precisely such left-wing intellectuals as Polanyi who are always weeping about the "Coca-Colanization" of the rest of the world and bemoaning the supposedly lost glories of "folk culture" in the undeveloped countries. For as soon as they get the chance, peoples all over the world, regardless of cultural tradition, abandon their supposedly beloved culture in order to adopt Western ways, Western clothes, get a Western-type job or serve Western tourists, and earn Western money—and drink Coca-Cola … (Rothbard, 2009, p. 133)

One version of the hermeneutics of suspicion often begets another. The opposing side also sought to discredit Hayek from the Left as presenting a mere shell for class power and privilege. As the economist Brad de Long insisted, 'Karl Polanyi's *Great Transformation* is certainly the right place to start thinking about "neoliberalism" and its global spread'.[7] A rather unimaginative version of Polanyite attacker tends to take its cue from the Lewis Powell memo to the Chamber of Commerce in 1971: 'There should not be the slightest hesitation to attack the Naders, the Marcuses and others who openly seek the destruction of the system. Nor should there be a reluctance to penalize politically those who oppose it'.[8] Other Polanyites endorse analyses of Marxists like David Harvey who openly indict Hayek and the neoliberals of providing ideological cover for U.S. strategic interests and corporate class warfare (Dale, 2010, pp. 209–210). A more scholarly cadre looks into the sources of organization and funding of the neoliberals, and diagnoses a change in the types of intellectuals that have taken up the mantle of Hayek:

> This is the context in which the huge investment by right-wing foundations in think tanks and policy organizations has proven so important. In the place of the earlier strata of organic intellectuals who had deep roots in actual business, these organizations have promoted and recruited new cohorts of 'business intellectuals' whose primary ideological commitments are to market fundamentalism. (Block and Somers, 2014, p. 215; see also Phillips-Fein, 2009)

Curiously enough, some of Hayek's disaffected fellow-travellers in the Mont Pèlerin Society (MPS), such as Frank Knight, also felt this way:

> I have gone along with these groups largely 'for the ride' ... [I] am interested in the cause of freedom, but within judicious limits, and these people seem to think of just giving everybody their own way, notably businessmen and property owners.[9]

So with respect to both of our protagonists there appears to have been a symmetry in the cast of characters and a similar posited asymmetry of ethos. Perhaps there abides one more symmetry, although it often gets far less airplay. In the period immediately after 1944, neither figure was wildly popular with the general public. Granted, *The Road to Serfdom* was a best-seller in America (though not Britain) and it is true that Hayek enjoyed a triumphal book tour there in 1945. Yet, nevertheless, Hayek later bemoaned the fact that, 'In America, it was discussed mostly by people who had not read it' (1994, p. 104). He admitted in retrospect that his little popular book had tarnished his reputation amongst economists and academics more generally. The move to Chicago in 1950 thus constituted a kind of retreat, a licking of wounds after a very public drubbing by Keynes and his students;[10] and the convening of the MPS in 1947 was another. In both cases Hayek had sought to create a special space where he could pursue his inclinations among a small coterie of like-minded scholars, sheltered from larger intellectual currents. Partly, this was due to the fact that his political position in *The Road to Serfdom* was rather amorphous and self-contradictory – the politics of neoliberalism still had to be worked out – and it was a task that would take decades.[11] *The Great Transformation* had made no comparable splash and eventually Karl Polanyi had to retreat to the discipline of anthropology because his account of the modern world harboured some thorny contradictions that he suspected needed clarification. He did enjoy a faculty position at Columbia from 1947–1957 but the space it seemed to open up for this Austrian émigré scholar seemed strangely confining, as did the culture of the world capital of finance. Rather than work through the various problems of his nascent alternative to neoliberalism, more and more Polanyi seemed to try and make his points with arcane disquisitions on so-called 'primitive economies', a problematic guaranteed to evade almost all serious scrutiny by those concerned with postwar politics.

If I may briefly indulge in a personal sidelight, I was trained by some followers of Polanyi as an undergraduate. They seemed to think that Polanyi had provided suitable support for a revival of institutional economics in America and that the behaviour of ancient or marginalized peoples, either contemporary or historical, would reveal deep truths about the nature of humanity and its encounters with the market. It will come as no surprise that their hopes were badly misguided and sadly dashed and, indeed, even economic anthropology soon repudiated their home Polanyite version of an alternative social science of markets.[12] So if we grant both sides an urge to treat their protagonists symmetrically as successful public intellectuals, it has to be admitted up front that Hayek's posse of supporters in the MPS first ambushed and then easily won out over the remnants of institutionalists in the subsequent decades. But that is *not* the Aristotelian arc I want to explore in this paper.

I would instead like to explore the possibility that their respective ideas were in fact far closer than this simple dramedy of pitiless conflict could suggest. They both posited dichotomies that were inherently unstable and, in one particular case, one might venture to suggest it was very nearly the same dichotomy. Only in the last decade have a few commentators begun to trip over that possibility.[13] They both sought to diagnose what in the economy had caused the breakdown of order in the 1930s, leading to the rise of totalitarianism. Polanyi and Hayek also both made bold predictions about the future that were wildly off-base, facts which their respective followers still seem unable to take to heart. Instead, they keep lobbing the same old canards at each other: 'market fundamentalism' or 'closet fascists'. If we can get past some of that and possibly come to see these polar positions as more alike than opposed, we might (with a little luck) be able to imagine a discussion of markets which might actually move beyond the repetitive and ancient antimonies.

A budget of polarities

The set of customary oppositions between Karl Polanyi and Friedrich Hayek are readily sketched. I will set out by naming them but then I will return to pick away at them, in a poor man's version of deconstruction, to call into question the supposed hierarchy of oppositions that seem to undergird much political thinking.

Politics

The first thing that everyone thinks they know about Polanyi is that he was a 'socialist', whereas those on the Left tend to characterize Hayek as a 'market fundamentalist'. Labels such as these are often irrepressibly volatile. Anyone who deals in them responsibly knows that they must qualify them almost immediately. Kari Polanyi Levitt, his daughter, insists Karl was 'all his life a socialist', but of course, that meant something different to someone who grew up in Hungary and Red Vienna. She thus continues,

> His socialism was neither that of traditional European social democracy, nor that of centralized communist planning. It was more akin to the third stream of European socialist tradition—the populist, syndicalist, quasi-anarchist and corporativist one. Other important influences included Robert Owen and English guild socialism; the democratic functional socialism of Otto Bauer; Max Adler's insistence on the socialist mission of the working class to raise the cultural level of society … and last but not least, a rereading of *Capital* which brought to the fore Marx's alienation critique of capitalism. (Polanyi Levitt, 2013, p. 39)

Whatever one might say about that last component, it is pretty clear that Polanyi was not a Marxist by any stretch of the imagination. Gareth Dale (2010, p. 14) goes so far to suggest he subscribed to neoclassical value theory; something for which I believe there is very little evidence after he moved to the U.S. It may not be too far off to call him a 'market socialist', a fairly common position on the Left in the 1940s and 1950s.[14] Kari Polanyi Levitt plumps instead for the label Christian Socialist, which has the virtue of stressing the moral insistence of his vision. If anything, Polanyi's vision coquetted with the transcendent: 'Socialism is the tendency inherent in an industrial civilization to transcend the self-regulating market by consciously subordinating it to a democratic system' (Polanyi, 1957, p. 234).[15]

Hayek, on the other hand, was relatively cagey about his own position. Nevertheless, the one common denominator of his intellectual trajectory was his opposition to the 'socialists'. Numerous commentators before me have insisted that *The Road to Serfdom* is a slippery book and not only because it predicts the eventual downfall of civilization due to the nefarious planning of socialists, but because it strives to tie them inexorably to the 'Nazis and the Fascists'.

> [S]ocialists everywhere were the first to recognize that the task they had set themselves required the general acceptance of a common Weltanschauung, of a definite set of values. It was in these efforts … that the socialists first created most of the instruments of indoctrination of which Nazis and Fascists have made such effective use. (1944, p. 113)

If he had to name his comrades, he frequently had recourse to the term 'liberals' – another label which had lost all effective content over time, since it had less and less to do with actual classical liberalism. He explicitly renounced the epithet 'conservative', and seemed to revel in praising fusty outré figures like Adam Ferguson and Francesco Guicciardini; one suspects him of the practice of *épater le bourgeois* when he said, 'I'm becoming a Burkean Whig' (1994, p. 141). But readers should take it to heart when he wrote in *The Road to Serfdom* that, 'Probably nothing had done so much harm to the liberal cause as the wooden insistence of some liberals on certain rough rules of thumb, above all the principle of laissez faire' (1944, p. 17). Polanyites like to accuse Hayek of 'market fundamentalism', but that epithet is far too evocative of religious slurs to capture the subtlety of Hayek's position; and worse, I think, it distracts from any serious understanding of the neoliberal movement to which Hayek gave impetus. Hayek ultimately does appeal to a kind of 'faith', but it is grounded in a very bleak vision of human epistemology, not some providential market eschatology. Really, the 'neo' in neoliberalism is most apt because it signals an awareness of the internal tensions of liberalism upon which Polanyi based his case.

Hayek, by comparison with Polanyi, wanted to transcend the weaknesses of the supposedly self-defining and self-sufficient market by consciously subordinating it to the political interventions of a group dedicated to the construction of what they considered a more robust market society. Curiously, Polanyi sometimes asserted something similar about the early British liberals, only with the codicil that they lusted after a Utopia that could never actually exist.[16] The later Polanyi then seemed to believe he could refute the doctrine that eventually congealed as neoliberalism once and for all by insisting people really were not selfish in a way he thought was presumed by his opponents. Where Polanyi was sadly mistaken was that he didn't realize that concerted organization and political imagination could trump the need for any fixed final ideal, or indeed any philosophical anthropology. Success was not to be measured relative to some ultimate goal, but rather, through the provisional defeat of their opponents from one local contest to the next. The appeal to some magical pie-in-the-sky 'spontaneous order' by the neoliberals was mainly effective in keeping the attention of the populace directed away from the pitiless war of ideas and policies on the ground.

Embeddedness, society

The second thing that everyone thinks they know about this duo was that Polanyi believed that markets were 'embedded' in society, whereas Hayek believed there was no such thing as society. As Fred Block maintained,

THE UTOPIAN SPRINGS OF MARKET ECONOMY

Because Thatcher's 'there's no such thing as society' is no longer merely an omen but an established ideological fact (though not, to be sure, a social one), Polanyi's plea for us to recognize the reality of society is just as compelling today [as in 1944].[17]

But venture beyond the slogans, and things rapidly become murky. Insistence upon the 'economy' being 'embedded' in something larger sounds nice and cozy, but amongst his acolytes that tenet is precisely where some of the worst intellectual problems begin to emerge.[18] Polanyi is all over the place about whether or not the economy is or can be detached from society; or in what sense markets were or ever could become 'disembedded', what constitutes the bedframe and the bedding of 'society', whether or not this is just the old Tönnesian formulation of Gemeinschaft and Gesellschaft in trendier bedclothing, and so forth. For example, is the so-called 'double movement' a faltering failed attempt to get out of bed? Is the distinction between market and society really a woolly attempt to reduce the world into two classes: current commodities and the things that money can't buy now but soon will? The notion that economy and society could become estranged from one another was a hallmark Polanyian theme well before *The Great Transformation*. In an article written for the Austrian weekly '*Der Volkswirt*' [The Economist], Polanyi summed up the situation at the beginning of the 1930s: 'Between the economy and politics an abyss has opened. That is in meagre words the diagnosis of the age. The economy and the political sphere ... have made themselves independent and wage war against each other' (Polanyi, 2002, pp. 138–9). This was also the theme of his 1940 lectures:

> In post-war Europe [i.e. post 1918] the separation of economics and politics developed into a catastrophic internal situation. The captains of industry undermined the authority of democratic institutions, while democratic parliaments continuously interfered with the working of the market mechanism. A state of affairs was reached when a sudden paralysis of both the economic and the political institutions of society was well within the range of the possible. (Polanyi, 2017, p. 6)

At minimum, one has to concur with Fred Block when he asks: Why didn't Karl Polanyi return to clarify the concept of embeddedness after *The Great Transformation*? (Block and Somers, 2014, p. 95). Indeed, it seems Polanyi had also given up on any attempt to even characterize 'socialism'. Maybe this had something to do with the reified, or at least severely undertheorized, concept of 'society' itself?

Enter Hayek. The older Hayek went on a rant about the very existence of 'society' starting in the late 1950s, later reduced to an epigram by Mrs. Thatcher, although I must acknowledge that neoliberals often warn against taking *The Fatal Conceit* too seriously in retrospect, because allegedly the editor took excessive liberties with the text.[19] In any event, Hayek 'wrote' there:

> The more the range of human cooperation extends ... the more 'social' comes not to be the key word in a statement of the facts but the core of an appeal to an ancient, and now obsolete, ideal of general human behavior .... Thus the word 'society' has become a convenient label denoting almost any group of people, a group about whose structure or reason for coherence nothing need be known—a makeshift phrase people resort to when they do not quite know what they are talking about. (Hayek, 1988, pp. 112–113)

There is a bit of a temporal translation problem here, because the German term *sozial* bears the connotation of serving the public good and supporting the weaker members of society, rather than the more neutral term *gesellschaftlich*, closer in meaning to the English term. There is also the further consideration that Hayek was seeking to position himself as critical of the term 'social market economy' coined by Ludwig Müller-Armack in 1947 as a political slogan for Hayek's erstwhile allies the ordoliberals. Hayek began attacking the uses of the notion of the social in an essay of 1957 (in Hunold, 1961) and continued to elaborate upon it up until Volume 2 of his *Law, Legislation and*

Liberty. Subsequently, sneering at the very existence of society became something of a neoliberal quirk.

The younger Hayek, circa 1946, was nowhere near so crotchety, however. In an exercise to explain his own rather qualified notion of individualism to his audience, he suggested that 'in order to contribute to our understanding of society', it would be a prerequisite to be 'starting from men [*sic*] whose whole nature and existence is determined by society' (Hayek, 1948, p. 6). Although he disdained any recourse to aggregates, he equally admitted people were malleable, continually being formed and shaped by their experiences. After his foray into psychology, Hayek would subsequently come to posit that knowledge itself might exist outside the consciousness of individual agents, which could qualify as the return of the 'social' with a neoliberal vengeance. Later members of the Neoliberal Thought Collective like the ordoliberals also seemed to be unable to dispense altogether with 'society' as a useful concept, without adding much more in the way of clarification. One might not particularly find it edifying, but the Chicago School subsequently took to asking with gusto whether 'culture' might influence economic growth by the insertion of variables such as religious affiliation, ethnic background, political beliefs and a raft of quasi-social variables in baroque regression equations purportedly explaining economic growth, the prevalence of entrepreneurs, preferences for redistribution by the state, and much else (Guiso, et al., 2006; Mirowski, 2011). Sociologists seem nervously apologetic about endorsing an 'over-socialized man', but the neoliberals don't seem all that bothered one way or another.

Thus I would tend to agree with the following Austrian assessment of their theoretical commitments:

> Both Hayek and Polanyi share a similar vision in terms of their relationship between the individual and the institutional structure. They both believe the agent and structure have an interactive relation that is not deterministic ...

> If Hayek was concerned with the danger posed by organizational reform that hindered the market, Polanyi criticized the emergence of rules that eliminated organizational and institutional buffers between the economic and the social spheres and that eradicated and scattered the very bounds of human life, like family, safety and living within a familiar culture and environment. (Migone, 2011, pp. 366, 357)

However, one has to temper this similarity to concede that subsequent members of the hard right of the Neoliberal Thought Collective tended not to grant any validity to the market/society distinction, in contrast to Hayek. Both the libertarian and intransigent Chicago wings took the position that Polanyi was wrong because there was nothing that the market could not organize:

> The market, therefore, is preeminently social; and the rest of the social consists of other voluntary, friendly, nonmarket relations, which also, however, are best conducted on the basis of a spiritual exchange and mutual gain. (Isn't it better if A and B are both friendly to each other, than if A is friendly to B but not vice versa?)

> The market, then, far from being a disrupter of society, is society. What, then, would Polanyi use to replace the market? The only relation aside from the voluntary is the coercive; in short, Polanyi would replace the market by the "social" relation of force and violence, of aggression and exploitation. (Rothbard, 2009, p. 135)

Role of nature

The third thing that everyone knows about Hayek and Polanyi is that Hayek believed that markets were in some sense 'natural', whereas Polanyi insisted that they were in some other sense 'unnatural'.

I have been struck upon re-reading *The Great Transformation* just how clearly Polanyi makes the case that economics became disengaged from philosophy and the other social sciences precisely by indulging in a heightened naturalism, artificially isolating the market into an ontological sphere of its own and then patterning its explanation upon some contemporary natural science. Here it is not that the market in itself is disembedded, but rather that dominant theories about the market undergo artificial isolation predicated upon the model of the deterministic science. He makes the case for population biology as the wellspring of inspiration, dating it from Joseph Townsend's 1786 *Dissertation on the Poor Laws*, and extending it on through Malthus and thenceforth through to Darwin, positing that the laws of nature were identical to the laws of the market. Polanyi wrote,

> The biological nature of man appeared as the given foundation of a society that was not a political order … What induced orthodox economics to seek its foundations in naturalism was the otherwise inexplicable misery of the great mass of producers [in the Industrial Revolution]. (Polanyi, 1957, pp. 115, 123)

While the interplay of theories of the human body and classical political economy is now taken as a fairly commonplace trope (see Gallagher, 1986; Mirowski, 1989), it seems to me that Polanyi had missed out on the natural appropriation that had already hit the jackpot in terms of cultural credibility, namely, the origins of neoclassical price theory in the energy physics of the mid-nineteenth century. The marginalist revolution, with its mathematics of constrained optimization and utility pattered upon potential energy, did not need to scream 'Nature!' quite so vehemently as the earlier Malthusian dogma; all it had to do was seduce wave upon wave of minions who became convinced that they were contributing to the first real 'science' of human behaviour. The Nature of energetics was a relentless pursuit of deterministic equilibrium; yet, at the same time, in the nineteenth-century it proudly sported the ambition to be a Theory of Everything. Indeed, one offshoot of the Polanyian insight was a research programme exploring all the myriad ways a backhanded dependence upon Nature to define the market could flourish, even amongst those too distracted to realize they were mimicking physics.[20]

The problem, however, was that a conceptual naturalization of market theory in economics was not at all the same thing as the purported absence of naturalization of markets in practice. Polanyi notoriously insisted that land, labour, and money were *fictitious* commodities, hinting that because they were 'unnatural', they were in some sense artificial or illegitimate. After claiming that, 'Commodities are here empirically defined as objects produced for sale on the market' (Polanyi, 1957, p. 72), he then proceeds to upend conventional wisdom by insisting labour and land are not actual commodities because they were not 'produced for sale' and, more curiously, he insisted money was not 'produced' at all, because it is just a token brought into existence by the banking system or state finance. Apparently, the market can only legitimately deal in the artifactual: things produced through human intentionally to be sold on the market. This weird insistence upon intentionality at the heart of his definitions constitutes Polanyi's own strangulated appeal to Nature: there, presumably, things only legitimately belong on the market because the relevant artisans designated them so destined. If Nature is (wrongly) defined as that which exists outside the realm of human intentionality and manipulation, then Polanyi begins to sound a bit like Rousseau, or maybe Henry George. His later reversion to the study of ancient and 'primitive' economies reinforced this impression. Indeed, the so-called 'double movement' in Polanyi was a dynamic where too many social phenomena became rendered 'unnatural' through some encroaching market development, prompting a reaction which restored something approximating a prior state of Nature. This potentially leads to all manner of paradoxical conundrums, such as slavery rendering labour a 'real' commodity, metallic currencies existing as the only 'real' money, children bred to provide for their parents in old age 'real' or legitimate labour. For someone who was apparently insisting upon the central place of law and custom, Polanyi's own commodity definition had brutally abstracted from law and established practice, in favour of a disguised appeal to the natural. Perhaps this is one reason he felt impelled to retreat into the realms of ancient and primitive economies in later life.

Hayek also had an uneasy relationship to Nature, but curiously, it was concerned not at all with the same reification as one encounters in the history of neoclassical price theory. I have sought to summarize this thesis elsewhere (see Mirowski, 2007a; Mirowski and Nik-Khah, 2017), so for the present purposes I will merely state the case in a relatively telegraphed manner. There were roughly three phases of Hayek's career, when one organizes it around his attitudes towards Nature. The first, which even most contemporary Austrians ignore, saw Hayek as a conventional Austrian economist of the 1920s and early 1930s: he was busy trying to shoehorn the notion of capital as embodied 'roundaboutness' into some tendentious story of business cycles. This programme was a dead end by the mid-1930s, with most Viennese jumping ship for something more plausible (see Klausinger, 2006). If this was all Hayek had ever done, we would not still be discussing him today. In the second phase, politics came to the fore: in the 1930s and 1940s Hayek began his famous reconceptualization of the market as information processor, but concurrently engaged in what he called his 'Abuse of Reason' project. Here, Hayek had recourse to a cobbled-together 'philosophy of the ineffable' to try and square his personal ambition to be a scientist, his hostility to socialism, the upsetting tendency of many natural scientists to portray socialism as scientific, and the failure of his previous 'Austrian' macroeconomic theory. From thenceforth, Hayek argued that the market was no longer a set of pipes channelling capital though roundabout channels, but rather an information processor, organizing and conveying the appropriate information to the relevant actors, by an instrumentality that could not be fully comprehended or manipulated by any central planner. Just as he began to assert in this period that the human mind could not come to an adequate understanding of its own operations, he also wanted to assert that 'Reason' could not on its own devices fully comprehend why markets are necessarily *the* superior format of social organization. Thus Hayek in this period became a kind of scold, denouncing most attempts to ground social thought in Nature as illegitimate 'Scientism', which he equated with a *hubris* born of believing one could plan and manipulate people the same way one planned and manipulated Nature.

A lot of neoliberals also regard this second phase of Hayek's as a bit of an embarrassment, since anyone who assumed an intransigent stance against Science was never going to get anywhere as a social scientist in the American Century. Luckily for them, sometime after 1947 or so, Hayek experienced a *volte-face* with regard to Nature, and decided he had to join the crowd in America naturalizing the market. The evocation of Nature happened at a number of different conceptual locations:

(a) Hayek would now acquiesce in the portrait of a single 'unified science', which he had been resisting for at least a decade or more. There was no open renunciation of his prior position; instead, he simply began to rely upon Karl Popper to inform people on what 'real science' looked like (Mirowski, 2007a).

(b) Hayek began to endorse various aspects of the 'cybernetics' project, which sought to reduce thought to mechanism. This was the source of his embrace of the 'sciences of complexity', which he derived from his reading of Warren Weaver (Mirowski, 2002, p. 175).

(c) With a lag, Hayek began to appeal to 'evolution' to explain how an ineffable complex order, which he simply equated with The Market, could have come about. The onus for ineffability was thus shifted from an earlier reliance upon Germanic philosophy to a more up-to-date biologistic metaphor. The conviction that a 'non-Darwinian evolution' could still support a

Naturalistic defense of the market was a precept more or less lifted from some of the cyberneticists, who were rather thick on the ground in postwar Chicago (Mirowski, 2011). The idea that evolution displays an unambiguous 'arrow of time' in the direction of greater complexity was another of their favoured doctrines, rapidly taken up by Hayek and the neoliberals.

Hence, Hayek struggled mightily with the heritage of Naturalism over the course of his career, but eventually capitulated to it, therefore ending up in a place nearer to Polanyi than either would care to admit.[21] For both, Nature came to represent something that existed outside the ambit of human intention and manipulation. The major difference was the valence each attached to it.

This flirtation with natural concepts proved salutary for the subsequent Neoliberal Thought Collective, if only because it suggested that there was a way to accomplish the impossible, to square the circle of preaching the virtues of a spontaneous order, all the while promulgating a political doctrine that the strong state must be commandeered to bring about the sorts of markets which constituted that order.

Markets as constructed vs. markets as spontaneous

The fourth thing that people think they know about Hayek and Polanyi is that Hayek believed markets worked fine left on their own, whereas Polanyi asserted that markets required constant intervention to be made to seem to work. Again, the polarity is illusory, but one needs some background to experience the Gestalt switch.

The place to start, as usual, was Vienna. It is *de rigueur* to note that a fierce critique of classical liberalism was happening around the time of Red Vienna, with all manner of thinkers seeking to unearth the internal contradictions of the *laissez faire* sensibility. One such critique that was developed in that hothouse was a notion that *laissez faire* was an *ignis fatuus*, in the sense that it posited a political state that could never actually exist. Karl Polanyi's most important intellectual contribution was to import those arguments into the English language context, in the guise that suggested all attempts to impose a market free of all governmental intervention was self-refuting:

> Just as, contrary to expectation, the invention of labor-saving machinery had not diminished but actually increased the uses of human labor, the introduction of free markets, far from doing away with the need for control, regulation and intervention, enormously increased their range. Administrators had to be constantly on the watch to ensure the free working of the system. Thus even those who wished most ardently to free the state from all unnecessary duties, and whose whole philosophy demanded the restriction of state activities could not but entrust the self-same state with the new powers, organs and instruments required for the establishment of *laissez faire*. (Polanyi, 1957, pp. 140–141)

Let us call this the 'unintended consequences' argument: all attempts to demote the state to night-watchman status end up augmenting the power and size of the state with respect to the market. On the same page, Polanyi indicts liberals 'Spencer and Sumner, Mises and Lippman' for perceiving the incongruity, but blaming it all upon 'impatience, greed, and shortsightedness' of the politicians, rather than anything specific about the free market itself, which is upheld as some sort of Platonic natural ideal. In other words, his opponents all realized that something paradoxical had happened to their political comrades when they sought to institute their programme of free markets, but they took it as adventitious, all written off to accidents and weakness of will. Less frequently do modern Polanyites acknowledge that Karl pressed the critique one step further, pushing home the irony:

> This paradox was topped by another. While *laissez faire* economy was the product of deliberate state action, subsequent restrictions on *laissez faire* started in a spontaneous way. *Laissez-faire* was planned; planning was not. (Polanyi, 1957, p. 141)

Let us call this the 'reverse English' argument: it upends the usual implications of the opponents' presuppositions. Reverting to his equation of the unintentional with the Natural, Polanyi therefore combines two arguments: one, unintended consequences, that liberal political attempts to actuate their vision of the market protected from the state just ends up making the state stronger; and two, 'reverse English', that this also sets in motion a 'Natural' rejection mechanism of political mobilization in the larger populace to restrict the market expansion. Notice how Polanyi is gratified that he can seemingly invert the commitments of his opponents, equating the spontaneous with the Natural, but then knock them askew by claiming natural provenance for his own political position of market skepticism and revanchist regulation. However, parenthetically, I would like to point out that there is very little specific empirical evidence cited to support these propositions, especially the second one.

What is intriguing and unexpected is the extent to which Hayek accepts much of this Viennese two-step.[22] Of course, one must acknowledge that large swathes of Hayek's later writings are taken up with a convoluted and rather boring series of attempts to insist there really is something called 'spontaneous order" in history and that it looks a lot like the market. However, those castles in the air have very little to do with the practical political precepts that have been subsequently developed within the Neoliberal Thought Collective. It is not some "spontaneous order" that is conjured at Heritage Action or the Frasier Institute or the Institute of Public Affairs. If Hayek really was so supremely confident in the inherent spontaneity of the market, there would be no rational earthly motivation behind the elaborate political mobilization theorized and then implemented by the neoliberals, especially from the 1970s onwards.[23] Indeed, it is in taking this contradiction to heart that the neoliberals have distinguished themselves from the earlier classical liberals. The confession already rears its head in *The Road to Serfdom*: 'In no system that could be rationally defended would the state do nothing. An effective competitive system needs an intelligently designed and continuously adjusted legal framework' (1944, p. 39). Hayek's opponents interpreted these lines as concessions to their belief in the inevitability of the 'mixed economy', but they were sadly mistaken.[24] In effect, first Hayek, and then to a more elaborate extent the later neoliberals, affirmed the first half of Polanyi's Viennese two-step – although without crediting him personally in any manner. 'The neoliberals recognized early on that the creation of new markets is a political process, requiring the intervention of an organized power' (Rodrigues, 2012, p. 1008). History taught them that the political will to impose 'good markets' resulted in a strong state and elaborate regulation; then, so be it. The neoliberals would accept the unintended consequences argument, but rather than taking it as a refutation of their ambitions, they would absorb it as a blueprint for achieving their ultimate ends, by intentional embrace.

The state would necessarily need to expand in economic and political power over time. The only codicil to the trend would be that the neoliberals themselves would need to seize state power and rewrite the regulations so that they could create the kind of market society they believed was progressive. The unintended consequences of expansion of state power would be overcome through redoubled intentionality, political organization, and conscious intervention. Ideal markets had to be imposed; they wouldn't just happen. Hayek at certain junctures in his career ranted against the evils of the 'constructivist' mentality, but it is difficult to regard this neoliberal embrace of the strong state as anything other than constructivist. This frame tale is now widely accepted as the correct interpretation of eighty years of the history of the Neoliberal Thought Collective.[25]

How about the second half of the Viennese two-step, the 'reverse English' argument? Hayek realized that the great democratic masses might not accept the imposition of the New Neoliberal Order from above; especially in a democracy, neoliberal gains might be quickly reversed at the ballot box. Hayek often complained that the socialists thought they knew what was best for the masses, often absent their consent, but in this regard, effectively, the neoliberals were no different.[26] The one place where Hayek diverged from Polanyi was that he could not ever allow that the blowback from markets could ever be a 'natural' response of the masses. At various points, Hayek would blame the recalcitrance of the populace to 'market reforms' on the scurrilous class of intellectuals, or on the self-interest of the politicians, or even upon the fundamental ignorance of the populace about the consequences of their preferences. But the eventual solution favoured by the bulk of the Neoliberal Thought Collective was to render democracy so hamstrung and ossified that it would never prove capable of neutralizing neoliberal market structures erected by the strong state (see Cornelissen, 2017). Their strong state had to come cladded with strong defenses against the will of the governed. 'I doubt whether a functioning market has ever newly arisen under an unlimited democracy, and it seems likely that unlimited democracy will destroy it where it has grown up' (Hayek, 1979, p. 77). This was the watchword of the later Hayek, of Bruno Leoni, of James Buchanan and the Virginia public choice school, of the 'Washington consensus', and the architects of the WTO and the European Union and the independence of central banks.

It's the things they share that have led us astray

I conclude bearing a perhaps unexpected and unwelcome message: it is the presuppositions that Karl Polanyi and Friedrich Hayek shared that bracket them as intriguingly paired in the intellectual history of neoliberalism, perhaps as much or more so than the oppositions and polarities for which they are more conventionally known. Given their Viennese backgrounds and early involvements with the Austrian School of Economics, some consilience of fundamentals might have been expected as a matter of course. The similarities might not have persisted more than a curiosum, however, except for the fact that a comparable set of unexamined presuppositions often inform modern political disputes and, consequently, often tend to further strengthen the cultural dominance of neoliberalism.[27]

The deep presuppositions that we have identified have to do with the ways both figures ground each discourse concerning markets in cultural themes that bear much of the emotional charge of their respective political stances. The three most germane to our duo are (1) their appeals to Nature; (2) their respective endorsements of a constructivist stance; and (3) their commitments to a certain particular ontology of markets. One reason that Hayek and Polanyi remain fascinating, in a way no modern orthodox economist has ever managed to approximate, is that they were engaged in disputation over the most basic ontology of what a market *is* and, by implication, what dictates the most important functions a market performs.

As already mentioned, for both Polanyi and Hayek, Nature, suitably interpreted, should tell us what an ideal social organization should look like and, simultaneously, undergird the appropriate political stance towards markets. This is a very ancient cultural preoccupation, nowhere near novel in 1944. But Polanyi and Hayek were dissatisfied with the answers on offer in their youth and struggled to provide some alternatives. Polanyi denounced the naturalism of the economists, only to replace it with a naturalism of his own: there were *fictitious* commodities, and then there were 'true' commodities, things produced consciously for the market and intended for sale. The class of fictitious commodities tended to get conflated with strong moral convictions about classes of phenomena which should never be subject to sale, sometimes gathered together under the portmanteau of 'community' or 'society', a natural formation under stress, and this lent a crusading tone to Polanyi's system. Such locutions permitted the portrayal of the so-called 'double movement' as itself Natural: 'the extension of market organization in respect of genuine commodities was accompanied by its restriction with respect to fictitious ones' (Polanyi, 1957, p. 76). This awkward paradox still makes contemporary sociologists cringe but inspires popular philosophers like Michael Sandel to impoverish analysis of markets as though it were a mere dispute over 'values', thus demarcating the 'limits of markets' by identifying 'what money can't buy' with what Nature never intended.[28] This species of Nature-talk never goes out of fashion but perhaps one of the reasons it is evergreen is that it never leads anywhere of political consequence.

Per contra, once Hayek got over his mid-career phase of denouncing 'scientism', he realized that modern images of the market needed to be updated, at least to the middle of the twentieth-century, to match emergent new images of Nature. Older mechanical notions embedded in neoclassical economics just wouldn't do; nor would classical political economy suffice. Just as with Polanyi, Nature was deemed to be something that stood outside the boundaries of human intentionality; but in his case, instead it was a market as a giant information processor, one that evolved beyond the understanding of the human participants, and knew things of which they themselves were unaware.

In the second instance and bucking the trend of contemporary economic commentary, both Hayek and Polanyi conceded that markets were constructed, and not born in immaculate conception, or else somehow always-already present back to when the world began. That some prior assembly was required was a stance which could have been found well established in the Germanic literature and Polanyi himself was heavily indebted to writers such as Thurnwald and Malinowski, as well as the Historical School. Both Polanyi and Hayek conceded the role of the state in this process of fabrication; but what they made of it was the locus where the friction between their renditions began. Polanyi sought to chase the fabrication back to some strained prelapsarian notion of origins and 'primitive economies'; whereas Hayek realized that any hope of controlling the process of construction meant neoliberal foot soldiers occupying the state, and proceeded to convene Mont Pèlerin to debate how this should be accomplished. It is significant that it was the neoliberals who took this version of constructivism as a personal injunction to mobilize politically and not the Polanyites, however much they may have considered themselves activists.

The third ontological principle shared by Polanyi and Hayek was that they would both retain the firmly established practice of characterizing The Market as a relatively homogeneous monolithic entity. This was the most telling legacy of their Austrian roots. Incongruously for both, they resorted to the language of evolution, but a strange sort of transmogrification which left the basic outlines and functions of the monolithic Market unchanged. For both, it was something that retained its identity and operation through vast stretches of time and space. Polanyi may have been skeptical that 'The Economy' referred to any stable phenomenon – in his later anthropological writings, he preferred to think of multiple modes of 'provisioning' physical sustenance – but his skepticism was never extended to what he called 'the market system' itself. For Hayek, The Market was effectively monolithic because it was the embodiment of an order which no human could possibly comprehend: 'the only alternative to submission to the impersonal and seemingly irrational forces of the market is submission to an equally uncontrollable and therefore arbitrary power of other men' (Hayek, 1944, p. 205). Yet this stark dichotomy was based on the notion that market forces were not 'arbitrary': that is, they performed the same operations in the same manner no matter what the circumstances. Thus 'The Market' for Hayek was monolithic not only because it was impenetrable to human understanding; but also because it reputedly performed its information conveyance towards all and sundry with no discrimination or favour. This purported impartiality was the centerpiece of Hayek's claim that The Market would transcend politics, in an environment of the rule of law.

At least up until now, I have never encountered an enthusiast for either Polanyi or Hayek who has realized that these three fundamental tenets of both neoliberalism and a non-Marxian market skepticism are not only shared, but also intrinsically self-contradictory, ushering both positions towards a political incoherence. Appeals to ground the economy in Nature have never sat very comfortably *vis-à-vis* the constructivist stance. We see this exacerbated in modern confusions over an 'information economy' and 'platform capitalism'. The constructivist stance essentially contradicts the possibility of an invariant uniform 'market system' existing though time: economists have tried to square this circle with their advocacy of 'market design'.[29] Finally, an ahistorical trans-global 'Market' is never sufficiently differentiated from a Society sporting an evolutionary Nature, which can only operate through an irreducible diversity of forms. The ontological presuppositions of both Polanyi and Hayek have always been irreconcilable.

Conclusion

Perhaps this reconsideration of the intellectual positions of Karl Polanyi and Friedrich Hayek could begin to get us past the widespread presumption that they offer the two main alternatives when it comes to political images of 'market' and 'society'. In fact, their shared Viennese heritage has bequeathed us a jointly incoherent set of images of Nature, a constructed society, and a monolithic Market. I might venture to suggest that, in a seriously revived Left, both of their systems, along with their shared ontologies, will have to be left behind.

Notes

1. This paper is based on a talk delivered at the workshop 'Questioning the Utopian Springs of Market Economy', University of Sydney/Australia (15–16 August 2014); thanks to the participants and referees for their comments.
2. There is one historian who bucks the trend: Innset (2017). Since that paper seems to anticipate some of the themes explored herein, I feel compelled to note that the author discussed these themes with myself numerous times, both at the workshop 'Questioning the Utopian Springs of Market Economy', at the University of Sydney (15–16 August 2014), and also afterwards. Delays in publication permitted his paper to appear first. I shall attempt to register where I diverge from his arguments in this paper.
3. The profound importance of the Socialist Calculation Debate for modern political economy is discussed in Mirowski and Nik-Khah (2017), see also Becchio (2007).
4. This is suggested by his daughter (Polanyi-Levitt, 2013, p.24).
5. Hayek, 'The Intellectuals and Socialism' (1949), in Hayek (1969, pp. 188–189). Also note footnote 3 in that paper, which paints Jews as especially susceptible in this regard.
6. Clark (2008). See also the work of Deidre McCloskey.
7. http://delong.typepad.com/sdj/2014/07/karl-polanyi-classical-liberalism-and-the-varieties-of-neoliberalism-virtual-office-hours-from-espresso-roma-ccxxvi-jul.html
8. See http://reclaimdemocracy.org/powell_memo_lewis/
9. Frank Knight to Theo Suranyi-Unger, 16 May 1965, Box 61, folder 12, Frank Knight Papers, Regenstein Library, University of Chicago.
10. This refers to the decimation of any legitimacy of Hayek's business cycle theory by Keynes and Piero Sraffa, such that it was no longer taken seriously within the economics profession. For a brief summary, see Kurz (2015).
11. Here again Keynes threw down the gauntlet, suggesting in a famous letter to Hayek concerning *Road* that liberalism necessarily would place restrictions on the competitive market, and "You agree the

line has to be drawn somewhere … But you give no guidance whatever as to where to draw it", quoted in Skidelsky (2000, p. 285).

12. I discuss this, particularly as it played out in the career of Marshall Sahlins, in Mirowski (1994).
13. See Rodrigues (2013); Samuels (2011); Migone (2011) and, of course Innset (2017).
14. His friend Jacob Marschak, who was instrumental in getting him to New York, was a prominent market socialist of that era, and another *Mitteleuropa* figure who got his start in the Socialist Calculation Controversy.
15. Even as early as 1940, Soviet Russia presented a problem for the definition of socialism: "It was the tragedy of Russia, and not of Russia alone, that in spite of the socialist forms of integration the democratic tendency succumbed in the long run to the totalitarian trend" (Polanyi, 2017, p. 9).
16. See Polanyi (2017) and Innset (2017, p. 683).
17. At: http://asociologist.com/2014/06/03/block-somers-qa/#more-2791
18. See, for instance, Krippner et al. (2004); Krippner and Alvarez (2007); Block and Somers (2014, pp. 91–95); and Dale (2010, Chap. 5).
19. For instance, Alan Ebenstein, "The Fatal Deceit" at: http://web.archive.org/web/20080622201757/http://libertyunbound.com/archive/2005_03/ebenstein-deceit.html
20. In that sense, much of my own work in the history of economics may have been suggested by my early exposure to *The Great Transformation*.
21. Here Innset (2017) stumbles, because he treats the 'Natural' as something generic, rather than the result of struggles with actual theories of Nature and intentionality.
22. Innset (2017, p. 680) glosses this as "Hayek in fact shared Polanyi's view that markets depended on state power," but without any analysis of the Viennese two-step.
23. This is documented in Mirowski (2013). "Hayek [is] much closer than Mises to Polanyi's (1944) characterization of the paradoxical relation between the state and markets in capitalism: the development of markets demands an expanding state with the power to impose the rules that markets require", see Rodrigues (2013, p. 1007).
24. One example of this can be found in Rodrigues (2012); another in Caldwell (2004).
25. McPhail and Farrant (2013), Peck (2010), Mirowski (2013), Rodrigues (2012, 2013), Shearmur (1996).
26. The similar stance of Hayek and the socialists is repeatedly stressed in Shearmur (1996, pp. 62, 103, 104).
27. Here lies my final divergence from Innset (2017).
28. See, for instance, http://ineteconomics.org/tags/michael-sandel, and especially https://www.ineteconomics.org/perspectives/videos/michael-sandel-on-inets-what-money-cant-buy-video-series. For critique, see Choat (2018).
29. This contradiction is discussed in detail in Mirowski and Nik-Khah (2017).

Disclosure statement

No potential conflict of interest was reported by the author.

References

Becchio, G. (2007). The early debate on economic calculation in Vienna. *Storia del Pensiero Economico*, 135–147.

Block, F., & Somers, M. (2014). *The power of market fundamentalism*. Cambridge: Harvard University Press.

Burgin, A. (2012). *The great persuasion*. Cambridge: Harvard University Press.

Caldwell, B. (2004). *Hayek's challenge*. Chicago, IL: University of Chicago Press.

Choat, S. (2018). Everything for sale? Neoliberalism and the limits of Michael Sandel's philosophical critique of markets. *New Political Science*, *40*(1), 1–14.

Clark, G. (2008, June 4). Reconsiderations: The great transformation. *New York Sun*.

Cornelissen, L. (2017). How can the people be restricted? The Mont Pelèrin society and the problem of democracy, 1947–1998. *History of European Ideas*, 43, 507–524.

Dale, G. (2010). *Karl Polanyi*. Cambridge: Polity.

Gallagher, C. (1986). The body versus the social body in the works of Thomas Malthus and Henry Mayhew. *Representations*, 14, 83–106.

Guiso, L., Sapienza, P., & Zingales, L. (2006). Does culture affect economic outcomes? *Journal of Economic Perspectives*, *20*(2), 23–48.

Hayek, F. (1944). *The road to serfdom*. Chicago, IL: University of Chicago Press.

Hayek, F. (1948). *Individualism and economic order*. Chicago, IL: University of Chicago Press.

Hayek, F. (1960). *The constitution of liberty*. Chicago, IL: University of Chicago.

Hayek, F. (1969). *Studies in philosophy, politics and economics*. New York, NY: Clarion.

Hayek, F. (1979). *Law, legislation and liberty*. Chicago, IL: University of Chicago Press.

Hayek, F. (1988). *The fatal conceit*. W.W. Bartley III (Ed.). Chicago, IL: University of Chicago Press.

Hayek, F. (1994). *Hayek on Hayek*. Stephen Kresge & Leif Wenar (Eds.). Chicago, IL: University of Chicago Press.

Hayek, F. (2011). *Collected works of FA Hayek*, vol. *17*. Ronald Hamowy (Ed.). London: Routledge.

Hunold, A. (Ed.). (1961). *Freedom and serfdom*. Berlin: Springer.

Innset, O. (2017). Markets, knowledge and human nature: Hayek, Karl Polanyi and 20th century debates on modern social order. *European History Quarterly*, 47, 670–700.

Klausinger, H. J. (2006). In the wilderness: Emigration and decline of the Austrian school. *History of Political Economy*, 38, 617–664.

Krippner, G. et al. (2004). Polanyi symposium: A conversation on embeddedness. *Socio-Economic Review*, 2, 109–135.

Krippner, G., & Alvarez, A. (2007). Embeddedness and the intellectual projects of economic sociology. *Annual Review of Sociology*, 33, 219–240.

Kurz, H. (2015). Capital theory, crises and business cycles: The triangular debate between Hayek, Keynes and Sraffa. *Journal of Reviews on Global Economics*, 4, 186–191.

McPhail, E., & Farrant, A. (2013). Hayek and the sorcerer's apprentice: Wither the Hayekian logic of intervention? *American Journal of Economics and Sociology*, 72, 966–982.

Migone, A. (2011). Embedded markets: A dialogue between FA Hayek and Karl Polanyi. *The Review of Austrian Economics*, 24, 355–381.

Mirowski, P. (1989). *More heat than light*. New York, NY: Cambridge University Press.

Mirowski, P. (1994). Tit for Tat: Concepts of exchange and barter in two episodes in economic anthropology. In N. de Marchi, & M. Morgan (Eds.), *Higgling* (pp. 313–342). Durham: Duke University Press.

Mirowski, P. (2001). Refusing the gift. In S. Cullenberg, J. Amariglio, & D. Ruccio (Eds.), *Postmodernism, economics and knowledge* (pp. 431–458). London: Routledge.

Mirowski, P. (2002). *Machine dreams*. New York, NY: Cambridge University Press.

Mirowski, P. (2007a). Naturalizing the market on the road to revisionism. *Journal of Institutionalist Economics*, 3, 351–372.

Mirowski, P. (2007b). Markets come to bits: Evolution, computation and markomata in economic science. *Journal of Economic Behavior and Organization*, 63, 209–242.

Mirowski, P. (2011). On the origins (at Chicago) of some species of neoliberal evolutionary economics. In R. van Horn, P. Mirowski, & T. Stapleford (Eds.), *Building Chicago economics* (pp. 237–278). New York, NY: Cambridge University Press.

Mirowski, P. (2013). *Never Let a serious crisis Go to waste*. New York, NY: Verso.

Mirowski, P., & Nik-Khah, E. (2017). *The knowledge we have lost in information*. New York, NY: Oxford University Press.

Peck, J. (2010). *Constructions of neoliberal reason*. New York, NY: Oxford University Press.

Phillips-Fein, K. (2009). *Invisible hands: The making of the conservative movement*. New York, NY: Norton.

Polanyi, K. (1957). *The great transformation*. Boston: Beacon Press.

Polanyi, K. (2002). *Chronik der großen Transformation I: Wirtschaftliche Transformation, Gegenbewegungen und der Kampf um die Demokratie* [Chronicle of the Great Transformation I: Economic Transformation, Reactions and the Fight for Democracy] M. C. Cangiani & Thomasberger (Eds.). Marburg: Metropolis.

Polanyi, K. (2017). *The present Age of transformation: Five lectures to Bennington college, 1940*. Montreal: Prime.

Polanyi-Levitt, K. (2013). *From the great transformation to the great financialization*. New York, NY: Zed.

Rodrigues, J. (2012). Where to draw the line between the state and markets? Institutionalist elements in hayek's neoliberal political economy. *Journal of Economic Issues*, 46, 1007–1034.

Rodrigues, J. (2013). The political and moral economies of neoliberalism: Mises and hayek. *Cambridge Journal of Economics*, 37, 1001–1017.

Rothbard, M. (2009). *Rothbard versus the philosophers*. Roberta Modugno (Ed.). Auburn, AL: Mises Institute.

Samuels, W. (2011). *Erasing the invisible hand*. New York, NY: Cambridge University Press.

Shearmur, J. (1996). *Hayek and after*. London: Routledge.

Skidelsky, R. (2000). *John Maynard Keynes: Fighting for Britain, 1937–1946*. London: MacMillan.

Polanyi's two transformations revisited: a 'bottom up' perspective

Sandra Halperin

ABSTRACT

In *The Great Transformation*, Karl Polanyi offers a 'top-down' analysis of the rise and demise of Europe's unregulated market system. He assumes that changes in the organization of the international economy provide particular kinds of opportunities for states to act which, in turn, shapes the extent to which social forces will be able to influence state policy. Consequently, his analysis focuses, first, on the international institutions created by the self-regulating market system; then on the 'liberal state' which these made possible; and finally on how the system impacts 'society as a whole'. The account which this analysis produces systematically underplays the social struggles which propelled and emerged from the rise of Europe's nineteenth century system and which ultimately led to its demise. In revisiting the two periods that are the focus of Polanyi's analysis, this article assumes that states and interstate systems reflect the interests of powerful social forces. Thus, working from the 'bottom up', it focuses on the class interests that produced Europe's market system, the state and international structures which reflected and supported them, and the social struggles that ultimately brought about the collapse of the system. What this 'bottom up' account reveals is the centrality of a 'double movement', not of market expansion and a protective countermove on the part of 'society as a whole', but of dominant classes monopolizing economic opportunities from global expansion, and a rising 'red tide' of disaffected workers. *This* double movement, it argues, better explains the demise of the system and the changes that ensued from it.

Two key transformations are the focus of Karl Polanyi's *The Great Transformation* (1944). The first occurred at the end of the eighteenth century with the *dis-embedding* of local markets and the rise of Europe's unregulated market system. As he was completing his magnum opus in the early 1940s, the second transformation had yet to occur. However, using the analytic framework on which he had based his account of the first transformation, he predicted the collapse of the unregulated market system in the course of the world wars and the outcomes that would ensue from it.

According to that framework, changes at the 'top' – in the organization of the international economy – provide particular kinds of opportunities for states to act which, in turn, shapes the extent to which social forces will be able to influence state policy. Thus, in his account of the first transformation, he focuses first on the establishment of a new liberal international order and the key institutions of this order. According to Polanyi, it was this overarching institutional order that enabled states to deregulate capital and to institute other changes that formed the basis of Europe's unregulated market system. Applying this same 'top down' analysis to the transformation he believed was imminent, Polanyi expected that, with the demise of Europe's nineteenth century market system, a new international opportunity structure would emerge that would enable states to introduce policies that would bring about a *re-embedding* of local markets.[1]

A few years after the publication of *The Great Transformation*, however, it became apparent that the outcomes that had emerged following World War II did not conform to his expectations. There had, indeed, occurred a great transformation as free markets and *laissez-faire* states gave way (in varying degrees) to regulated markets and interventionist states. However, the liberal international order had survived.[2] Moves to establish new international economic arrangements had been effectively blocked by efforts of the United States to restore a world economy based on the principles of the nineteenth-century system.[3] Thus, while local markets had been transformed in important ways, it was not, as Polanyi had assumed, as a result of changes at 'the top'.

There were other post-World War II outcomes that failed to conform to Polanyi's expectations. In *The Great Transformation*, Polanyi had argued that the rise of Europe's nineteenth century system was an unprecedented and once-and-for-all occurrence. He therefore expected that with the demise of that system following World War II, the consequent re-embedding of markets would represent a permanent change. However, by the 1970s there emerged a campaign to promote the dispersal of capital investment and production to foreign locations and, with this, there began a return to many of the features associated with Europe's nineteenth century system. Contrary to Polanyi's expectations, 'globalizing' trends that had characterized that system had re-emerged and were reversing post-World War II changes that Polanyi had assumed would be permanent.

Interestingly, though the return to more globally free capital in the 1970s violated a key assumption of *The Great Transformation*, the search for insight into the forces at work in the rise (once again) of a global market and its likely outcomes led to a resurgence of interest in the book. Much of this interest focused on one of its central features: the notion that, in the nineteenth century, the rise of the unregulated market system had triggered a simultaneous protective countermove to check its action with regard to labour, land, and money. Polanyi argued that this counter-move on the part of 'society as a whole' generated stresses and strains that ultimately culminated in two world wars and the collapse of the system. However, the rise of neoliberal globalization began some forty years ago and while it has engendered resistance and mobilized new social groups, it has yet to trigger a protectionist countermove by 'society as a whole'.

The failure of outcomes to conform to Polanyi's expectations warrants closer scrutiny of his assumptions about how the world economy, states, and social forces are interrelated. As was observed previously, his analysis of the rise of Europe's unregulated market system works from the 'top down': it focuses, first, on the international institutions created by the self-regulating market system – the balance of power system (which had made possible a 'Hundred Years' Peace' in Europe) and the gold standard – and on the 'liberal state'. It then explores the impact of the self-regulating market on 'society as a whole'. The sections which follow revisit the two periods that are the focus of *The Great Transformation*. However, in contrast to Polanyi's analysis, they assume that states and interstate systems reflect the interests of powerful social forces. Consequently, the analysis works from the 'bottom up'. It focuses, first, on the configuration of class power and interests that produced the system and the tensions and class struggles that the system generated (and that ultimately brought about its demise).[4] It then considers the state and international structures which reflected and supported those interests.

From this perspective, a quite different 'double movement' comes into focus than the one on which Polanyi's account centres. Polanyi argued that the basic dynamic shaping both the development of industrial capitalism in Europe and its transformation in the course of the world wars, was the antagonism which emerged between 'society as a whole' and the 'soulless institutions' of the self-regulating market system. In the 'bottom up' account which follows, what comes into focus is a 'double movement', not of market expansion and a protective countermove on the part of 'society as a whole', but of dominant classes pursuing global expansion in order to monopolize opportunities for economic gain and prevent the rise of new classes; and a rising 'red tide' fuelled by the disaffection of radicals and socialists of various sorts, trade unionists, and suppressed national minorities. It will argue that it was the stresses and strains generated by *this* double movement that led to crisis of the world wars and the changes that ensued as a result of it.

The first transformation: social forces in the rise and consolidation of Europe's nineteenth century market system

Polanyi begins his analysis of the rise of Europe's nineteenth century market system with the emergence of a new liberal international order, the key institutions of which, he claimed, enabled states to pursue liberal, non-interventionist policies and, thus, to establish free trade and free markets. While, previously, exchange relations had been governed by principles of economic behaviour (reciprocity, reallocation, and house-holding) that were 'embedded' in society, with the rise of Europe's unregulated market system, local markets were 'disembedded'.

Polanyi does not offer a detailed analysis of these changes. While he recognizes that there were social and economic interests associated with Europe's nineteenth century market system, he provides no account of the powerful political campaign which, by dismantling Europe's eighteenth century 'moral economy', paved the way for the rise of the unregulated market system. Missing, too, are the social conflicts that emerged as a result of these developments. Instead, the focus of the story that unfolds is the disastrous impact of the unregulated market system on 'society as a whole'. While nineteenth-century European observers had written prolifically about what they had considered to be the most characteristic aspects of their societies – domination, exploitation, inequality, and authoritarianism – in Polanyi's account, states are politically neutral, and societies appear as organic unities in which all are more-or-less equally victimized by the 'soulless institutions' of the self-regulating market system.

The account presented here begins, not with the overarching international institutional order, but with the social struggles that drove and shaped the changes that occurred at that time. A closer look at this chapter in Europe's industrial expansion shows that the dismantling of market regulations and systems of national welfare prevailing at that time in Britain, France, and elsewhere in Europe was evidence, not of the rise of new liberal commercial interests, but of the continuing power of rural, pre-industrial, and autocratic structures of power and authority.

The dismantling of Europe's eighteenth century 'moral economy'

Beginning in the sixteenth century, 'Absolutist' rulers in Europe had gradually been able to achieve sufficient autonomy to establish and maintain what later would be described as a 'moral economy'. Europe's 'moral economy' was characterized by 'the conviction that members of the community possessed certain rights, enforceable at law, including that of ... the rights to basic material security, protection from violence, theft and extreme oppression' (Thane, 1990, p. 7). Beginning in the sixteenth century, 'Absolutist' states in England,[5] France, and elsewhere in Europe were ensuring that these needs were met either through public or through private bodies, but with state oversight and enforcement.[6] States regulated markets on behalf of local people through legislation which ensured that local, face-to-face buying and selling was conducted through open transactions in the marketplace.[7]

In addition to ensuring communal control over economic life, states had pushed legislation to create new institutions for poor relief, and to establish a system of hospitals to provide medical care for paupers. This was a Europe-wide movement. By the beginning of the eighteenth century, England had a national welfare system.[8] Later in the century, *ancien régime* France established a nation-wide welfare system, and Prussia introduced measures establishing a cradle-to-grave welfare system that guaranteed every subject adequate food, sanitation, and police protection.[9] In addition to state regulation of markets, wage controls and other labour protections, and the provision of welfare, the fact that European economies at the time were still largely based on local markets and face-to-face relations between seller and consumer meant that workers were able to exercise power both as labourers and consumers.

In the eighteenth century, a revolution of consumption in Britain had fuelled the expansion of a domestic market for mass – produced consumer goods;[10] as a result, there was a marked improvement in the variety and quality of household furnishings, decorations, and 'luxury' items among artisans and farmers.[11] In fact, in Britain 'a greater proportion of the population than in any previous society in human history' was able 'to enjoy the pleasures of buying consumer goods' and 'not only necessities, but decencies, and even luxuries' (McKendrick, Brewer, & Plumb, 1982, p. 29). As the century progressed, elite anxiety grew as this 'democratization of consumption' appeared to increase social mobility and undermine class distinctions.[12] Had the production of mass consumption goods continued to fuel Britain's industrial growth, along with the mass purchasing power and internal market needed to support it, the class, land, and income structures on which the existing structure of social power in Europe rested would have been destroyed. Thus, despite the growth of the domestic market in the eighteenth century, and the fact that at the end of the Napoleonic Wars abundant opportunities remained for investment and the expansion of production for home consumption, in the nineteenth century, the gradual democratization of consumption that had taken place throughout Europe in the eighteenth century was halted and put into reverse. Instead, Europeans launched a brutal expansion of production-for-export that became a model for elites and ruling groups throughout the world.

The success of a campaign to dismantle regulations tying production and investment to local economies put an end to the expansion of domestic markets and broad-based industrial growth. This marked the culmination of a centuries-long struggle by those opposed to the price and wage controls, labour protections, and national welfare systems that had been introduced by Absolutist rulers in Britain, France, and elsewhere in Europe. Opponents of these changes attacked 'Absolutism' for its over regulation. However, the regulations that were the target of this attack were concerned with protecting the local population against monopoly and speculation, and shortages and high prices, and with ensuring that trade would be conducted inside open markets, by means of open transactions, and according to the rules and regulations which maintained fair practices and prices (Lie, 1993, p. 283).[13] Opponents of Absolutism were thus concerned with dismantling much of what today we would consider socially enlightened about 'liberal absolutism'. At the same time, they were committed to retaining much of what was not in a new guise. Consequently, the regulative, protective system of mercantilism was only selectively dismantled and, by the end of the nineteenth-century, there was a full-blown return to monopoly and regulation. Deregulation of markets and capital, the end of national welfare systems and 'moral economies', and the further de-industrialization of rural areas and concentration of production in cities, succeeded in 'dis-embedding' markets and. accelerating the globalization of capital.

The context for these developments was the quarter century of war that began with the French Revolution and ended in 1815. The dangers of a trained and compact mass army had been revealed in this period of war and revolutionary turmoil, and elites had drawn many analogies between the revolutionary currents unleashed by the mass army of soldiers that had been created for the Napoleonic Wars and the dangers of mobilizing a mass army of workers to expand industrial production. The French Revolution had also seen the birth of socialism, and its focus on eradicating private property – something for which dominant classes had struggled over the course of a century or more – seemed, in combination with the revolutionary ferment unleashed by the war, to threaten an anti-capitalist revolt of the masses. Thus, the central dilemma for dominant groups tempted to mobilize labour for the expansion of industrial production was how it would be possible both to mobilize – train, educate and, in other ways, empower – labour while, at the same time, maintaining its subordination to capital. Mass mobilization for industry (as for war) creates, out of the relatively disadvantaged majority of the population, a compact and potentially dangerous force. Thus, elites showed little interest in the expansion of industry at home.

This, then, was the context in which industrial expansion became externally-oriented and markets were 'disembedded'. Wherever industrial production expanded, whether of manufactured or agricultural or mineral goods, it was in order to increase exports. By expanding production largely for export, dominant classes obviated the need to provide labourers with the means to buy what they produced and deprived them of the ability to exercise power through consumer choice or boycott. Thus, while Europe at that time saw an increase in the scale of industrial production, involving a massive mobilization of human and material resources and a re-organization of production processes, this revolution of scale, as it might be called, involved neither a revolution in technology nor a transformation either of means or relations of production (see Halperin, 2014, Chapter 3).

In Europe, mechanization was introduced very slowly and selectively and methods of production were employed that deskilled workers and kept labour, as a whole, fragmented and poorly paid. The overall pattern of expansion that emerged was 'dualistic' – based on production principally for export to foreign ruling groups or areas of 'new' settlement abroad,[14] rather than on the growth and integration of local markets. It was based on developing purchasing power *abroad* (through loans and investment in infrastructure, railroads and armaments) and on repression and exploitation at home.[15]

In 1914, mechanization, skilled labour, and rising productivity and real wages in Britain (the 'first industrial nation') were found only in sectors producing for export. These sectors had only a limited impact on the rest of the economy. Little attempt was made to expand or mechanize industries producing goods for domestic household consumption. Britain's exports of capital provided purchasing power among foreign governments and elites. British built foreign railways, canals, and other public works, including banks, telegraphs, and other public services owned by or dependent upon governments, funded the development and transport of food and raw materials exports to Europe, thus creating additional foreign purchasing power and demand for British goods. At the centre of this expansion was the City of London which, like the advanced sector of a 'dependent' third world economy, worked to build strong linkages between British export industries and foreign economies, rather than to integrate various parts of the domestic economy.

The two central features of Europe's system of industrial expansion – internal repression and external expansion – generated what might be characterized as a 'double movement' of imperialist expansion abroad and the persistent opposition of disaffected and exploited classes at home.

Polanyi argued that the unfettering and expansion of the market triggered a simultaneous countermovement on the part of all groups within society. However, the disadvantageous consequences of the unregulated market in the nineteenth century were not experienced by 'society as a whole': some benefitted, some did not. Moreover, if dominant groups sought protection it was, not from the market, but from pressures for redistribution and reform that threatened their monopoly and privilege. As Polanyi himself observed (though without drawing the implications), industrialists demanded from the state that their property be protected, not from the market, but 'from the people' (1944, p. 225).

States and international structures

Polanyi argued that Europe's nineteenth century market system represented the victory of liberal interests and values. But industrial expansion in Europe was shaped, not by a liberal, competitive ethos, but by monopolism, protectionism, cartellisation and corporatism, and by rural, pre-industrial, and autocratic structures of power and authority.

Polanyi begins his account of the nineteenth century market system with an analysis of the institutions of what he calls a 'new liberal international order': the Concert of Europe, the balance of power and imperialist 'regimes', and the gold standard. He claimed that it was this international order that made possible the establishment of 'liberal' states and 'free' markets.

But states in nineteenth century Europe were not Liberal: they were exclusionary and nobilitarian. Dominant classes either controlled the apparatus of the state directly or had access to political leaders and could trade their political support, or the withdrawal of political opposition, for concessions from them. Consequently, landowners did not experience significant political setbacks with respect to tariffs, labour legislation, land reform, state allocations, tax policy, or internal terms of trade until after World War II.[16] Moreover, markets were not unregulated. States regulated markets for the benefit of the dominant classes. They adopted interventionist economic policies with regard to labour, industry, markets, and trade which enabled dominant classes to carry on an essentially coherent legislative, legal, military, and political assault on artisans, labourers, and peasants. They restricted the expansion of domestic markets because of their potential to increase social mobility and promote the growth of new commercial classes. They blocked land reform; monopolized domestic industry and international trade through the creation of cartels and syndicates, and through tariffs and various other controls; and placed further limits on competition by instituting corporatist arrangements of a discriminatory and 'asymmetrical' nature.

Europe's nineteenth-century balance-of-power system was maintained by a Concert of Europe which, Polanyi claimed, was dominated by a concern for the preservation of liberal, free-market institutions. Polanyi claimed that, in pursuit of this interest, Concert acted as an 'international peace interest' and this, he argued, resulted in what he saw as one of the most striking features of the new liberal international order: the 'Hundred Years' Peace' in Europe.

But, like all international institutions, the Concert and other nineteenth century international institutions were state-created and – supported; and these served the interests of states committed, not to free trade and free markets, but to the militant pursuit of foreign markets and repression at home.[17] Throughout the century the Concert remained committed, not to free markets and liberal states, but to protection, autocracy, and the defense of the existing sociopolitical order against revolutionary threats.[18] If the Concert helped to prevent multilateral great power conflicts in Europe, it was because Europe's aristocracies feared that such conflicts would call into use the mass armies that, during and immediately after the Napoleonic Wars, had triggered revolutionary upheavals throughout Europe. However, in spite of the Congress, European states were continually engaged in conflict with their own populations, with other European states and populations, and with territories and states outside of Europe. During the nineteenth century, dozens of wars were waged by European states: fourteen were fought in Europe between and among Britain, France, Germany, Spain, Russia,

Denmark, Austria, Italy, Greece, and Serbia; twelve were fought by Britain, France, Russia, Austria, against foreign populations in Europe. During that period, European states also fought some fifty-eight wars outside of Europe (see Halperin, 2004, Chapter 4). Far from being a period of peace gradually overtaken by the contradictions of the unregulated market, the nineteenth century was a century of social conflict and war. It was born in violence and remained violent throughout.

The great transformation

Polanyi argued that, with the unfettering of markets, there emerged a protective countermovement on the part of society as a whole, and that it was the stresses and strains generated by this countermovement which ultimately led to two world wars and to the collapse of the system. But, as the account developed thus far suggests, Europe's nineteenth century industrial expansion was characterized by a double movement of external expansion and internal repression, and it was this that, by generating recurring tensions and social conflicts, eventually led to social polarization, crisis, and the collapse of the system.

Throughout the nineteenth century, Europe experienced more or less continual conflict over the distribution of resources and the terms and conditions under which market forces operated. Conflicts involving labour were a continuous source of tension; and, as the century progressed, these increasingly overlapped with enfranchisement struggles and nationalist conflicts. Workers were not simply clamouring for protection, but struggling against monopoly and greed. Recurring conflict erupted for changes in property relations, higher wages, extension of the suffrage, redistribution of the national product: shorter hours of employment, and the right to secure bread at an affordable price, to organize, and to work in safe conditions.

By the end of the nineteenth century, the central features of Europe's industrial expansion – external expansion and internal repression – were coming into increasing conflict. A global depression and rising 'red tide', and a sharp escalation of imperialist rivalry combined to produce a multi-lateral war in Europe. Consequently, states were forced, for the first time since 1815, to mobilize the masses, both for war and for the expansion of industrial production needed to support it.

The unravelling of the nineteenth-century system

The unravelling of the nineteenth-century system began with the global Great Depression of 1873–1896 and the accelerated rise of a global 'red tide'. The depression had an immediate impact on industrial conflicts in Europe. The sharp increase in the number of strikes in Britain each year of that decade, shown below, was indicative of this and of the general trend (see Bevan, 1880, p. 37).

Strikes in the 1870s: Britain

1870 30	1875 245
1871 98	1876 229
1872 343	1877 180
1873 365	1878 268
1874 286	1879 308

Violent strikes continued right up to 1914.[19] As these stresses and strains escalated, European states sought to escape their increasingly polarized societies through a sharp escalation of imperialist expansion. As a result, after the 1890s, opportunities to expand overseas quickly diminished, and when they did, the expansionist aims of European powers began to focus, once again, on Europe itself. The tensions and rivalries this generated culminated in a multi-lateral great power war in

Europe.[20] This forced ruling groups to do precisely what a century of external expansion had enabled them to avoid: mobilize (and, thus, organize, train and, in other ways, empower) the masses. As numerous scholars have shown, war often produces social levelling, revolution, and shifts in the balance of social forces.[21] During the world wars this is what happened in Europe. The mobilization of increasingly politicised, radicalized and, as a result of the mobilization itself, organized masses to fight for a system that had, for decades, generated increasingly divisive social conflict, set in motion a social revolution that began in 1917 and, thereafter, swept through all of Europe.

Contrary to many contemporary observers, as well as to later accounts of this period, working-class participation in the war effort did not represent a victory of nationalism over Socialist solidarity.[22] Instead, workers' struggles continued during the war. Moreover, the wartime mobilization of urban working classes and peasant masses produced stronger, larger, more united and better organized labour movements. At the end of the war, Europe had 34 million trade unionists (Ogg, 1930, pp. 759–797).[23] As skilled and unskilled workers, workers of different occupations, anarchists and socialists, Social Democrats and Communists, revolutionaries and reformists closed ranks (Cronin, 1982, p. 139, 121), there was an explosive rise of trade union membership, peasant organization, socialist parties and socialist radicalism. Attempts to block the rising 'red tide' by a strategy of actively aiding and abetting the re-armament and expansion of Germany as a bulwark against Bolshevism led directly to World War II (see Halperin, 2004, Chapter 7).

The demand for labour, and need for its cooperation for a second European war, compelled a political accommodation of working-class movements that, in many aspects, represented a resumption of policies associated with Europe's eighteenth-century 'moral economies.[24] States adopted social democratic and Keynesian goals and policy instruments that, before the war, would never have been accepted by the wealthy classes (Schumpeter, 1950/1976, p. 218). State policies required capitalists to use the profits they realized from this to increase productive capacity and to allow labour to share in productivity gain, so that wages rose with profit and made possible higher mass consumption for new mass consumer goods industries. This more balanced and internally oriented development bought an end to the intense social conflicts and the great movements of colonialism and imperialism that had characterized nineteenth-century Europe.

The Napoleonic wars had been followed by restoration and a century of counter-revolution. But the vastly increased organizational strength and power of working classes and peasant masses and the need of capitalists to gain their cooperation in a resumption of the war against socialism, forced an historic class compromise – a political accommodation of working-class demands that made a restoration of the pre-war system impossible.

Conclusions

Many scholars see Karl Polanyi's analysis of Europe's nineteenth-century market system in *The Great Transformation* as offering key insights into contemporary trends of change. It has been and continues to be a source of inspiration for political-economists, international relations theorists, sociologists, and historians endeavouring to understand current transformations of national, regional, and global structures.

However, the 'top down' account that Polanyi offers of the rise and demise of Europe's nineteenth century market system is, in important ways, misleading. Because it largely ignores the class interests and politics that gave rise to the system, it misses what is perhaps the most crucial chapter in modern history for understanding contemporary globalization: the ultimately successful campaign to dismantle eighteenth-century Europe's systems of national welfare and regulated markets, and the social conflicts which emerged as a result of it. The centrality for Polanyi of the absence of multi-lateral great power conflict in Europe – what, in his account, he calls the 'hundred years' peace', and his focus on the impact of the unregulated market system on 'society as a whole', causes him to systematically underplay the recurring social conflicts and imperialist wars that characterized Europe's nineteenth-century industrial expansion, and ignore their role in bringing about and shaping the outcome of the great transformation which occurred following World War II. In contrast to Polanyi's analysis, a 'bottom up' perspective highlights the social struggles and political dynamics which drove and shaped both the rise of Europe's nineteenth century market system and the outcomes that ensured from its demise. It highlights, too, the emergence of a 'double movement', not of market expansion and societal protection, but of imperialist expansion and social repression.

Polanyi assumed that the collapse of Europe's nineteenth-century market system in the course of the world wars would make it possible for the economies of European societies to undergo a process of re-embedding and, in the view of many, European economies *were* re-embedded after 1945. A historic post-World War II 'compromise between capital and labour, saw the introduction of welfare reforms and the partial de-commodification of labour; and of market and industry regulation that made investment and production serve the expansion and integration of national markets. However, by the late 1970s a campaign had emerged to reverse this post-war compromise; and, since then, it has succeeded in bringing about the return of features of the dis-embedded capitalism that characterized nineteenth-century Europe.

In Europe, markets, it seems, were embedded until the end of the eighteenth-century; they were then dis-embedded and remained so throughout the nineteenth-century. The conclusion of a 'compromise' between capital and labour led to the re-embedding of European economies after World War II. However, in recent decades, concerted efforts have been made to reverse this compromise and to return, once again, to the dis-embedded capitalism that characterized nineteenth-century Europe. It appears, then, that in the history of capitalism there have been phases of nationally embedded and global free market capitalism – periods when capital is relatively more, and relatively less, free from national state regulation.

To draw the implications of this history for current trends of change requires an account of the political struggles which drove and shaped these phases. The changes of recent decades, like those that gave rise to Europe's nineteenth-century system, might be seen as part of an on-going struggle over the distribution of costs and benefits of industrial capitalism. It is a struggle that began with the deregulation and reorganization of economic relationships at the end of the eighteenth-century and with the aggressive external expansion and internal disenfranchisement which ensued. A closer reading of this struggle than that found in *The Great Transformation*, may offer important insights into the forces at work in the rise (once again) of a global market, as well as the forces of resistance that may be capable either of reversing it, or shaping it in less destructive ways.

Notes

1. A year after the publication of *The Great Transformation*, Polanyi invoked this analytical schema in an article on the transformation of liberal capitalism. To understand the transformation of liberal capitalism, he argued, we must look, first, to the international environment, 'since it is in the international field that the methods of private enterprise have broken down—as shown by the failure of the gold standard; and it is in that field that adherence to such methods constitutes a direct obstacle to practical solutions' (Polanyi, 1945, p. 89).
2. The hybrid system that this created was later characterized by John Ruggie as one of 'embedded liberalism' (Ruggie, 1982).

3. See Polanyi's article, 'Our obsolete market mentality' (1947), reprinted in Polanyi (1971, pp. 59–57). For insightful analyses of U.S. policies at this time, see, e.g. Block (1977), van Der Pijl (1984, pp. 50–137).

4. While endeavouring to write class struggles back into the analytical narrative, the focus is not on working classes and labour mobilization, but on the broad configuration of class forces and structures which included both dominant and working classes.

5. Some argue that England did not have an absolute monarchy because it was constrained by parliament. But, as Brian Manning points out, England's parliament played an essential part in the establishment of the absolute state under Henry VIII and Elizabeth I, and was an integral part of it (Manning, 1965, pp. 250–251; see, also, Anderson, 1979, pp. 113–142).

6. In England, state regulations prevented middlemen merchants from bypassing or cornering the market, ensured quality control, a 'just price', and an adequate domestic supply of goods; and market courts enforced them (Lie, 1993, p. 282).

7. This approximates to what Polanyi characterizes as 'embedded' markets. For a comprehensive discussion of the various interpretations of what, for Polanyi, 'embedding' and 'disembedding' constitute, see Dale (2011).

8. In her study of this system, Pat Thane concludes that 'There is a real question as to whether the vastly richer Britain of the twentieth century is relatively more or less generous to its poor than the England of the seventeenth and eighteenth centuries' (Thane, 1998, p. 55).

9. The legal measures were never fully implemented, however, because of resistance from aristocratic office-holders whose job was to apply them

10. Initially, the impetus to industrial growth in Britain was the home market. 'Between 1750 and 1780, the overseas market did not play a major role in providing the justification of the expansion for the country as a whole. If for some sectors, and some areas, exports were already vitally important, this certainly was not known to those responsible for the conduct of other sectors' (Eversley, 1967, p. 221; see, also, Mathias, 1983, p. 16, 94).

11. During the eighteenth century, Britain's industrial output quadrupled, and the bulk of this output was mass consumption goods. As McKendrick, Brewer, and Plumb have argued, it is 'extremely improbable that all this extra consumption could be absorbed by the top layers of income' (McKendrick et al., 1982, p. 29).

12. Sumptuary laws, official documents, records of elite complaints, and public pronouncements about excessive popular consumption attest to the ubiquity of this concern throughout the world.

13. These reforms were similar to those which, today, we associate with the welfare state and with progressive liberalism. Attempts to capture this contradiction in terms are seen in such phrases as 'enlightened despotism' and 'liberal absolutism'. However, the word survives as a key analytic term in the study of early modern Europe, together with its negative connotations and the hostility that it was originally meant to express.

14. Between 1830 and 1914 about 50 million Europeans, 30 per cent of Europe's population in 1830, immigrated to the Americas. The Americas provided markets for European products *overseas, rather than locally*, thus enabling Europeans to expand production without dangerously impacting social relations at home.

15. The building industries grew by expanding employment rather than by introducing innovations in organization or technology. In the 1930s, half the industry's workforce still practiced 'their traditional handicrafts, especially in house building, largely untouched by mechanization' (Benson, 1989, p. 20). By 1913 the output of Britain's electrical industry was little more than a third of Germany's (Hobsbawm, 1968, p. 180). Before World War II, the great majority of those employed in the transport sector worked for a small employer or were self-employed (Benson, 1989, pp. 22–23). It was only in the 1890s that automatic machine-tools production was introduced there and as a result of the desire of employers 'to break down the hold of the skilled craftsmen in the industry' (Hobsbawm, 1968, p. 181). Gas manufacture was mechanized late and as a result of pressure from trade unions. Coal production increased—from 49 million tons in 1850 to 147 million in 1880—not by introducing labour saving techniques, but by increasing the numbers of coalminers. In the 1930s, 'more than 40% of British coal was cut and practically 50% conveyed without the aid of machinery' (Benson, 1989, p. 16). Though Britain had pioneered major innovations in steel production, she was slow to apply the new methods and failed to keep up with subsequent improvements. Though British industrialization was based on the expansion of capital goods

production for railway building, rapid technical improvement came, even here, only when compelled by military competition and the modernizing armaments industry.

16. The absence of agrarian reform, the social and political isolation of agrarian labour, low agricultural land taxes (which offset price controls and taxes on agricultural exports when they were unavoidable), the monopolization of domestic industry and international trade through the creation of cartels and syndicates, attest to this.

17. Externally-oriented expansion requires a system of stable exchange rates, and the gold standard system was developed to provide this. It was stable, between 1871 and 1914, because the absence of effective democratic representation in European societies meant that working classes were unable to put pressure on governments when restrictive monetary policies created unemployment.

18. It was this concern that motivated it to sponsor numerous anti-revolutionary military actions in Europe.

19. And at the same time, trade-union movements increased exponentially. This occurred not only in Europe, but in Africa, the Americas, Asia, and the Middle East. European workers, found in all the large cities of the world, cooperated with indigenous workers and promoted trade unionism, see Stoler (1989), Comaroff and Comaroff (1985, 1986), Gordon and Meggitt (1985), Breman (1987), Callaway (1987), Kennedy (1987), Ingelson (1981), Orr (1966).

20. The scope of these expansionist ambitions was detailed in the set of treaties concluded by all the belligerents in the war that began in 1914, treaties which clearly expressed their hope of achieving vast extensions of their territories, both within and outside Europe, as a result of the war. These treaties were published in the official journal of the Soviets, and in the *Manchester Guardian*. A good summary is found in Baker (1922, I, Chapter 2).

21. See, Marwick (1980, Chapter 11), Titmuss (1958, p. 86), Andreski (1968, pp. 33–38), Sorokin (1927).

22. See Braunthal (1967, p. 355), Schumpeter (1950/1976, p. 353), Carr (1945, pp. 20–21) and, for other works, Doyle (1997, pp. 317–319 and especially 318n.9).

23. Trade union membership doubled in Britain from 4 to 8 million (Geary, 1981, pp. 151–155), in Italy, having doubled during the war, it nearly doubled again by 1920 (Maier, 1975, p. 47).

24. Fascism and the sacrifices entailed in defeating it effectively discredited the old right throughout Europe. Thus, even where workers were not mobilized for the war effort as, for instance, in France, the balance of political power after the war shifted in their favour.

Disclosure statement

No potential conflict of interest was reported by the author.

References

Anderson, P. (1979). *Lineages of the absolutist state*. London: Verso.

Andreski, S. (1968). *Military organization and society*. Berkeley and Los Angeles, CA: University of California Press.

Baker, R. S. (1922). *Woodrow wilson and world settlement*. New York, NY: Doubleday.

Benson, L. (1989). *The working class in britain, 1850–1939*. London: Longman.

Bevan, G. P. (1880). On the strikes of the past Ten years. *Journal of the Royal Statistical Society, 43*, 35–54.

Block, F. (1977). *The origins of international economic disorder*. Berkeley and Los Angeles: University of California Press.

Braunthal, J. (1967). *History of the international, Vol. I: 1864–1914*. (H. Collins & K. Mitchell, Trans.). New York, NY: Praeger.

Breman, J. (1987). *Taming the coolie beast. Plantation society and the colonial order in Southeast Asia*. Delhi: Oxford University Press.

Callaway, H. (1987). *Gender, culture and empire: European women in colonial Nigeria*. Oxford: Macmillan Press.

Carr, E. H. (1945). *The soviet impact on the western world*. New York, NY: Macmillan.

Comaroff, J., & Comaroff, J. (1985). *Body of power, spirit of resistance*. Chicago, IL: Chicago University Press.

Comaroff, J., & Comaroff, J. (1986). Christianity and colonialism in South Africa. *American Ethnologist, 13*(1), 1–22.

Cronin, J. E. (1982). Coping with labour, 1918–1926. In J. E. Cronin, & J. Schneer (Eds.), *Social conflict and the political order in modern Britain* (pp. 113–145). New Brunswick: Rutgers University Press.

Dale, G. (2011). Lineages of embeddedness: On the antecedents and successors of a Polanyian concept. *The American Journal of Economics and Sociology, 70*(2), 306–339.

Doyle, M. W. (1997). *Ways of War and peace: Realism, liberalism, and socialism*. New York, NY: W.W. Norton & Co.

Eversley, D. E. C. (1967). The home market and economic growth in England, 1750-1780. In E. L. Jones & G. E. Mingay (Eds.), *Land, labour, and population in the industrial revolution* (pp. 209–252). London: Arnold.

Geary, D. (1981). *European labour protest, 1848–1939*. London: Croom Helm.

Gordon, R., & Meggitt, M. (1985). The decline of the Kipas. In R. Gordon & M. Meggitt (Eds.), *Law and order in the New Guinea highlands* (pp. 39–70). Hanover: University Press of New England.

Halperin, S. (2004). *War and social change in modern Europe: The great transformation revisited*. Cambridge: Cambridge University Press.

Halperin, S. (2014). *Re-Envisioning global development: A 'horizontal perspective'*. London: Routledge.

Hobsbawm, E. (1968). *Industry and empire*. London: Weidenfeld and Nicolson.

Ingelson, J. (1981). Bound hand and foot: Railway workers and the 1923 strike in Java. *Indonesia, 31*, 53–88.

Kennedy, D. (1987). *Islands of white: Settler society and culture in Kenya and southern Rhodesia, 1890-1939*. Durham: Duke University Press.

Lie, J. (1993). 'Visualizing the invisible hand: The social origins of 'market society' in England, 1550-1750'. *Politics & Society, 21*, 275–305.

Maier, C. (1975). *Recasting bourgeois Europe*. Princeton: Princeton University Press.

Manning, B. (1965). The nobles, the people, and the constitution. In T. Ashton (Ed.), *Crisis in Europe, 1560-1660* (pp. 247–270). London: Routledge & Kegan Paul.

Marwick, A. (1980). *Image and reality in Britain, France and the U.S.A. since 1930*. London: Collins.

Mathias, P. (1983). *The first industrial nation*. (2nd ed.). New York, NY: Methuen.

McKendrick, N., Brewer, J., & Plumb, J. H. (1982). *The birth of a consumer society: The commercialization of eighteenth century England*. London: Europa.

Ogg, F. A. (1930). *Economic development of modern Europe*. New York, NY: Macmillan.

Orr, C. A. (1966). Trade unionism in colonial Africa. *The Journal of Modern African Studies, 4*(1), 65–81.

Polanyi, K. (1944). *The great transformation: The political and economic origins of our time*. New York, NY: Farrar and Rinehart.

Polanyi, K. (1945). Universal capitalism or regional planning? *London Quarterly of World Affairs, 10*, 86–91.

Polanyi, K. (1947). Our obsolete market mentality. *Commentary, 3*, 109–117.

Polanyi, K. (1971). *Primitive, archaic, and modern economies: Essays of Karl Polanyi*. In G. Dalton (Ed.). Boston: Beacon Press.

Ruggie, J. (1982). International regimes, transactions, and change: Embedded liberalism in the postwar economic order. *International Organization, 36*(2), 379–415.

Schumpeter, J. A. (1950/1976). *Capitalism, socialism and democracy*. London: Routledge.

Sorokin, P. (1927). *Social mobility*. London: Harper.

Stoler, A. L. (1989). Rethinking colonial categories: European communities and the boundaries of rule. *Comparative Studies in Society and History, 31*(1), 134–161.

Thane, P. (1998). Histories of the welfare state. In W. Lamont (Ed.), *Historical controversies and historians* (pp. 49–64). London: UCL Press.

Thane, P. (1990). Government and society in England and Wales, 1750-1914. In *The Cambridge social history of Britain, 1750-1950, Vol. III: Social agencies and institutions* (pp. 1–62). Cambridge: Cambridge University Press.

Titmuss, R. M. (1958). *Essays on the welfare state*. Boston: Beacon Press.

van Der Pijl, K. (1984). *The making of an Atlantic ruling class*. London: Verso.

ᵈ OPEN ACCESS

'Our world was made by nature': constructions of spontaneous order

Gareth Dale ⓘ

ABSTRACT
This article explores the concepts of spontaneity and spontaneous order, in particular their deployment by Friedrich Hayek and Karl Polanyi. Although in many respects these thinkers were poles apart, the article identifies a point of convergence. They both mobilize the concept of spontaneity in a manner that naturalizes a particular social process: for Hayek, the market economy, for Polanyi, society's protective movement that arises in reaction against the market economy. To contextualize the uses of spontaneity by Hayek and Polanyi, I trace its evolution, with reference to Leibniz, Mandeville, and the thinkers of the Scottish Enlightenment. Having sketched the ways in which earlier thinkers understood spontaneity, I turn finally to Hayek and Polanyi. I argue that their invocations of spontaneity and spontaneous order contribute to a downplaying of relations of domination and exploitation. While Hayek sees the market system as the exemplar of spontaneous order, for Polanyi, the concept of spontaneity underpins his belief that the protective countermovement is a 'natural' reaction to the evils of market society; as such, power relations pass beneath the radar.

This article attempts a critical investigation of spontaneity and spontaneous order, concepts that have long played a role in social thought, and in particular their deployment in the work of Friedrich Hayek and Karl Polanyi. Although in most respects these two thinkers were poles apart, I identify one point of convergence. They both mobilize the concept of spontaneity in a manner that naturalizes a particular social arrangement: for Hayek, the market economy, for Polanyi, society's movement of social protection that arises in reaction against the market economy.

To understand the meaning of spontaneity in Hayek and Polanyi's work, I trace its development in earlier social theory, with reference to Leibniz, whose use of spontaneity aligns it with the lack of coercion, to Mandeville and thence to the thinkers of the Scottish Enlightenment, from whom Hayek took inspiration. While Hayek constructs the idea of spontaneous order as a clear-cut tradition, advanced by Hume, Smith and Ferguson much as by Hayek himself, I explore aspects of their interpretations that jar with his. I then turn briefly to the nineteenth-century sociologist Herbert Spencer, whose conception of spontaneous order is rather closer to Hayek's in its integration of themes from Darwinian evolutionary theory, but also in its crude dichotomy of 'militant' and 'industrial' forms of society.

Having sketched the ways in which earlier thinkers understood spontaneity, I turn finally to Hayek and Polanyi. I argue that their invocations of spontaneity and spontaneous order contribute

---

This is an Open Access article distributed under the terms of the Creative Commons Attribution-NonCommercial-NoDerivatives License (http://creativecommons.org/licenses/by-nc-nd/4.0/), which permits non-commercial re-use, distribution, and reproduction in any medium, provided the original work is properly cited, and is not altered, transformed, or built upon in any way.

to an underplaying of relations of domination and exploitation – in Hayek's case egregiously, in Polanyi's case subtly. In Hayek, this occurs through the antithesis he establishes between freedom and coercion, with the former associated strongly with markets and the latter with states, and through his defence of social inequality in capitalist society as indispensable to spontaneous social progress. In Polanyi, it occurs through his acceptance of some key liberal ideas on the spontaneous self-ordering tendencies of the market system, and his downplaying of exploitation in statist economies. In both cases, the concept of spontaneity is a contributory factor. Hayek sees the market system as the exemplar of spontaneous order, one that allows individuals to freely find their role. For Polanyi, the concept of spontaneity underpins his belief that the protective countermovement is a 'natural' reaction to the evils of market society; as such, power relations pass beneath the radar.

'Lawfulness without a law'

In several areas of social and economic theory, including studies of social movements and of market order, 'spontaneity' figures prominently. It is a concept that matters. But it is frustratingly – or intriguingly – rubbery. It gathers connotations of free will, naturalness, self-generation, and randomness. Its ambiguities are as striking as its associations are heterogenous (immediacy, nature, the 'genuine' self). Is spontaneous activity unforced, unintended or undetermined? Is it unpredictable yet law-governed? When applied to human beings, does spontaneity refer to sincerity and authenticity (the consonance between one's words and feelings, between head and heart), or to acts in which conscious deliberation is absent, or to expressions of unconstrained autonomy, or somehow to all of these? When referring to willed behaviour, does it denote something unconscious (especially if habitual or contagious), or behaviour that is intentional but yielding of unintended consequences?

Concepts with similar profiles to spontaneity, and even 'spontaneous order,' go back a long way. In the fourth century BC the Chinese philosopher Zhuang Zhou observed that 'good order results spontaneously when things are let alone' (Hamoway, 1987, p. 6). Several centuries later the Epicurean philosopher Lucretius penned *De Rerum Natura* (The Nature of Things) which contains the following lines:

> Our world was made by nature, when
> atoms, meeting by chance, spontaneously,
> and joined in myriad useless, fruitless ways,
> at last found patterns, which when thrown together
> became at once the origin of great things –
> earth, sea, and sky, and life in all its forms.

In Europe, 'spontaneous' was in use from the thirteenth century, to refer to people acting of their own accord, but it did not enter common usage until the 1650s. It was not always positively freighted, yet its increased popularity was striking. What were its causes? And why did the breakthrough occur in the mid-seventeenth century? At least in England, a transformation in religious subjectivity played a part. In the theological flux of the revolutionary decades, Protestants, including some Puritans and many other Dissenters, downgraded liturgy or even castigated it as sinful. This of course did not open them to an embrace of spontaneity as a general principle of behaviour. Puritanism instilled a rigid order into the conduct of its adherents through educating them to a continuous self-monitoring and detailed control of their lives, and to the repression of libido – 'the destruction of spontaneous, impulsive enjoyment,' in Max Weber's description (1905/1992, pp. 119–126). But within the compass of the believer-deity relationship the new emphasis was on its sincerity, performed and affirmed through spontaneous prayer and other forms of 'enthusiastic' worship. Lori Branch (2009, p. 4) refers to this as the new 'spirituality of spontaneity, with its ethos of free prayer, emotional self-scrutiny, and evangelism.' Spontaneous emotional effusion came to be understood 'as *evidence* of the condition of one's heart, when that heart came to be conceived of as an object of investigation, appraisal, and exchange like so many others in the given world.' It is best interpreted, she suggests (2009, p. 87), as the product of the era's transformed epistemological *and economic* discourses, and also as 'a constellation of resistances borne of this subjection.'

The same era also witnessed a burgeoning interest in what would later become known as spontaneous order. The demotion of the deity from an executive to a merely legislative role, from puppet master to instruction-manual author, against a backdrop of wrenching social change and political tumult, all this called for new ways of conceptualizing social order: its foundations, dynamics and complexity. In an earlier age, for example that of Calvin, providence had been a moral doctrine: the belief that God is at work in the world. Faith, not knowledge, was its object (Sheehan & Wahrman, 2015, p. 18). But in the mid-seventeenth century, philosophers such as Gassendi blended the theological concept of providence together with Lucretian materialism to confect a providential naturalism. In this view, God had created atoms, infusing them with energy and a tendency to order (Sheehan & Wahrman, 2015, p. 30). So conceived, providence was the key to understanding the universe; it was now an epistemological and ontological doctrine, not merely a moral one. Moreover, philosophers reasoned, the Bible teaches that God commanded the ground to bring forth plants and living creatures, perhaps, therefore, God's blueprint for creation still existed in matter such that, in the right conditions, new life could be spontaneously produced. This idea underpinned, also in the 1650s, a renaissance, now in Christian colours, of the ancient doctrine of the spontaneous generation of life from inanimate matter. In London, the illuminati of the Royal Society attempted to prove the spontaneous generation of life by showing the 'creation' of insects from cheese (Ginzburg, 1976, p. 57; Ziman, 1991, p. 57).

The new language of spontaneous sentiments, Branch suggests, jibed with 'the languages of experimental discovery and with mercantile and emerging consumer discourses of being current and up-to-date,' in comparison with which the old practices of ritual and repetition appeared as superstitious, authoritarian and out-of-date, smothering of 'the natural responses of the soul' (Branch, 2009, p. 4). One type of ascendant discourse was associated with the revolution in the sciences – notably, the belief that the natural world is governed by Newtonian principles, with order emerging spontaneously from the interaction of nature's myriad corpuscles. Another was the concern for individual autonomy and self-determination, and it, in turn, connected to the new paradigm of market and contract. Whereas the market, as it had operated in earlier centuries was, in Foucault's words (Foucault, 2008, p. 30), 'essentially a site of justice,' by the mid-seventeenth century it was coming to be regarded as 'something that obeyed and had to obey "natural," that is to say, spontaneous mechanisms.' In comparison with previous forms of absolutism, Terry Eagleton suggests (1990, p. 27), a shift occurred in the balance between coercion and consent: where individuals in their economic lives required a substantial degree of autonomy, power, to be effective, had to be 'inscribed in the minutiae of subjective experience.' In the nascent bourgeois order, individuals found themselves isolated and rivalrous in their economic existence; at the political level they appeared to be connected by little but abstract rights. This is why the realm of pieties, intuitions, sentiments, affections and 'spontaneous bodily habits' gained such importance: to it fell the task of cohering 'an otherwise abstract, atomized order.' The individual authentication of power in the new order required the construction, within the subject, of 'a new form of inwardness,' one that would perform 'the unpalatable

THE UTOPIAN SPRINGS OF MARKET ECONOMY

work of the law.' Law, then, could in effect dissolve into custom and habit, such that 'to transgress that law would signify a deep self-violation' (Eagleton, 1990, p. 20). Philosophers began to speak of 'lawfulness without a law' (Kant) and 'authority which is not an authority' (Rousseau), as ways of envisaging a new kind of universal law, one that 'lives wholly in its free, individual incarnations,' the law being ultimately nothing but 'an assembly of autonomous self-governing particulars working in spontaneous reciprocal harmony' (Eagleton, 1990, p. 21).

The embedding of the idea (or ideology) of spontaneity within a broader and increasingly secular culture was a task, first and foremost, for philosophy (Branch, 2009, p. 89). In Britain, the pioneers were moral philosophers: the Earl of Shaftesbury, who knitted the ethos of spontaneous benevolence and spontaneous 'natural affection' together with those of gentility, emotional sincerity and moral sensitivity (Branch, 2009, p. 3, 10), and the Scottish moralists, on whom more below. In Germany, the same period saw spontaneity receive sustained scrutiny from Gottfried Leibniz. In his writings, spontaneity is positioned in immediate proximity to self-determination, and therewith close to the Enlightenment grail: the perfection of all things and all humans. The natural changes to which each monad is subject, Leibniz proposed (in Sgarbi, 2012), 'come from an internal principle,' and the more that substances 'are determined by themselves, ... the more perfect they are' (Leibnitz, 1692/2010, p. 94). Human freedom, in his definition, is the 'spontaneity of someone endowed with intellect,' with spontaneity itself defined as 'contingency without coercion' (Leibnitz, 1692/2010, p. 94). Leibniz attempted, further, to categorize spontaneity into subgroups: willed and involuntary, for example. 'Everything voluntary is spontaneous,' he reasoned (in Losonsky, 2001, p. 174), 'but there are spontaneous actions which are not chosen and therefore are not voluntary' – a ball set in motion would be a case in point. Kant was later to elaborate on Leibniz' taxonomy. He differentiated among different types of spontaneity, including 'absolute,' 'relative,' and 'automatic.' (The latter is seen 'when a machine moves itself according to an inner principle, e.g. a watch' (Kant, in Sgarbi, 2012, p. 76)). And, like Leibniz before him, Kant aligned spontaneity with the idea of the essential self-activity of the subject, or self-determination – a move that was taken up by the idealist philosophers Fichte, Schelling and Hegel; they steered it toward a new, Romantic philosophy of subjectivity.

After the bubble

In its broad-brush summary of a centuries-long set of developments, the above survey may give the impression that developments followed one another smoothly and logically. But they did not. There were multiple non-synchronicities and contradictions. Not the least of these was that the age was punctuated with wars, revolutions, social tumult and economic crisis, even as the dominant Cartesian philosophy was depicting the universe as governed by regular and mechanistic laws – this was the period in which God was first imagined as the divine watchmaker (Durant & Durant, 1963, p. 618).

It is a contradiction that has piqued the interest of two historians of early modern Europe, Jonathan Sheehan and Dror Wahrman. In *Invisible Hands*, they trace the novel conceptualizations of the law-governed character of human society that grew from the dissatisfaction with the simplicity and predictability of the Cartesian universe. A seminal decade was the 1720s. It was then, particularly in Britain, that *self-organization*, in the sense of reflection on the existence of forms of order beyond the worldview both of the mechanical philosophers and traditional providence, emerged as a recognizable cultural phenomenon. The world, as it was now envisaged, was 'vulnerable to the operations of chance,' because not manipulated in detail by a divine architect, but it nonetheless appeared to be 'organized by unseen and powerful forces.' Imagining this algebra of social order 'required new appreciations for complexity, new understandings of causality, and new functions for the divine hand.' In response to the question of what *did* guarantee order, contemporaries came up with a novel notion: that, when left to their own devices, complex systems generate order immanently, without external direction, through self-organization (Sheehan & Wahrman, 2015, p. x).

Why was it specifically the 1720s that saw the emergence of this new concept – of complex self-organizing social patterns ('order') arising as the unanticipated outcome of unconnected, random, atomic acts? The precipitating cause, Sheehan and Wahrman suggest, were the Mississippi and South Sea financial bubbles of 1719–1720 and their aftermath. This thesis is speculative, but *Invisible Hands* brings together an array of evidence in its support. The argument begins with the bubbles. These bouts of financial hyperactivity and hyperinflation provoked within Britain's upper echelons an obsessive interest, and an unsettling sense of disorder (Sheehan & Wahrman, 2015, p. 99). When a bubble bursts, a contemporary explained, it brings

> a prodigious Number of Sellers to the Market, one Man selling alarms another, and makes him sell, and thus the Stock has run down insensibly, till all the People are put in a Fright; and such has been the panick Fear, that it has brought great Confusion along with it. (Sheehan & Wahrman, 2015, p. 106)

A bubble brings chaos, suddenly and very visibly. But in each case order swiftly returned – and at least in Britain's experience of the South Sea Bubble, even its deflation exerted only a small impact on bankruptcy levels (Knafo, 2013, p. 116).

These periods, of ferment and turbulence followed by a rapid return to order, inspired a growing doubt in the sufficiency of inherited models of causality. The vision of Newtonian order – that consequences follow causes in linear and stable fashion – was disrupted. Regularity crumbled into chance. Was each bubble caused by Providence? Was it conspiracy? Some contemporaries explained it away in these terms. Others identified Whiggish over-ambition as the culprit. (The Tory propagandist Daniel Defoe, for example, charged John Law, chief architect of the Mississippi Bubble, with having

> screw'd up the adventurous Humour of the People by starting every Day new Surprizes, new Oceans for them to launch out into; so supporting one Chimera by another, building Infinite upon Infinite, which it was evident must sink all at last into infinite Confusion. (in Wennerlind, 2011, p. 237))

Still others, however, groped towards a new view, an embrace of nonlinearity and the invisibility of cause-effect relations within a new framework of order: market order emerging from the random, even chaotic, behaviour of a multitude of actors (Sheehan & Wahrman, 2015, p. 96, 104, 118).

A pivotal figure was Richard Cantillon. His own outlook could be described as Newtonian, at least inasmuch as his economic theory postulated a system of interacting and logically functioning parts that tend to equilibrium (Lewis, 2014, p. 68). The economy, accordingly, was held to be 'constantly adjusting to basic changes in population, production, tastes, and so forth,' whereby the drive of the adjustment process was 'the self-interested pursuit of profit' – a motive of such ubiquity that it takes the position in Cantillon's inquiry 'that Newton's "universal principle of attraction" (i.e. gravity) took in his' (Ekelund & Hébert, 2013, p. 78). In applying scientific principles to economic behaviour, Cantillon has received accolades. His *Essai* was for William Stanley Jevons 'the first systematic treatise on economics' (Ekelund & Hébert, 2013, p. 78). Joseph Schumpeter bracketed him together with David Hume as the first to have definitively theorized equilibrium in international trade (Dumont, 1977, p. 35), and Hayek hailed him as 'the originator of the self-adjusting price specie flow mechanism' (in Sheehan & Wahrman, 2015, p. 131).

In his conception of the economy as a system of interconnected markets that tend to equilibrium, Cantillon anticipated Adam Smith's invisible hand. The engine and guarantor of equilibrium is the 'free play of self-interested entrepreneurs,' as Robert Ekelund and Robert Hébert (2013, p. 79) paraphrase Cantillon; it 'keeps the system in adjustment by their conduct of "all the exchange and circulation of the State."' Therefore the economy can function perfectly well without intervention in its internal mechanisms; indeed, government regulation will breed perverse effects (Maucourant, n.d.). Although crucial to establishing equilibrium, however, entrepreneurs occupy only a middling rank in Cantillon's economic hierarchy. At the top are the gentry, for as landowners the entire population depends upon them. (Land, in Cantillon's cosmology (1755/2001, p. 92), is the source of all wealth.) Particularly striking in Cantillon – and altogether neglected in the literature, except by Michael Perelman – is his theorization of the free play of market competition as the mechanism by which the social hierarchy is fixed into place. Cantillon was the first to see clearly, Perelman suggests (1983, p. 71), that market competition mediated by the price mechanism can produce essentially the same social outcome as the systems of direct command over labour found in a feudal economy; in other words, market relations function as 'an effective means of control.'

Cantillon, a stock-market speculator, was intimately involved in the 1719–20 bubbles and he wrote his famous *Essai* in the 1720s (Sheehan & Wahrman, 2015, p. 130). As such, he is the key witness in Sheehan and Wahrman's case: that reverberations in society's upper echelons as the bubbles burst and order resumed formed a crucial catalyst of the entire tradition of thought that conceives of the market system in terms of spontaneous self-organization (the 'invisible hand'). It is I think a persuasive thesis. It requires some exaggeration, or at least some overlooking of the degree to which a spontaneous order paradigm had made inroads in the previous century (in the work of economists such as Dudley North) and in Mandeville's *Fable* of 1714. However, there is no doubt that the paradigm took wings with Cantillon, or that it reached its acme with the Scottish moralists (who drew on Cantillon), before its vulgarization in subsequent centuries by the likes of Herbert Spencer and Friedrich Hayek.

Spontaneous order, from Mandeville to Spencer

Hayek saw himself as inheritor of the tradition founded by Mandeville and the thinkers of the Scottish Enlightenment, but in several respects the positions they developed are quite unlike his. Take for example Mandeville. His *Fable of the Bees* is credited by Hayek (in Schneider, 1984, p. 36) as the first to display 'all the classical paradigmata of the spontaneous growth of orderly social structures: of law and morals, of language, the market and money, and also the growth of technological knowledge.' There's certainly something to this. Mandeville's recipe for social order was to put a number of selfish people together, shake it all about, and watch as an ethical society spontaneously crystallizes (Sheehan & Wahrman, 2015, p. 6). He theorized social institutions as the products of an evolutionary process that developed as the unintended outcome of countless individual actions, and he marvelled at the marriage between demand and supply of labour in particular trades that arises 'spontaneously from the Nature of every large Society' (quoted in Hamoway, 1987, p. 9). Yet Mandeville was rather more of a mercantilist, more of a dirigiste, than Hayek allows (Petoulas, 2001, p. 100). He repeatedly compared societal harmony to the workings of a well-regulated machine. Even the most complicated clock, he reasoned, will 'work with the minimum of supervision … once the internal mechanism is discovered and the various parts are put together.' Correspondingly, once the legal system of a society has been developed and its laws 'brought to as much Perfection, as Art and Human Wisdom can carry them, the whole Machine may be made to play of itself, with as little Skill, as is required to wind up a Clock' (Mandeville, in Petoulas, 2001, p. 96). Such analogies gesture towards the idea of spontaneous order, but in the invocations of human art and wisdom they connote, too, artifice and the 'made' order.

More than Mandeville, it was the Scots who adumbrated a theory of spontaneously emerging social order. Moralists before they were economists, the guiding question of Hume, Smith, Adam Ferguson *et al.* was how to achieve virtue and social cohesion in an atomized commercial society in which the temptations of private gain lure individuals to egotism and corruption (McNally, 1988, p. 163). The institutions of modern society, they argued, are too complex to be constructed brick by brick under the command of a directing intelligence; they arise instead from the interaction of myriad individual acts – whether habitual or intentional. Hume, for example, argues that rules of property, as well as the rules and conventions of justice, money and language, evolve spontaneously, and his *History of England* invokes a developmental process that one commentator has dubbed 'the invisible hand of politics' (Louis Schneider quoted in Hamoway, 1987, pp. 10–13. Cf. Varoufakis, 2012). Hume is of additional relevance to my argument because he theorized the religious enthusiasm of the previous century as a prerequisite for the social framework of spontaneous order that flowered in his own. His 'Of Superstition and Enthusiasm' comes down firmly in favour of the latter. Whereas superstition 'renders men tame and abject and fits them for slavery,' enthusiasm, 'being the infirmity of bold and ambitious tempers, is naturally accompanied with a spirit of liberty' (Hume, 1967, p. 177). As such, and despite his distaste for Puritanism and his condescension toward Quakers, Hume saluted enthusiasm as a critical factor in the evolution of the spontaneously organized bourgeois habitus.

For Hume, and for Smith too, spontaneity characterizes the formation of institutions in an overarching sense – as the pattern that characterizes the social process as a whole (life evolves spontaneously from nature; property rights arise spontaneously, and on that basis the market economy spontaneously arises). Smith's focus in *Wealth of Nations* was economic order: the magic of the invisible hand, which weaves social order and the public good, and economic growth, from the disparate skeins of private self-interest. In *Theory of Moral Sentiments* (2009, p. 275), he had earlier made a not dissimilar case with the help of a different metaphor: of the legislator who is 'so enamoured with the supposed beauty of his own ideal plan of government' that he imagines 'he can arrange the different members of a great society with as much ease as the hand arranges the different pieces upon a chess-board,' failing thereby to consider that whereas 'the pieces upon the chess-board have no other principle of motion besides that which the hand impresses upon them,' in 'the great chess-board of human society, every single piece has a principle of motion of its own, altogether different from that which the legislature might chuse to impress upon it.' Continuing this complex extension of the mechanical metaphor, Smith argues in the same book (2010, Section III, Chapter 1) that society exists in harmonious self-regulation, like Newton's universe, or 'like a great immense machine, whose regular and harmonious movements produce a thousand agreeable effects.' And behind this machine lies another: human beings perceive a divinity, whose benevolence and wisdom has 'contrived and conducted the immense machine of the universe, so as at all times to produce the greatest possible quantity of happiness' (Smith, 2012, p. 237). For Smith, then, 'the ultimate ground of economic reality,' as Thorstein Veblen remarked (2018, p. 85), 'is the design of God.' The invisible hand or the market was 'attached to God's invisible arm' (Henwood, 1998).

Smith was more sympathetic than his Austrian disciple to the possibility that spontaneous order was providentially enabled, and he was more relaxed on the question of government intervention. The scale and operations of the state, Smith maintained, would grow in tandem with the rise of commercial society. (He has even been described as a structuralist development economist *avant la letter* (Muller, 2002, p. 76; Rostow, 1990, p. 50)). And he was famously wary of the commercial spirit and of its bearers, the mercantile and manufacturing classes. Any proposal emanating from these groups and claiming to be in the public interest should be treated with the utmost suspicion:

> it comes from an order of men, whose interest is never exactly the same with that of the public, who have generally an interest to deceive and even to oppress the public, and who accordingly have, upon many occasions, both deceived and oppressed it. (Smith, in Davidson, 2012, p. 76)

Hence Ludwig von Mises' lament (in McNally, 1993, p. 45) – that the author of the *Wealth of Nations* 'could not free himself from the standards and terminology of traditional ethics that condemned as vicious man's desire to improve his own material conditions.'

This same complaint would presumably apply with greater force to Ferguson. Much as in Smith, Ferguson (1995, p. 110) identifies spontaneous social behaviour as the means by which society tends to progress. Despite the human disposition to form 'projects and schemes,' he argues, the actions of most people most of the time are governed in fact

> by the circumstances in which they are placed; and seldom are turned from their way, to follow the plan of any single projector. Every step and every movement of the multitude … are made with equal blindness to the future; and nations stumble upon establishments, which are indeed the result of human action, but not the execution of any human design.

For Ferguson, society's tendency to progress is conceived as providentially inspired yet manifested in the form of a spontaneous process consisting of myriad private acts of innumerable actors through time (Hill, 1997, p. 678). As the central engine of progress he identifies the market system, and yet he was plagued by the tensions between commerce and virtue. His *Essay on the History of Civil Society* abounds with reservations about the 'polished' society of expanding commerce exhibited by England, which paradoxically, he held, contained the seeds of its own destruction (Hill, 1997, p. 681; Hirschman, 1977/1997, p. 107; Wood, 2012, p. 283, 311). If for Smith the accent is on the 'spontaneously cohesive' structures of commercial society, Ferguson is more sceptical (Eagleton, 1990, p. 37). In his reading, the commercial age, while a natural product of the workings of spontaneous order, had brought luxury, egotism, decadence and a weakening of the civic spirit, all of which bring the danger of social collapse (Hill, 1997, p. 681).

From the Scottish moralists onward, the theme of spontaneous order can be traced through left Smithians such as Tom Paine, for whom the self-organizing resilience of the social order allows for political experiments and ruptures, and through right Smithians (or Humeans) such as Edmund Burke, for whom the evolution of political order, being gradual, planless and the product of a multitude of human customs and conventions, is necessarily conservative; ergo its laws and institutions should not be rashly tampered with (Sheehan & Wahrman, 2015, p. 279). From Burke, through Herbert Spencer and then Hayek, the concept assumed an increasingly vulgar stamp. In Spencer's case the vulgarity consisted in his bolting the idea of spontaneous order onto a simple dichotomy of 'militant' versus 'industrial' society. In a polemical simplification of the spontaneous order thesis, Spencer bundles the policy regime that Smith opposed, mercantilism, together with all pre-commercial stages of society, in opposition to commercial (in Spencer's lexicon 'industrial') society. Primitive militant societies are characterized by command and control, with governments or chieftains calling the shots; the result is economic backwardness, social tension and international conflict. In industrial society, by contrast, individuals work for one another, motivated by a blend of egotism and sympathy (Bowler, 1989; Spencer, 1884/92/1969, p. 134). The mechanism that enables this felicitous outcome is the market. It embodies the principle of evolutionary spontaneous order, which permits free enterprise and individual initiative to flourish, with peace, prosperity and progress as the civilizational consequences.

Michael Polanyi and Friedrich von Hayek

In the twentieth century, Spencer's dichotomy was adapted and developed. A milestone arrived in 1948 with Michael Polanyi's essay on 'Planning and Spontaneous Order.' The distinction Polanyi made was between *spontaneous* and *corporate* orders. The former is a horizontal arrangement in which each individual decides how to act, adjusting their actions to the outcomes of others, allowing the system to evolve through agents' decisions and mutual adaptation. The latter, exemplified by a ship's crew, a firm, or an army, exhibits a pyramidal structure, with descending lines of authority. Such organizations are commanded by an executive, which plans strategy. Typically, the plan is guided by a single overarching goal. The two types, Polanyi notes, are not radically separate. Market actors, for example, interact on their own initiative but are subject to laws laid down by government (Jacobs, 2000, pp. 57–59).

Like Michael Polanyi (and indeed Karl Polanyi), Hayek's economic philosophy was informed by ethical individualism. A 'free society,' he held (1960/2006, p. 63), requires that 'its members regard it as right that each individual occupy the position that results from his action and accept it as due to his own action.' In turn, this necessitates a system of absolute private property. The exclusive right of owners to determine the use of their property encourages individual responsibility, enabling each to make full use of his knowledge and possessions in the interests of himself and the wider community (Hayek, 1936/2009, p. 20). On this basis, a spontaneous, 'endogenously' grown, evolutionary order – or *cosmos* – arises, featuring unintended yet coherent networks of relations through which actors pursue their heterogenous aims regulated only by common procedural rules. It is defined in opposition to *taxis*: 'exogenously' constructed, artificial orders, where purposive organizations such as governments, families, farms and corporations seek to realize substantive collective goals (Jacobs, 2000, p. 51).

For Hayek, as for the Scottish moralists, commercial society brings about a civilized order – an order, in other words, that facilitates social progress. For him it is 'civilization,' with Western market society at the pinnacle, that 'distinguishes man from beast' – far more than language, culture, tool use, or the many other human qualities that flourish in 'pre-civilized' societies (Hayek, 1960/2006, p. 37). In making this argument, Hayek is at pains to detach spontaneity from its associations with 'natural instinct.' Primitive peoples, whose ethical systems are geared to norms of 'solidarity' and 'altruism,' are in his cosmology closer to beasts, for their social organization consists of 'made' orders: they are 'guided by innate instincts to pursue common perceived goals' (Hayek, in Papaioannou, 2012, p. 103). History's 'vanguard' societies, by contrast, are those that pioneered the market economy and imposed it on the rest. They learned to embrace the open society, with its abstract rules, and that for Hayek is the road to civilization and progress.

What, Hayek asks next, is progress? It is above all the growth of knowledge, and the accumulation of capital. 'The market system,' he argues in *Law, Legislation and Liberty* (2012, p. 275), is the spontaneous, evolutionary, progressive order *par excellence*. It

> leads not only to the creation of an order, but also to a great increase of the return which men receive from their efforts. ... It is a wealth-creating game, that is, one that leads to an increase of the stream of goods and of the prospects of all participants to satisfy their needs.

And how to ensure that economic growth continues? One must encourage the rich – the 'vanguard' of civilization – by ramping up inequality, for their gains will eventually 'become available to the rest'; indeed, all rational hopes 'for the reduction of present misery and poverty rest on this expectation' (Hayek, 1960/2006, p. 46). Here Hayek's position may usefully be compared with that of Smith and Ferguson. Not unlike Smith, for Hayek economic growth figures as a key index of social progress, but whereas Smith nurtured the (illusory) hope that over time capitalist growth would equalize incomes, Hayek celebrates its tendencies to income polarization. And whereas Ferguson worried about the corrosive impact of commerce and self-interest on public virtue, when Hayek writes about virtue, he tends to praise the market for producing distinctly commercial virtues.

Hayek's schema has been subjected to critique from various angles. One is identified by the political theorist William Connolly. Connolly shares Hayek's fascination with sophisticated and multifarious self-organizing systems in the natural world and in the market economy. But the market economy, he points out, is not the only social system 'that displays moments of *creative* spontaneity and differential degrees of self-organizing power.' These creative traits are found in other spheres of social life in which Hayek displayed negligible interest, notably 'spontaneous social movements.' A corollary of this blind spot is that Hayek tended to exaggerate 'the self-organizing power of markets by implicitly deflating the self-organizing powers and creative capacity' of other systems – certainly social movements, and also politics. These, Connolly proposes (2013, p. 66), should be included 'within the domain of creative spontaneity' as opposed to the Hayekian 'desire to contain democratic politics.'

A second critical observation is that Hayek maps the cosmos/taxis couplet onto a set of dichotomies: endogenously grown vs. exogenously designed, evolutionary rationalism vs constructivist rationalism, market vs planning, freedom vs despotism, individualism vs collectivism, capitalism vs socialism, liberalism vs totalitarianism, and so on. With this move, a dichotomy with suggestive uses as a social-scientific model becomes a manifesto, a credo that counterposes coercive, lumbering and inevitably over-reaching statist centralism to the realm of individual initiative, private enterprise, the spontaneously evolving and smoothly self-adjusting market *cosmos,* and the rule of law (which Hayek believes to be the spontaneously achieved corpus of rules, which, being abstract and impartially applied, are antithetical to coercion and belong instead in the realm of freedom (Connolly, 2013, p. 31; Hayek, 1960/2006). Of course, Hayek (and Michael Polanyi) recognize that spontaneously ordered systems in practice include organized corporate parts – just as firms, in a formulation of Dennis Robertson, exist as 'islands of conscious power in an ocean of unconscious cooperation, like lumps of butter coagulating in a pail of buttermilk.' And they accept that actions in a corporate order are not necessarily merely responses to the diktat of one's superordinates. However, they, and Hayek in particular, etch a sharp line between the two types of order, such that an entity must be of one type or the other. They recognize interaction but exclude fusion, or hybrids. It is a Manichean procedure in that, in the worldview it defines, order exists either as cosmos or taxis (Petoulas, 2001, p. 12). It is a distinction, moreover, that cannot bear much weight because, as Timothy Sandefur has shown (2009), the difference between spontaneous and constructed orders tends to collapse on close examination. What some perceive to be the application of a spontaneously evolved rule appears to others as constructivist intervention. In *The Road to Serfdom,* Hayek (1944/ 1986, p. 71) reveals that his attitude 'toward society is like that of the gardener who tends a plant.' What this elides, Sandefur argues (2009), is that the gardener stands outside the garden 'with an exogenous idea of how it ought to look, and he rationally constructs it, prudently allowing plants to grow in some ways and pruning back others.' In Hayek's understanding (1960/2006, p. 141), the spontaneous order requires a 'lawgiver' whose task it is 'induce' the establishment of order by creating conditions 'in which an orderly arrangement can establish and ever renew itself.' The market system relies on a strong state with a deliberately designed constitution, and to that extent it is itself constructivist.

In Hayek's dichotomy, then, there is little scope for seeing an order as 'buttermilk' from one vantage point, 'butter' from another. Consider the signing of a wage contract: a spontaneously achieved agreement between private citizens *and* a document of corporate serfdom. Or consider the politburo of the GDR. From one line of sight its decrees were a classic case of 'constructing order'; from another, it was a participating actor within, and buffeted by, a multitude of 'spontaneous' forces – geo-economic, balance of power, consumer industrial struggle, and so on. Moreover, Hayek's schema obscures the tendency of the market order to permit monopoly logics and the transmutation of market success into economic power – in which corporations 'can first enact initiatives on their own in the market and then use funds, lobbying power, campaign contributions, collusion, and bribery to consolidate those advantages through the state' (Connolly, 2013, p. 62). Such phenomena cannot be separated out from the market order and reduced to policy and politics – the 'made order.'

Hayek regarded his thoughts on spontaneous order as a continuation in more sophisticated form of the Smith-Hume lineage, but as suggested above, his position was in several respects blunter and cruder. And whereas the Austrian placed enormous emphasis on trial and error in competitive conditions and *independently* of human understanding as the means by which institutions develop and adapt, with the Scots there is also a pronounced emphasis, in their explanations of the origins and evolution of private property and political institutions, on rational deliberation, intentional experimentation and the active comprehension of actors (Petoulas, 2001, p. 137). In their approach, a good deal of 'selection' is not trial-and-error but deliberate, and led above all by virtuous public-spirited gentlemen. As noted above, articulations of market and command are largely elided in Hayek's work. Throughout, Hayek overstates the element of spontaneity in the evolution of the market order, and understates the deliberate construction work undertaken by policymakers and officials. Of this, few were more acutely aware than Karl Polanyi.

Karl Polanyi: against 'spontaneous spontaneity'

The political philosophies of Polanyi and Hayek could hardly have been more different. Polanyi was a socialist. But how did this affect his approach to spontaneity? In the era in which he came of age, the term was much used in the socialist vocabulary, and with a polysemy not unlike that discussed above. For example, in his infamous (because editorially bowdlerized) Introduction to Marx's *Class Struggles in France*, Friedrich Engels (1895) brings spontaneity into play in a positivist way, in an allusion to the German workers' movement's inevitable tendency to progressive evolution and ultimate triumph: 'Its growth proceeds as spontaneously, as steadily, as irresistibly, and at the same time as tranquilly as a natural process.' For a later generation of Marxists, Rosa Luxemburg for example, spontaneity was more likely to be used to refer to the mass activism and political learning processes of working people: the processes through which social movements arise and through which actors gain consciousness of their collective self-identity, their interests, and so on (Borch, 2012, p. 90). The young Polanyi was no follower of Luxemburg; he was drawn rather to her arch-antagonist on the 'revisionist' right of social democracy, Eduard Bernstein, in whose view history was evolving inevitably toward ever greater democracy. It was in a Bernsteinian critique of Karl Kautsky that we find Polanyi's first use of 'spontaneous.' Kautsky, he charges, 'is unable to understand the new forms of democracy that are welling up from the spontaneous life of labour' (Polanyi, 2016).

It was in later life, in the 1940s, that 'spontaneity' entered Polanyi's work in a more systematic way, most notably in an essay on Rousseau – a philosopher who is to Polanyi as Hume is to Hayek (Tamás, 2006). Rousseau (1979) partook of a Romantic sensibility that counterposed civilization to nature, and the external law-governed motions of the planets to the internal 'spontaneous' movements of living creatures. The Genevan thinker's critique of modern civilization – cruel, frenzied, competitive and harsh, in opposition to primitive gentleness, idleness, abundance and

THE UTOPIAN SPRINGS OF MARKET ECONOMY 49

spontaneity – was echoed by Polanyi (1947/1968, pp. 59–60) in his critique of 'industrial civilization, with its paralyzing division of labour, standardization of life, supremacy of mechanism over organism, and organization over spontaneity.'

Polanyi deployed the concept of spontaneity within a framework that is broadly Romantic but within the standard Enlightenment parameters: spontaneity must be guided. This can be seen in Polanyi's essay on Rousseau. It begins with Rousseau's quandary over freedom, which Polanyi phrases as the conflicting imperatives of individualism and totalitarianism. The totalitarian element 'derives from the naturalistic law of survival' (every human society 'behaves in such a fashion as to ensure its survival, irrespective of the will of the individuals composing it') while its individualistic counterpart 'derives from the normative principle of natural law' (every free society 'bases its behaviour on the wills of the persons constituting it') (Polanyi, n.d.). The Rousseauian *volonté générale* is, then, in a sense 'simply the principle of survival (Polanyi, 1943).' But if that is the case, how is freedom possible? Polanyi did not suppose that Rousseau had resolved the paradox but he had at least pointed toward the solution. Crucially, it was Rousseau who first discovered the *reality of society*. Through social bonds (or the 'social contract') each citizen is pledged to support her fellows, and receives 'the same pledge from all, in exchange.' In recognizing political society as real, 'i.e. subject to laws of nature and morality,' Rousseau had demonstrated the limits to 'illusions and wishful thinking,' in particular the belief that 'freedom is a principle on which society can be safely based and that individuals will spontaneously conform to all demands.' Through these insights, Rousseau had discovered the path toward freedom in modern, 'complex' society, with freedom understood as rational self-direction, a path that can only be realized through the collective control of the common life, a reconciling of individual freedom with the reality of society. He had demonstrated, in other words, that there exists 'no "best form of government"; no spontaneous spontaneity, no natural freedom which can make a society survive.' In order to reconcile the dictates of survival and freedom, the dispositions of the people, enabled by processes of collective self-education and moral discipline, must be 'such that they will spontaneously work their institutions in such a way as to allow society to survive' (Polanyi, n.d.).

Like Rousseau, Polanyi (1955) found lessons for modernity in societies of antiquity – for example Old Assyria, where economic behaviour, in his interpretation, was regulated simply by law, which ensured that there was

> no bureaucracy, no administration, no command, no shifting of responsibility: instead the organization of trade is free, spontaneous, undirected *but* within an institutional frame which leaves it to the individual to act at will as long as he keeps to the law.

This sort of mediated spontaneity was quite unlike the modern market society that had been called into being by the ideologues of spontaneous economic order. In *The Great Transformation,* Polanyi takes the Smith-Hayek lineage to task for its veneration of spontaneous progress. 'Nowhere,' he thunders,

> has liberal philosophy failed so conspicuously as in its understanding of the problem of change. Fired by an emotional faith in spontaneity, the common-sense attitude toward change was discarded in favor of a mystical readiness to accept the social consequences of economic improvement, whatever they might be. … A blind faith in spontaneous progress had taken hold of people's minds, and with the fanaticism of sectarians the most enlightened pressed forward for boundless and unregulated change in society. The effects on the lives of the people were awful beyond description.

The belief in spontaneous progress, he continues, had blotted out

> the role of government in economic life. This role consists often in altering the rate of change, speeding it up or slowing it down as the case may be; if we believe that rate to be unalterable—or even worse, if we

deem it a sacrilege to interfere with it—then, of course, no room is left for intervention. (Polanyi, 1944/2001, p. 35, 39, 79)

In his defence of radical state intervention and national planning, Polanyi and Hayek's views were antithetical, but on certain matters of relevance to this article they were close. Polanyi found inspiration in the economics of the Austrian school, including Böhm-Bawerk, Schumpeter, and above all its founding father, Carl Menger (of whom Hayek was also a great admirer, in particular for his theorization of the spontaneous generation of social institutions). Polanyi defined the capitalist market economy, as Alexander Ebner (2011, p. 31) points out, in the Austrian manner: 'almost exclusively as a domain of exchange, contract and profit.' He referred to it as the 'self-regulating market,' the 'market economy' or the 'market system' – terms that, as J. K. Galbraith (2004, pp. 6–8) has argued, distance contemporary society from the unsavoury associations of capitalist power. With Hayek, Polanyi identified the late nineteenth century as the juncture at which liberalism's political, economic and intellectual decline commenced, and, with Hayek, he viewed the interwar corporatist shift in economic policymaking as propitious to, if not direct evidence of, a transition to socialism. This was a leitmotif in *The Great Transformation* and in Hayek's contemporaneous *The Road to Serfdom*, which suspected the hydra of socialism in almost every act of planning or direct economic intervention. Both books, Hüseyin Özel (n.d.) observes, use 'similar models to explain the working of capitalism.' Despite differences of terminology, they analyse capitalism's institutional structure in much the same way.

This combination of analytical similarity and normative antithesis is strikingly apparent in respect of the theorization of spontaneous/constructed orders. Here, Polanyi's position is the very mirror of Hayek's. For the Austrian, macro-economic steering and overambitious social policy represent the trespass of *taxis* onto the terrain of *cosmos*. *The Road to Serfdom* (1944/1986, p. 14) warns against those who advocate restrictions on markets, whether in the form of 'socialism in its more radical form or merely "organisation" or "planning" of a less radical kind.' For the Hungarian, the collectivist countermovement arises *spontaneously,* in resistance to the artificial market machine. Even government intervention, the 'legislative spearhead' of the countermovement 'as it developed in the half century following 1860, turned out to be spontaneous, undirected by opinion, and actuated by a purely pragmatic spirit' (Polanyi, 1944/2001, p. 147).

Like Polanyi, the sharp line Hayek draws is between the liberal market economy (or 'extended order') and any form of regulated society (or 'tribal order'), but for the Austrian the polarity is reversed: a regulated society is anathema, liberal capitalism the ideal. If nineteenth-century liberalism suffered from a single shortcoming it was that its triumphant progress had encouraged hubris – a perfectionist, even utopian, overreach – that excited the romantic instincts of its enemies, socialism and fascism, which thereupon joined it in battle. In this way, it may well have been

> that the very success of liberalism became the cause of its decline. Because of the success already achieved man became increasingly unwilling to tolerate the evils still with him, which now appeared both unbearable and unnecessary. (Hayek, 1944/1986, p. 16)

For Hayek, the utopian aspect is not intrinsic to liberalism but is an irrational and unjustifiable leap beyond it. For Polanyi, by contrast, that element is irrational but also inherent: economic liberalism is necessarily utopian for it brings into being an artificial institutional assemblage against which society, understandably and rationally, reacts. The 'disruptive strains' that emerged around the time of his birth and which then led to the dismantling of liberal institutions in those interwar decades in which the ideas of *The Great Transformation* were germinating were the dragons' teeth sown, inevitably and as a product of its nature, by classical liberalism itself. In this way, Polanyi inverts a well-rehearsed right-wing charge against socialism: that it represents a utopian exercise in social engineering, inhuman in its suppression of catallactic spontaneity. In Polanyi's schema the tables are turned: economic liberals are the utopian extremists; their opponents merely the bearers of the inevitable and spontaneous reaction of social protection.

Conclusion

'Spontaneity' has come to occupy a privileged niche in social-theoretical vocabulary and little wonder. A feel-good word, when applied to bourgeois society spontaneous order connotes freedom, the *demos*, and the natural, as contrasted with terms ('market anarchy,' 'organized capitalism,' etc.) that evoke disorder, or the whip, and the chain of command. In Hayekian theory the emphasis is on webs of transactions through which individuals negotiate their business affairs, responding and adapting all the while to the new information provided by market prices (Petoulas, 2001, p. 37). This presumes that market-mediated transactions produce order rather than 'spontaneous *disorder*' – with its implication of the need for interventionist policies (Tieben, 2012). And it elides the 'abode of production' in which labour is subject to despotism. So for example when Hayekians describe Facebook as a 'superb example of Spontaneous Order' (Easterly, 2011), we can be sure that the owners and designers, not to mention the unslakeable thirst for biopolitical power, are discreetly shaded from view.

In contradistinction to Hayek, Karl Polanyi proposed that the market system is an artificial construct, and whereas Hayek, following Ricardo, postulated that if the state seeks to intrude arbitrarily into the market mechanism anonymous social forces will resist, he proposed the converse: the foisting of the market mechanism upon society will elicit a protective response, or 'countermovement.' The 'laissez-faire economy,' in Polanyi's words, was 'the product of *deliberate* state action.' In this, he was voicing an argument shared by other interwar socialists. Antonio Gramsci (1971, p. 160), for example, saw the self-regulating market as politically engineered:

> a form of State 'regulation,' introduced and maintained by legislative and coercive means; ... a deliberate policy, conscious of its own ends, and not the spontaneous, automatic expression of economic facts. ... Laissez-faire liberalism is a political programme designed to ... change the economic program of the state itself.

But what is peculiar to Polanyi is that he counterposed (artificial) liberal economics to the 'subsequent restrictions on it' which 'started in a *spontaneous* way.' Where the market system was socially engineered, society '*unconsciously* resisted any attempt at being made into a mere appendage of the market' (Polanyi, 1944/2001, p. 141). The myriad impulses behind collectivist interventions, in short, had arisen spontaneously in resistance to the market machine. Polanyi's 'counter-movement' is society's spontaneous rebuke to the 'made' market order.

In his reaction against liberal apologetics that contrast the market economy as spontaneous and functional with the constructedness and dysfunctionality of state intervention, Polanyi (1944/2001, p. 141) reversed the polarity, emphasizing the 'extreme artificiality' of the market system. The historian Mohammad Nafissi (2005, p. 168) has put the point pithily, in a paraphrase of Polanyi:

> Market society had to collapse not so much because its opponents appeared to have gained the upper hand in the 1930s, but because it violated human nature which in turn explains why its opponents had gained the upper hand.

Polanyi's conception of human nature, I would add, was Christian-inflected. In this regard, 'providence', in the broad sense that a divine force exists conducive to social harmony, is present in his outlook in a manner that the Scottish moralists would have recognized, but not Hayek, who seeks to obscure the centrality of providence to the tradition he seeks to inherit.

Polanyi's dichotomy of 'artificial liberalism' and 'natural protectionism' in one sense echoes Hayek's. Both theorists regarded the modern market system as a clear departure from earlier economic arrangements that had expressed the communitarian instincts of human beings. In another sense it is antithetical to Hayek. In Hayek's dichotomy, the positive attributes are heavily on the liberal-market side; in Polanyi's the weight is on the statist and protectionist side. Both thinkers play down relations of exploitation. In Hayek's case (1960/2006) this is achieved by constructing a freedom-coercion dichotomy in which coercion is identified strictly with the direct application of state power and by way of his justification of social inequality in market society. In Polanyi's case it is achieved by understating the oppressive and exploitative relations in 'redistributive' societies, from Mesopotamia to Dahomey to the Soviet Union and, in general, through a neglect of conflict, competition and power relations. The weight of explanation invariably falls upon the pattern of economic integration and rarely if ever upon the exercise of control over productive property and the systematic relationships of inclusion and exclusion that flow from it. In creating these blind spots, the concepts of spontaneity and spontaneous order play an active part. For Hayek, the market system is defined as a manifestation of spontaneous order in which individuals are able to flourish in a coercion-free realm. For Polanyi, a Romantic-tinged concept of spontaneity affirms the thesis that the protectionist countermovement is a 'natural' response by 'society' to the depredations of the market system, allowing relations of power to remain under-specified.

Acknowledgements

This article was first presented at the Research Colloquium 'Crowd Dynamics and Financial Markets,' Copenhagen Business School, October 2015. It also draws on materials I presented at the workshop 'Questioning the Utopian Springs of Market Economy,' University of Sydney/Australia (15-16 August 2014). I thank the participants at both events, and the anonymous reviewers, for their comments.

Disclosure statement

No potential conflict of interest was reported by the author.

ORCID

Gareth Dale http://orcid.org/0000-0003-4991-6063

References

Borch, C. (2012). *The politics of crowds: An alternative history of sociology.* Cambridge: Cambridge University Press.
Bowler, P. (1989). *The invention of progress: The Victorians and the past.* Cambridge: Blackwell.
Branch, L. (2009). *Rituals of spontaneity: Sentiment and secularism from free prayer to Wordsworth.* Waco: Baylor University Press.
Cantillon, R. (1755/2001). *Essay on the nature of commerce in general.* Somerset: Transaction.

Connolly, W. (2013). *The fragility of things: Self-organizing processes, neoliberal fantasies, and democratic activism*. Crowhurst: Duke University Press.

Davidson, N. (2012). *How revolutionary were the bourgeois revolutions?* Chicago: Haymarket.

Dumont, L. (1977). *From Mandeville to Marx: Genesis and triumph of economic ideology*. Chicago: The University of Chicago Press.

Durant, W., & Durant, A. (1963). *The story of civilization: The age of Louis XIV, 1648–1715*. New York: Simon and Schuster.

Eagleton, T. (1990). *The ideology of the aesthetic*. Cambridge: Blackwell.

Easterly, W. (2011). *Complexity, spontaneous order, blah, blah, blah … and wow*. Retrieved from http://aidwatchers.com/2011/01/complexity-spontaneous-order-blah-blah-blah-and-wow/

Ebner, A. (2011). Transnational markets and the Polanyi problem. In C. Joerges & J. Falke (Eds.), *Karl Polanyi, globalisation and the potential of law in transnational markets*. Oxford: Hart.

Ekelund, R., & Hébert, R. (2013). *A history of economic theory and method: Sixth edition*. Long Grove: Waveland Press.

Engels, F. (1895). *Introduction*. Retrieved from www.marxists.org/archive/marx/works/1850/class-struggles-france/intro.htm

Ferguson, A. (1995). *An essay on the history of civil society*. Cambridge: Cambridge University Press.

Foucault, M. (2008). *The birth of biopolitics: Lectures at the Collège de France, 1978–79*. Basingstoke: Palgrave.

Galbraith, J. K. (2004). *The economics of innocent fraud*. Boston: Houghton Mifflin.

Ginzburg, C. (1976). *The Cheese and the Worms: The cosmos of a sixteenth-century miller*. Harmondsworth: Penguin.

Gramsci, A. (1971). *Selections from the prison notebooks*. London: Lawrence & Wishart.

Hamoway, R. (1987). *The Scottish enlightenment and the theory of spontaneous order*. Carbondale: Southern Illinois University Press.

Hayek, F. (1936/2009). *Individualism and economic order*. Auburn: Ludwig von Mises Institute.

Hayek, F. (1944/1986). *The road to serfdom*. London: ARK Paperbacks.

Hayek, F. (1960/2006). *The constitution of liberty*. London: Routledge.

Hayek, F. (2012). *Law, legislation and liberty: A new statement of the liberal principles of justice and political economy*. London: Routledge.

Henwood, D. (1998). *Wall street*. London: Verso.

Hill, L. (1997). Adam ferguson and the paradox of progress and decline. *History of Political Thought, XVIII*(4), 677–706.

Hirschman, A. (1977/1997). *The passions and the interests: Political arguments for capitalism before its triumph*. Princeton: Princeton University Press.

Hume, D. (1967). Of superstition and enthusiasm. In L. Schneider (Ed.), *The Scottish moralists on human nature and society* (pp. 170–183). Chicago: University of Chicago Press.

Jacobs, S. (2000). Spontaneous order: Michael Polanyi and Friedrich Hayek. *Critical Review of International Social and Political Philosophy, 3*(4), 49–67.

Knafo, S. (2013). *The making of modern finance: Liberal governance and the gold standard*. London: Routledge.

Leibnitz, G. (1692/2010). *The shorter Leibniz texts: A collection of new translations*. London: Bloomsbury.

Lewis, C. (2014). *A coincidence of wants: The novel and neoclassical economics*. London: Routledge.

Losonsky, M. (2001). *Enlightenment and action from Descartes to Kant: Passionate thought*. Cambridge: Cambridge University Press.

Maucourant, J. (n.d.). *The ambiguous birth of political economy—a discussion of the work of Montchrestien and Cantillon*. Manuscript in possession of the author.

McNally, D. (1988). *Political economy and the rise of capitalism: A reinterpretation*. Berkeley: University of California Press.

McNally, D. (1993). *Against the market: Political economy, market socialism and the Marxist critique*. London: Verso.

Muller, J. (2002). *The mind and the market: Capitalism in modern European thought*. New York: Alfred Knopf.

Nafissi, M. (2005). *Ancient Athens and modern ideology; value, theory and evidence in historical sciences*. London: Institute of Classical Studies.

Özel, H. (n.d.). *The road to serfdom in the light of the great transformation: A comparison on the basis of unintended consequences*. Retrieved from http://yunus.hacettepe.edu.tr/~ozel/HayekvsPolanyi.pdf

Papaioannou, T. (2012). *Reading Hayek in the 21st century: A critical inquiry into his political thought.* Basingstoke: Palgrave.

Perelman, M. (1983). *Classical political economy, primitive accumulation and the social division of labor.* Totowa: Rowman & Allanheld.

Petoulas, C. (2001). *Hayek's liberalism and its origins: His idea of spontaneous order and the Scottish enlightenment.* London: Routledge.

Polanyi, K. (1943). To Misi, 29 September, Michael Polanyi Papers, University of Chicago, Box 17, Folder 10.

Polanyi, K. (1944/2001). *The great transformation.* Boston: Beacon Press.

Polanyi, K. (1947/1968). Our obsolete market mentality. In G. Dalton (Ed.), *Primitive, archaic and modern economies: Essays of Karl Polanyi* (pp. 57–73). Boston: Beacon Press.

Polanyi, K. (1955). KPA-49-4, Letter to John, 5 January.

Polanyi, K. (2016). Karl Kautsky and democracy. In G. Dale (Ed.), *Karl Polanyi: The Hungarian writings* (pp. 114–117). Manchester: Manchester University Press.

Polanyi, K. (n.d.). Polanyi, 'Jean Jacques Rousseau,' Karl Polanyi Archive, Concordia University, Box 18, Folder 24.

Rostow, W. (1990). *Theorists of economic growth from David Hume to the present.* Oxford: Oxford University Press.

Rousseau, J.-J. (1979). *Emile.* New York: Basic Books.

Sandefur, T. (2009). Some problems with spontaneous order. *The Independent Review, 14*(1), 5–25.

Schneider, L. (1984). *The grammar of social relations: The major essays of Louis Schneider.* Somerset: Transaction.

Sgarbi, M. (2012). *Kant on spontaneity.* London: Continuum.

Sheehan, J., & Wahrman, D. (2015). *Invisible hands: Self-organization and the eighteenth century.* Chicago: University of Chicago Press.

Smith, A. (2009). *Theory of moral sentiments.* Harmondsworth: Penguin.

Smith, A. (2010). *Theory of moral sentiments.* New York: Harriman House Limited, Section III, Chapter 1.

Smith, A. (2012). *The theory of moral sentiments.* North Chelmsford: Courier Corporation.

Spencer, H. (1884/92/1969). *The man versus the state.* Harmondsworth: Penguin.

Tamás, G. M. (2006). *Telling the truth about class.* Retrieved from www.gerlo.hu/kommunizmus-vita/tgm/telling_the_truth_about_class.pdf

Tieben, B. (2012). *The concept of equilibrium in different economic traditions: An historical investigation.* Cheltenham: Edward Elgar.

Varoufakis, Y. (2012). *Why valve? Or, what do we need corporations for and how does valve's management structure fit into today's corporate world?* Retrieved from http://blogs.valvesoftware.com/economics/why-valve-or-what-do-we-need-corporations-for-and-how-does-valves-management-structure-fit-into-todays-corporate-world/

Veblen, T. (2018). *The place of science in modern civilization.* London: Books on Demand.

Weber, M. (1905/1992). *The protestant ethic and the spirit of capitalism.* London: Routledge.

Wennerlind, C. (2011). *Casualties of credit: The English financial revolution, 1620–1720.* Cambridge: Harvard University Press.

Wood, E. (2012). *Liberty and property: A social history of western political thought from renaissance to enlightenment.* London: Verso.

Ziman, J. (1991). *Reliable knowledge: An exploration of the grounds for belief in science.* Cambridge: Cambridge University Press.

Market/society: mapping conceptions of power, ideology and subjectivity in Polanyi, Hayek, Foucault, Lukács

Nicola Short

ABSTRACT
In light of discussions around the common anniversary of the publication of Karl Polanyi's *The Great Transformation* and F.A. Hayek's *The Road to Serfdom,* this article puts these texts – iconic representations of social democratic and neoliberal political theory – into conversation with Michel Foucault's subsequent, influential critique of neoliberalism, *The Birth of Biopolitics.* There are interesting points of contact in the way each text constructs its argument, even as they arrive at distinct positions *vis-à-vis* the material and subjective nature of market society, while nevertheless sharing an opposition to Marxian approaches. Yet the work of Polanyi and Hayek's Marxian contemporary, Lukács' *History and Class Consciousness,* offers precisely a critical framework for understanding the relationship between markets, liberty and society in which the material and the subjective need not be read as antagonistic. It is thus also examined here, in an effort to shed light on how discussions of contemporary neoliberalism are framed.

Karl Polanyi's *The Great Transformation* and F.A. Hayek's *The Road to Serfdom* represent two of the most iconic interpretations of the economic crisis of the early twentieth-century and its consequences, written in the same year from radically different positions that continue to resonate today. That the anniversary of their publication occurred in our times against the background of the reappearance of global economic crisis puts the opposition of these texts and the broader positions they represent—social democracy and neoliberalism—into new relief.

Polanyi and Hayek address the 'utopian springs' of *laissez-faire* differently. The former sought to demystify the ideological pretense of a spontaneous order by illustrating its origins as a political project. The latter recognized the vulnerability it represented to liberal thought and sought to reconstruct the paradigm on new foundations, a shift that formed a central element of Foucault's influential theorization of neoliberal governmentality. Polanyi and Foucault, in fact, both examined the 'birth of political economy' as the moment in which new agencies ('society' and 'population' respectively) that established limits on the scope of government action could be identified, though reaching very different conclusions about the nature and political implications of such forces. Indeed, these two positions arguably represent the dominant positions of critique of neo-liberalism: Polanyi the materialist/social democratic and Foucault the subjectivist/post-modern.[1] This division of labour has been read as both antagonistic and complementary, but the two find consensus in rejecting Marxism's 'economism'. Yet the oft-neglected work of Polanyi and Hayek's Marxist contemporary, Georg Lukács' *History and Class Consciousness,* in fact offers precisely a critical position on what would later be understood as the neoliberal reading of the relationship between markets and liberty in which the material and the subjective need not be read as antagonistic.

The discussion that follows thus examines the points of contact and divergence between the broader theoretical traditions symbolized by these four classic texts: Polanyi's social democratic *Great Transformation*, Hayek's neoliberal *Road to Serfdom*, Foucault's subjectivity-oriented 'postmodern' *The Birth of Biopolitics* and Lukács' Marxian *History and Class Consciousness*. In so doing, it hopes to shed light on the intellectual history of how discussions of contemporary neoliberalism are framed and to contribute to a deeper understanding of how it functions.

Laissez-faire was planned

Polanyi's *The Great Transformation* is iconic for its careful historical elaboration of how '*laissez-faire* was planned', documenting the state's role in its emergence contra dominant liberal representations of a spontaneous market order. He outlines the evolution of public policy in response to specific historical conditions, particularly *vis-à-vis* the administration of poverty and its consequences for the advent of a labour market in England. He argued that the proposals for *laissez-faire* emerged from those industries that had once relied on government protectionism and that continued to use the state for promoting free trade when that was more advantageous to their interests. *Laissez-faire* not only involved deregulation in those cases, as one would expect, but a broad expansion of the administrative capacity and functions of the state. In sum, this work sought to demystify the central claims of liberal thought, particularly to illustrate that there is no natural, 'spontaneous', or state-less foundation for a liberal order as per the ideological claims of its own political theory; rather, *laissez-faire* involved significant state intervention and indeed the expansion of the state itself.

Yet just as *The Great Transformation* was making the case that *laissez-faire* was planned, Hayek's *Road to Serfdom* argued that *laissez-faire* was not the true foundation for liberal thought in any case, in what would later be understood as an archetypal *neo*liberal defense of market society. For Hayek, privileging *laissez-faire* mistook 'passively accepting institutions as they are' for the true aim of liberalism, which should be creating the conditions for competition, the only real guarantee for individual liberty (Hayek, 2001 (1944), p. 18). Hayek suggested that the general historical trajectory above all in 'western civilisation' was towards an increase of human liberty, ultimately grounded in the logic of commerce (Hayek, 2001 (1944), pp. 14–15). In so doing, he rearticulated the grounds on which liberal policies such as free trade should be defended: not because of the naturalness of the market, but for explicitly normative reasons: a duty to the value of liberty.

Foucault's *The Birth of Biopolitics* suggested that the displacement of *laissez-faire* as one of the pillars of liberal thought is a central feature of the distinction between classical and neoliberal political theory. For him, the emergence of neoliberal political-economic theory was not just a response to the need to justify the liberal state in the context of necessary post-war government spending for reconstruction, but was symptomatic of a deeper epistemological shift in the evolution of social and political theory away from arguments grounded in natural law (the classical sovereign order) towards a recognition of the socially-constructed nature of human affairs (a correlate to the emergence of 'governmentality'). The *neoliberal* argument against *laissez-faire*, he suggested, is that it involves 'a naive naturalism', faith in a 'given of nature, something produced spontaneously' (Foucault, 2008, pp. 119–120). Indeed, neoliberal governmentality involves a reversal of a key aspect of classical liberal thought in at least two related registers. The purpose of government no longer involves establishing a sphere in which the non-economic interests of society might be protected from market forces, but rather involves protecting the market from the anti-competitive effects of society. This shift occurs in parallel at the level of individual political subjectivity: under neoliberal governmentality, the individual is no longer a subject of (political) 'right' but a subject of (economic) 'interest', whereby the role of government is no longer to protect the natural rights of 'pre-given' citizens but to construct market subjects, *homo economicus.*

The birth of political economy: the 'discovery' of society and (neo)liberal governmentality

Polanyi and Foucault both foreground the 'birth of political economy' in their analyses and each associated it with the emergence of a particular agency that disciplines state action. Polanyi argued that it was only with the birth of political economy that society was 'discovered' as an autonomous force that subjugated the state – in its spontaneous reaction to policies that would dis-embed it from its natural foundations – rather than the other way around. For Foucault, the birth of political economy was associated with the emergence of 'population' as the object of government and of market 'veridiction' as a regime of power/knowledge that structured the logic and evaluation of government action. In his account it is not 'society' that disciplines the state, but the internalization of a new discipline on the part of the state itself, the reconstruction of *raison d'état* towards a new, market-oriented objective. While Polanyi grounded his arguments in an interpretation of the material consequences of the emergence of a commodified labour market in England, Foucault followed a genealogical approach to discourses of liberal governance as expressions of the evolution of sovereignty and state power. Thus, despite many points of contact within a common concern, Polanyi and Foucault arrive at radically different conclusions: the former that there is a material limit to the logic of market society, which may be expressed in a spontaneous 'societal' reaction when things go too far, and the latter that market logics completely reconstitutes the social in its image: that contemporary subjectivity has become that of a neoliberal *homo economicus.*

Polanyi on the 'discovery' of society

In the same way that the French Revolution had informed political theorists such as Voltaire and Rousseau, Polanyi argued, debates over the Poor Laws of 1834 structured the nineteenth-century understanding of political economy across the ideological spectrum (Polanyi, 1957, p. 84). These were grounded in a number of intellectual developments that transformed the foundations for understanding state and society, with reference to the problematic of 'political economy'. (Polanyi, 1957, pp. 84, 103). The nineteenth-century 'discovery of society' marked a shift, from 'the inventors of the state' to the awareness of 'the existence of a society that was not subject to the laws of the state, but, on the contrary, subjected the state to its own laws', *via* (the indeed opposing positions within) the work of Ricardo and Hegel (Polanyi, 1957, p. 111). The discovery tracked the conditions of the day, which seemed to operate independently of the state and thus became easily attributable to natural and biological explanations (Polanyi, 1957, p. 115).

In reaction to the Elizabethan Poor Laws, which established classifications for the poor and demanded those that could work do so to be eligible for public subsidies, the Speenhamland 'law' of 1795 that, in fact, was not formally legislated but widely adopted, established the principle of the working poor's 'right to live', i.e. a minimum income based on the price of bread, regardless of one's wage (Polanyi, 1957, pp. 83–84). Yet Speenhamland, unintentionally had an effect opposite to its purpose: it led to the destitution of the countryside, as wages dropped under its broad subsidization while labour remained compulsory to attain any benefits. Thus, it produced conditions in which the need for reform was widely accepted, even if the specific solution – the Poor Laws of 1834 – ultimately would prove to be enormously unpopular. These abolished Speenhamland's principle of the right to live, and in so doing provided the material and intellectual foundations for a competitive labour market (Polanyi, 1957, pp. 83–84).

The Great Transformation examines the development of liberal theory in this period, which from varied positions read as natural the conditions produced by Speenhamland, a development that had given the appearance of a capitalist labour market before one actually existed. Speenhamland united the otherwise methodologically and politically distinct positions of Townsend, Malthus and Ricardo, Bentham and Burke in opposition: 'What made economic liberalism an irresistible force was this congruence of opinion between diametrically opposed outlooks; for what the ultrareformer Bentham and the ultratraditionalist Burke equally approved of automatically took on the character of self-evidence' (Polanyi, 1957, p. 127). In other words, there was a material foundation for the ideological convergence for the commodification of labour, though one that suffered from a misunderstanding of the historical circumstances that produced it.

Foucault on the emergence of governmentality

Foucault's analysis of the emergence of political economy and how it established population and economy as the standard of for the evaluation of government in *The Birth of Biopolitics* (his 1978–9 lectures at the *Collège de France*) has certain interesting parallels with Polanyi's argument. Foucault, like Polanyi, is concerned with the shift to understanding market mechanisms as 'natural' and 'spontaneous'. However, for Foucault, political economy represents the eighteenth-century coupling of 'a regime of truth and a new governmental reason', an example of the coupling of claims of truth articulated to law that he called 'veridiction' (derived from '*dire le vrai*'). As such a regime of *veridiction*, political economy stands independent of the content of specific political programmes, i.e. it is not one paradigm among others to be potentially chosen by policy makers or a consideration around which interest groups might pressure policy makers, but the very field of government itself.

Foucault's conception of 'governmentality' is in fact introduced and elaborated in the previous lecture series, collected in *Security, Territory, Population* (2007). The triad of the title represent the three elements constitutive of governmentality, a logic of power that emerges in the eighteenth-century, 'which has as its target population, as its principal form of knowledge political economy, and as its essential technical means apparatuses of security' (Foucault, 2003, p. 244). There he makes an argument that appears to echo Polanyi's, with respect however to 'population' rather than 'society', i.e. that the 'birth of political economy' relied on the constitution of a new subject, 'population', associated with a shift from 'a regime dominated by structures of sovereignty to one ruled by techniques of government' (Foucault, 2003, p. 242).

The governmentality framework foregrounds an analysis of power read to a large extent as a question of 'administration', in which the population as an object of government represents both a concern whose welfare becomes a standard for the judgement of power and a target of security and discipline. In *The Birth of Biopolitics*, Foucault elaborates that the significance of political economy is that it provokes a shift in government reason from a concern with rights to one of effects and outcomes, understood to be the product of discernable, knowable mechanisms, and situates this reading of power as an extension of his previous theorisations (Foucault, 2008, pp. 16, 186).

In Polanyi, the interaction of material and political-legal produce new 'truths' that establish an 'ecumenical' liberal hegemony. Foucault's governmentality *qua* veridiction involves a greater focus on the latter two elements in a more ideological register, or as he put it, 'taking up a history of truth that is coupled, from the start, with a history of law' (Foucault, 2008, p. 35). He eschews 'universal' historical methods in favour of establishing 'a polygonal or polyhedral relationship' between certain elements understood to be significant in the transformations of the eighteenth-century: currency, demography, agriculture, technology, 'the access to governmental practice of a number of technicians who brought with them both methods and instruments of reflection' as well as 'a number of economic problems being given a theoretical form' (Foucault, 2008, p. 33). For Foucault, there is no *one* cause by which the market becomes 'an agency of veridiction' and thus it would be foolish to look for one. Rather, to analyze 'this irruption of the market as a principle of veridiction, we should simply establish the intelligibility of this process by describing the connections between the different phenomena [referred to above]' (Foucault, 2008, p. 33).

For both Polanyi and Foucault, albeit on different grounds, the 'birth of political economy' signals the emergence of a new conceptual framework for the governance of capitalist market society. Polanyi observed the emergence of a broad, liberal ideological hegemony in the 'common sensical' reaction to the unintended, pernicious effects of anti-poverty measures. Foucault's analysis saw the birth of political economy as an 'epistemological' development that produced 'population' as the new political subject/object and the market as a new form of 'veridiction', a new standard of truth by which government would be organized and judged.

Market / society: commodity fictions, freedoms, effects

The articulation of market and society in *The Great Transformation*, *The Road to Serfdom* and *The Birth of Biopolitics* can be considered through 'the commodity', which appears as a central concern in all three texts. Polanyi grounded his arguments about the social as an inherent limit to the market in his conception of 'the commodity fiction'. In direct opposition to such concerns, Hayek argued that precisely those features of the market that Polanyi read as 'disembedding' constituted the foundation for liberty: i.e. the subject's *autonomy* from the social afforded by the nature of capitalist exchange. Foucault argued that the neoliberal turn had in fact destroyed the 'commodity effect', replacing exchange with competition.

Polanyi: commodity fiction and the double movement, the social as natural limit to the market

Polanyi distinguished the emergence of market society in Britain from other, historically 'natural', socially-embedded market societies in its turn to understanding money, land and labour as commodities, denying the fundamentally non-economic, social nature of these entities in what he termed the 'commodity fiction'. In his view, the historical record demonstrated that markets had always been accompanied by restrictions (Polanyi, 1957, p. 68). The emergence of a market society based on self-regulation was an anomaly specific to nineteenth-century society resulting from two liberal ideological fallacies associated with the commodity fiction: the claims that the economic and the political can be institutionally separated, and the related premise that the economic can be disembedded from the social (Polanyi, 1957, p. 71). These positions are untenable, because, classically:

> labor, land, and money are obviously not commodities; the postulate that anything that is bought and sold must have been produced for sale is emphatically untrue in regard to them. In other words, according to the empirical definition of a commodity they are not commodities. (Polanyi, 1957, p. 72)

The commodity fiction involves a mis-representation/-recognition of labour, land and money that denies their true natures.

Polanyi formulated the commodity fiction to posit certain spheres as possessing organic, natural characteristics, *contra* the Marxian understanding of the commodity fetish, though he does not elaborate the nature of the distinction. In a footnote he states: 'Marx's assertion of the fetish character of the value of commodities refers to the exchange value of genuine commodities and has nothing in common with the fictitious commodities mentioned in the text' (Polanyi, 1957, pp. fn 3, 72). Indeed, Polanyi reads Marx as not in fact diverging sufficiently from liberal thought ('*Das Kapital* implied the commodity theory of money, in its Ricardian form' (Polanyi, 1957, p. 25)). These two statements suggest a lack of appreciation of how Marx included the social relations of capitalism in his definition of the commodity form, discussed further below (cf: Dale, 2010; Selwyn & Miyamura, 2013, p. 15).

The effects of the commodity fiction – the disembedding of land, labour and money from their natural functions – provokes a spontaneous, counter-vailing impulse towards their protection, which Polanyi termed the 'double movement'. The social history of the nineteeth-century involved such a 'double-movement' restricting the expansion of market organization vis-à-vis 'fictitious commodities', as the massive expansion of global trade was accompanied by powerful institutions regulating the markets associated with labour, land and money (Polanyi, 1957, p. 76). Though the commodity fiction represented at its core a kind of ethical failure (the 'wrongful' commodification of fictitious commodities), Polanyi did not see the double movement per se in normative terms: it could reflect either a progressive or regressive societal response, and indeed fascism was an expression of the latter in his view (Polanyi, 1957, p. 133). This dimension of Polanyi's thought is associated with a second critique of Marxism, that it errs in positioning class rather than society as the central referent for economic history (as well as then ultimately privileging the state over society as a transformative agency (Polanyi, 1957, pp. 151–152, 108)). Polanyi suggested that here too Marx followed Ricardo in ostensibly defining class in economic terms, arguing that the Marxian preoccupation with exploitation should be distinguished from commodification and that it obscured the problem of 'cultural degeneration' (Selwyn & Miyamura, 2013, p. 17). As an alternative, Polanyi in fact relied on a highly sociological (essentially occupational, distinctly non-Marxian) understanding of class (Polanyi, 1957, p. 152; see also: Selwyn & Miyamura, 2013, p. 6).

Hayek: exchange and commodities as freedom

Interestingly, at one point in the *Road to Serfdom*, Hayek appears to argue, like Polanyi, that the political and the economic cannot be separated. Yet he did so with an entirely distinct agenda: to discredit positions that suggest government intervention into the economy could remain limited to that sphere alone (Hayek, 2001 (1944), pp. 91–92). Indeed, Hayek could not sustain the claim to understanding the political and the economic holistically: the rest of the discussion makes clear that his theory relies on the autonomy of the economic as a means to achieve non-economic ends (Hayek, 2001 (1944), pp. 91–92). Hayek ultimately grounds his concept of liberty in the (capitalist) market: for him, freedom of choice can only be found in the system of abstract equivalence that money (*qua* commodity-based exchange) implies. He makes this argument with reference to a broad trajectory in European history, but ultimately it is the commodity form of money that represents 'one of the greatest instruments of freedom ever invented by man' (Hayek, 2001 (1944), p. 93). Anyone in possession of money, even a poor person, is afforded a degree of autonomy of choice that could not otherwise exist (Hayek, 2001 (1944), pp. 15, 93). Other forms of privilege, whatever they might entail, ultimately deny the recipient the agency of being able to select one's specific preference (Hayek, 2001 (1944), p. 93).

Hayek, like Polanyi, argues against 'economism', though here too on different grounds, via the claim that when the economic is properly established as the (abstract) means to achieving our ends, it does not have any value for its own sake, it becomes only the mechanism by which our interests are evaluated against each other (Hayek, 2001 (1944), p. 94). When we are deprived of such decision making, we lose our autonomy to establish our own values and place them in the hands of 'economic planners' (Hayek, 2001 (1944), p. 95). Of course, Hayek constructs this conception of liberty specifically as a response to those concerned with the disciplinary nature of markets, arguing that the perception of liberty and control even over very scarce resources is more important than any concerns over the potentially negative social impacts of markets.

Hayek's understanding of liberty as grounded in the commodity form informs his conception of government *qua* Rule of Law. For him, the question is not 'government or no government', but what principles of government can be established to preserve best competition in society. It is a question of strictly dictating the sphere of government intervention rather than its scale. Hayek argued that contra nineteenth-century discussions that miscast the dilemma as one of 'liberty versus law' ('as John Locke had already made clear, there can be no liberty without law'), the real question for liberals is properly 'what kind of law?', to which the answer must be the Rule of Law,

> general principles laid down beforehand, the 'rules of the game' which enable individuals to foresee how the coercive apparatus of the state will be used, or what he and his fellow-citizens will be allowed to do, or made to do, in stated circumstances. (Hayek, 2001 (1944), pp. fn1, 86)

The Rule of Law establishes the scope for government rule-making, which under liberal theory must be 'formal', established in advance, entirely divorced from specific outcomes or the interests of any particular people (Hayek, 2001 (1944), pp. 76–77). The moment the state attempts to affect specific outcomes it becomes partisan or discriminatory (Hayek, 2001 (1944), p. 80).

The Rule of Law thus implies enormous limits to the legislative authority of government, excluding any 'non-formal' government policies designed for specific outcomes that might differentially affect groups or individuals (Hayek, 2001 (1944), p. 87), though it does not preclude the expansion of a strong state in the name of competition. As he underscores: 'The important thing is that the rule enables us to predict other people's behaviour correctly, and this requires that it should apply to all cases – even if in a particular instance we feel it to be unjust' (Hayek, 2001 (1944), p. 83). This standard is one that can be continually invoked, furthermore, to structure and discipline government action: liberalism, Hayek argues, 'does not deny, but even emphasises, that, in order that competition should work beneficially, a carefully thought-out legal framework is required, and that neither the existing nor the past legal rules are free from grave defects' (Hayek, 2001 (1944), pp. 37–38).

In sum, in radical opposition to Polanyi, for Hayek the market is the basis for liberty precisely due to the way in which abstract equivalence 'disembeds' the individual from societal contexts that deny his autonomy. He extends this notion to his conception of the state, which to maintain this logic of non-discrimination must itself follow a parallel conception of the Rule of Law: the Rule of Law extrapolates the principle of individual liberty via the logic of rational calculation to defend a government organized around the principle of competition.

Foucault: neoliberalism as the end of the 'commodity effect'

Building on his reading of Hayek and others, Foucault argued that the neoliberal turn towards competition displaced altogether the 'commodity effect'.

The society regulated by reference to the market that the neo-liberals are thinking about is a society in which the regulatory principle should not be so much the exchange of commodities as the mechanisms of competition. It is these mechanisms that should have the greatest possible surface and depth and should also occupy the greatest possible volume in society. *This means that what is sought is not a society subject to the commodity effect, but a society subject to the dynamic of competition.* Not a supermarket society, but an enterprise society. The *homo oeconomicus* sought after is not the man of exchange or man the consumer; he is the man of enterprise and production. (Foucault, 2008, p. 147, emphasis added)

Like Polanyi, Foucault outlines an argument about the subordination of society to the economy, not however in terms of the imperative against commodifying natural entities, but rather through the reconstruction of political subjectivity from the subject of right to that of interest, reflected in the redefinition of *homo economicus* from the subject of exchange to the subject of competition.

Foucault argued that the neoliberal move to understanding subjectivity in terms of the calculation of interest was constitutive of the shift that allowed it to be seen as responsive to external conditions rather than naturally given. Further, via this move neoliberalism also posits all rationality as tantamount to economic calculus; for it 'Homo oeconomicus is someone who accepts reality' (Foucault, 2008, p. 269). Neoliberalism's 'behaviouralist' shift moves the subject of market society from classical liberalism's 'man of exchange' to an understanding of *homo economicus* as an entrepreneur of himself (Foucault, 2008, p. 252).

Associated with such assumptions, the *raison d'état* of neoliberal governmentality becomes the generalization of the logic of market competition in all spheres of public policy, assuming and producing citizenship defined by (the neoliberal) *homo economicus*. The evolution of neoliberal political theory over the twentieth-century from the early post-war *Ordo* school in Germany to the Chicago School in the U.S. some decades later involves an intensification of the role of the state in constructing *homo economicus* and subordinating 'society' to the economic. As Lemke summarizes the argument:

> Whereas the *Ordo*-liberals in West Germany pursued the idea of governing society in the name of the economy, the U.S. neo-liberals attempt to re-define the social sphere as a form of the economic domain. The model of rational-economic action serves as a principle for justifying and limiting governmental action, in which context government itself becomes a sort of enterprise whose task it is to universalize competition and invent market-shaped systems of action for individuals, groups and institutions. (Lemke, 2001, p. 197)[2]

Foucault includes Hayek's conception of law and state in his analysis of the transformation of neoliberal subjectivity, though always referring to it in terms of 'Rule of law *in the economic order*', giving the impression that Hayek's project involved rules specific to administering the economic sector rather than a fully formal theory of law and state (Foucault, 2008, p. 169). This is interesting because it forecloses a full analysis of the 'commodity form of law' that Lukács' Marxian analysis does not (discussed below).

In *The Birth of Biopolitics*, Foucault diverges from Marx in a number of explicit and implicit ways that underscore the 'ideational' rather than material nature of his commitments.[3] On a fundamental level, Foucault used the categories of production and consumption in an extremely broad sense, with no direct relationship to material labour: 'The man of consumption, insofar as he consumes, is a producer. What does he produce? Well, quite simply, he produces his own satisfaction' (Foucault, 2008, p. 252). Foucault casts this as a qualitatively new condition, beyond the scope of both classical political-economic (including Marx, presumably) as well as sociological theory, which 'have no value in relation to an analysis of consumption in the neo-liberal terms of the activity of production' (Foucault, 2008, p. 252). He continues, 'So, even if there really is a return to the idea of *homo oeconomicus* as the analytical grid of economic activity, there is a complete change in the conception of this *homo oeconomicus*' (Foucault, 2008, p. 252). The production/consumption metaphor is in fact an expression of neoliberal rational calculus, and thus public policy can also be cast in the same terms (Foucault, 2008, p. 256).[4]

Foucault indeed argued that the neoliberal turn evidenced capitalism had moved beyond the conditions of Marx's analysis: 'if there is something like a return in neo-liberal politics, it is certainly not a return to the governmental practice of *laissez-faire*, and it is not a return to the kind of market society that Marx denounced at the beginning of Book I of Capital' (Foucault, 2008, p. 147). However, the limitations of Marxism extend back further, to the 'Weberian turn' associated with the 'movement from capital to capitalism, from the logic of contradiction to the division between the rational and the irrational' (Foucault, 2008, p. 105). In not following that turn per se, Marxian analysis missed the significance of the 'institutional', which Foucault credits neoliberals with understanding in their attention to social construction (Foucault, 2008, p. 176).

Foucault's most fundamental critique of Marxism in *The Birth of Biopolitics*, however, would seem to be its 'singularity', associated with a kind of economic determinism, which forecloses its potential to examine the institutional and the juridical:

> ... if we accept that in a Marxist type of analysis, in the broadest sense of the term, it is the economic logic of capital and its accumulation that is determinant in the history of capitalism, then you can see that in fact there can only be one capitalism since there is only one logic of capital. There can only be one capitalism which is defined precisely by the single necessary logic of its economy and regarding which all we can say is that this institution has favored it and this other institution has impeded it. (Foucault, 2008, p. 164)

Foucault juxtaposes this 'capitalist singularity' to the dynamic of 'economic-institutional transformations, which open up a field of possibilities for it' (Foucault, 2008, p. 165). These concerns can be found in Foucault's argument that Marxism (more importantly than potentially failing to have a theory of state) lacks a theory of 'governmental reason' or 'the definition of what a governmental rationality would be in socialism, that is to say, a reasonable and calculable measure of the extent, modes, and objectives of governmental action' (Foucault, 2008, pp. 91–92).

In sum, Foucault argues in *The Birth of Biopolitics* that neoliberalism represents an evolution of ideational and institutional factors that signal capitalism has moved beyond the parameters of 'the commodity effect' of classical Marxist analysis, which is limited in its appreciation of the relationship between subjectivity/rationality (particularly vis-à-vis the logics of its socially constructed dimensions), the institutional and the political-economic.

Market / society in Lukács' history and class consciousness

Lukács' *History and Class Consciousness* offers yet a fourth position on the problematic of market society, one that predates and in many ways anticipates the concerns of the other works discussed here. It shares Polanyi's concern with the material effects of commodification; and like Foucault, it is concerned with the (re)construction of individual subjectivity under market society. However, in contrast to the incommensurate positions these two critiques establish methodologically, Lukács does not consider the material and the subjective unrelated concerns and, indeed, his analysis of their articulation offers insight into Hayek's work and its political purchase. The key to this relationship is a Marxian appreciation of the social relations immanent to the commodity form.

Lukács offers a consideration of the processes, nature and implications of the generalization of commodity fetishism beyond the initial stages of capitalist exchange. He argued that there is a qualitative difference between the presence of the commodity form as one among many *in* society and the commodity as the *universal structuring principle of society*. Drawing on Marx's arguments in volume one of *Capital*, he uses the trope of 'reification' to capture the historically 'molecular' transformations of commodification in reconstructing societies towards capitalist social relations. Barter and exchange in pre-capitalist societies begin a process of abstracting things from their 'use-values' to their 'exchange-values', which begins to have a 'disintegrating' effect on community, a process that gradually transforms the social fabric as the commodity structure moves from being particular to specific objects to the universal social form (Lukács, 1967, p. 85). The commodity then, classically, becomes the embodiment of the inversion of the social and material relations: the social relations between labourers appears 'objectively' as the things they have produced, while the objective relationship between such products appears as a social relation in the act of exchange (Lukács, 1967, pp. 86, drawing on Marx (1990/1867)).

The process by which commodities move from being an element within society to its universal form is a function of both the material and the ideological/subjective development of capitalism. On the material side, the process of commodification follows a self-reproducing logic that no one person can affect, not even when armed with the awareness it is happening.

> The laws governing these objects are indeed gradually discovered by man, but *even so they confront him as invisible forces that generate their own power*. The individual can use his knowledge of these laws to his own advantage, but *he is not able to modify the process by his own activity*. (Lukács, 1967, p. 87, emphasis added)

These social relations in turn affect individual subjectivity: confronted with the ways in which the commodity form abstracts the product of work from the labourer and subjects it to the logic of market exchange, the individual understands his or her own activity through the commodity form (Lukács, 1967, p. 87). The mutually constitutive material and subjective dimensions of the commodity form that Lukács' work illuminates may be associated to at least two corollaries significant to the discussion above. The first involves a critique of the logic of Polanyi's commodity fiction for failing to understand the structural consequences of the commodity form for capitalist social relations. The second involves an implicit critique of Foucault's conception of neoliberal *homo economicus* understood to signal a stage of capitalism beyond the commodity effect; on the contrary, for Lukács, the transformation of liberal thought is precisely an expression of the commodity effect in its full significance.

The material imperatives of commodification

Lukács followed Marx in his critique of Proudhon, and by extension Polanyi's concept of the commodity fiction, in arguing that the process of commodification has an irreducible material dimension that cannot be overcome by 'normative fiat'. Polanyi, in positing two kinds of commodities, real and fictitious, seeks to separate the bad, *laissez-faire* capitalism (which wrongly commodifies 'uncommodifiable' fictitious commodities) from a good, social democratic capitalism (see Polanyi's discussion of Owen 1957, pp. 129, inter alia). His critique of Marxism was that it fell into liberal economism in accepting that land, labour and money could be commodified. The Marxian rejoinder is that the fact that land, labour and money are commodified under capitalism occurs not by the normative choice of any particular agent but is the result of a material logic that reproduces itself structurally. Thus, as Marx sought to illustrate in his critique of Proudhon, attempts to 'cheat' the logic of commodification, e.g. by replacing money with substitutes such as work-time coupons, are doomed to failure because they would ultimately end up turning effectively into money themselves, differing in name only ('and all the previous contradictions would return in force' (Marx, Grundrisse vol. 28, p. 180, in: Jameson, 1990, pp. 95–96)). Put another way, though the Proudhonists and later Polanyi were able to identify certain systemic contradictions in bourgeois ideologies, they failed to appreciate the full material logic of and foundations for such ideologies, targeting the symptoms rather than the causes.[5]

In fact, Lukács addresses his work equally to liberal and vulgar Marxist political-economists: both groups, he argued, fail to understand that knowledge itself reflects its embeddedness in historically constituted social relations (Lukács, 1967, p. 33). For Lukács, 'consciousness' is rooted in historical-material conditions, and the discovery of society is a product of the way the commodity form structures capitalist social relations; the presumption of formal equality in the exchange relation allows for the progressive disembedding of 'man' [sic] from nature and only then is 'society' properly a phenomenon that can be recognized as such (Lukács, 1967, p. 19). The implications of this point might thus be framed as: analogous to the way in which Polanyi correctly identifies the symptoms of the commodity fiction but misses a full account of the structural nature of the commodity form, his emphasis on the discovery of society through political economy focuses on its emergence in bourgeois thought (the 'symptom') rather than its true material origins in the formal equality of abstract exchange (the real cause).

The material foundations of bourgeois ideology

This conception of knowledge as historically embedded extends to other concepts associated with the emergence of capitalist social relations and the formal equality of abstract exchange; most importantly for the discussion here, bourgeois conceptions of freedom and equality, which are also 'real and objective and are organically generated by the market system itself' (Jameson, 1990, p. 96). In this sense, from Lukács' perspective, there is some validity to Hayek's argument about the relationship between liberty and the commodity form: capitalist social relations displace feudal society with a 'substantive' appeal to freedom that is at once ideological *and* material. And while the bourgeois notion of freedom at work with this transformation is ultimately unsatisfactory to Lukács because it involves a hyper-individualized, alienated subject, neither can it be addressed through Polanyi's appeal to a transhistorical notion of the 'social'.

Indeed, Lukács anticipates Hayek's arguments for the 'commodity form of law' in drawing on Weber's argument that rational calculation becomes a formal requirement for the juridical under modern capitalism. Weber argues that the structure of modern legal reality, whatever its specific origins in particular jurisdictions, is the development of a system 'formally capable of being generalised so as to relate to every possible situation in life and it is susceptible to prediction and calculation.' (Weber cited in Lukács, 1967, p. 96). The universalization of rational calculation expresses, for Weber, the organizational foundation of modern capitalist production, which also demands the bureaucratic state and corresponding juridical system. From this perspective, when Hayek makes the argument for the Rule of Law he is merely giving voice to the intensification of the 'commodity effect': articulating a reconciliation of liberal legal principles to more profoundly reified, commodified social relations.

The material logics of homo economicus

Lukács' discussion thus suggests Foucault misunderstands Marx in casting him as relying on a 'rational actor' to the exclusion of a Weberian problematic of 'irrationality': both are immanent to

Marx's work and indeed capitalist social relations. This tension is a structural feature of capitalism in the sense that on the one hand, the environment proscribes that individual actors pursue 'rational', 'private economic calculation' to meet their own needs; at the same time, at the systemic level, accumulation occurs through competition, which requires an 'irrational' degree of unpredictability: a fully rational system would eliminate the possibilities for such competition. As Lukács clarifies:

> This irrationality - this highly problematic - 'systematisation' of the whole which diverges, *qualitatively and in principle* from the laws regulating the parts, is more than just a postulate, a presupposition essential to the workings of a capitalist economy. It is at the same time the product of the capitalist division of labour. (Lukács, 1967, pp. 102–103)

He continues, in sympathy with Polanyi's concerns, 'It has already been pointed out that the division of labour disrupts every organically unified process of work and life and breaks it down into its components' (Lukács, 1967, p. 103).

Reading rationality/irrationality as a systemic quality of capitalism poses a certain challenge to Foucault's periodization of *homo economicus,* which is grounded in a perceived shift from the former to the latter. The idea that there is no break in such periodization underscores the most fundamental implication of Lukács' work *vis-à-vis* Foucault's: that the transformation of *homo economicus,* far from moving away from the commodity effect, reflects its intensification, or more properly in Lukács' framework, the ongoing reification of subjectivity under capitalist social relations. For Lukács, the subject of capitalism, is inherently (has always been) the subject of interest, as the process of commodification operates on subjectivity from the outset to produce that result. His description of those effects, which does lead towards a 'classical Marxian' conception of alienation, nevertheless also captures something close to Foucault's rendering of *homo economicus.*

> [The evolution of the commodity relation] stamps its imprint upon the whole consciousness of man; *his qualities and abilities are no longer an organic part of his personality, they are things which he can 'own' or 'dispose of' like the various objects of the external world.* And there is no natural form in which human relations can be cast, no way in which man can bring his physical and psychic 'qualities' into play without their being subjected increasingly to this reifying process. (Lukács, 1967, p. 100, emphasis added)

Parallel to Polanyi's confusion of 'symptom' and 'disease' with respect to the nature of commodification, one might say that Foucault's analysis, in implicitly attributing agency to changing liberal discourses in reconstructing the subjectivity of *homo eocnomicus,* confuses the symptom (liberal discourses of ideological justification) for the cause (the process of reification acting on subjectivity). To be clear, such a metaphor of symptom and cause should not be read with respect to Lukács' work as one of crude positivist (or vulgar materialist) cause and effect. Rather, in the same way that Hayek's articulation of the Rule of Law expresses a certain logic immanent to capitalist social relations at a formal level that had not yet been, and may never be, realized 'purely' in historical practice, the rearticulation of 'classical' liberal rights as neoliberal interests reflects a logic immanent to the longstanding role of competition in capitalist social relations.[6]

Conclusions

The point of departure of this discussion was a conference on the common anniversary of the publication of *The Great Transformation* and *The Road to Serfdom* in the context of a recurrence of global economic crisis. Both of these texts illustrated the limitations of 'classical' *laissez-faire* liberalism, Polanyi with an eye to discrediting liberalism while Hayek sought to rescue it, rearticulating it in what would become understood as neoliberal theory, by making a case that the foundations of liberty ultimately lie in a competitive market society, established though a highly 'formal' conception of the Rule of Law. Before the 2008 global economic crisis, the academic literature critical of 'neoliberalism' articulated as such arguably saw a preponderance of attention to Foucauldian concerns of subjectivity and governmentality. The recurrence of crisis offered new ground for other positions critical of neoliberalism, particularly those concerned with the relationship between the material logics of accumulation and crisis, such as Polanyi's conception of the double movement. Indeed, the Foucauldian and the social democratic would now appear to represent the dominant spectrum of critique of neoliberalism, and express many common concerns (the historical emergence of markets, the 'epistemological' consequences of the 'birth of political economy' for governance), though they ultimately construct a division of labour around the material and the subjective through distinct methodological approaches. Such methodological differences certainly support the conclusion that these positions are incommensurate, yet their reception by critics of neoliberalism appears more complicated. While in some quarters they may be seen as wholly antagonistic, they are also often implicitly or explicitly combined under an apparent acceptance of the need for a methodological division of labour with respect to the material and the subjective.

Lukács' neglected work, however, recovers Marxian analysis from vulgar readings, sympathetic and hostile, and challenges the proposition that the subjective and the material are beyond methodological unification. Through an account of the historically-situated construction of knowledge, his approach in fact offers insight into the political traction that Hayek's arguments about liberty have in the context of reified capitalist social relations. Such understanding represents a blind spot for Polanyi and related approaches because of the way in which the ambivalent dimensions of capitalist social relations are externalized into a 'good' version of social-democratic market society that does not commit the error of the commodity fiction and the 'bad' *laissez-faire* capitalism that does, rather than appreciating the ambivalence is immanent to capitalism itself.

Further, Lukács' provides a framework for reading Hayek's conception of law as a formal / 'logical' expression of reification of the commodity form, a parallel blindspot, one might argue, in Foucault's conception of law *qua* veridiction. Here, too, the key lies in appreciating the ambivalent quality of law. For Lukács it indeed functions ideologically to naturalize certain 'limits of the possible'; while necessary for the state's legitimacy and its capacity to rule without constantly resorting to force, it also introduces a standard of judgement against which state power is assessed as more or less in accordance with the true nature of the existing socio-economic order. To wit, Lukács cites the role natural law played as a precursor to the bourgeois revolutions in providing the theory that was able to articulate the greater 'truth' of the emerging social order vis-à-vis the one it was in the course of displacing, both reflecting new circumstances and contributing their historical realization (Lukács, 1967, p. 257). Thus, *contra* Foucault, the law ultimately finds a potential limit in its correspondence to socio-material conditions, rather than functioning in a purely disciplinary capacity articulated to an ideational regime of truth.

Most fundamentally, however, Lukács offers the tools to consider the material and subjective effects of neoliberalism in a methodologically holistic manner, both facets of the process of reification immanent to capitalist social relations. In his analysis, commodification is not a normative problem to be addressed 'ethico-politically', but a material process that defies being so contained, though his analysis does not deny the grounds for a critique of the anti-social nature of its disembedding effects. Furthermore, Lukács' work offers an account of how the 'commodity effect' structures subjectivity from the outset, placing *homo economicus* in historical material context, by reading competition as immanent to capitalist exchange relations even if these are instantiated in a molecular fashion over time.

Notes

1. Here 'post-modern' is used heuristically to signal a tradition of critique predominantly concerned with the question of subjectivity and that propose alternatives to 'modern' approaches to historiography, both characteristics of Foucault's reading of neoliberalism. Debates about the exact parameters of postmodernism and questions of how *The Birth of Biopolitics* should be read within his oeuvre overall, lie outside the scope of this paper.

2. In Foucault's own words:

   > ... American neo-liberalism seeks instead [of the German emphasis on the state regulation of prices] to extend the rationality of the market, the schemas of analysis it offers and the decision-making criteria it suggests, to domains which are not exclusively or not primarily economic: the family and the birth rate, for example, or delinquency and penal policy. (Foucault, 2008, p. 323)

   In other words, there is an intensification of the role of the state precisely because it becomes an agent for the promotion of market logic within society (Foucault, 2008, p. 247), and in the expansion of the exercise of state power through the Law ('there is an inflation of forms and bodies of knowledge, of discourse, a multiplication of authorities and decision-making elements, and the parasitic invasion of the sentence in the name of the law' (Foucault, 2008, p. 250)).

3. The nature of this discussion involves focus on a specific text and space does not permit a comprehensive examination of the now sizable literature on the relationship between Foucault and Marx. Yet, given its focus on neoliberalism, I would suggest that *The Birth of Biopolitics* represents a particularly interesting text for considering Foucault's reading of Marx / Marxism. Broadly, in any case, the discussion here is sympathetic to Étienne Balibar's conclusion that of the four paradigms for considering the relationship between Marx and Foucault – articulation (borrowing from each), subsumption (reading one through the other), 'meta-theory' (the proposition that 'the oeuvres of Marx and Foucault the expressions of one same underlying theory, and as this theory is brought to light Marx and Foucault are shown to be variations on the same problematic') and the notion that they are irreconcilable, the last is most compelling (Balibar, 2015, as cited in; Keucheyan, 2016) (see also, inter alia: Bidet, 2016; Macherey, 2014).

4. Foucault did ask a question in the concluding lecture that seems to run counter to his previous assessment of Marxism:

   > Similarly, we can say that government regulated according to the truth also has not disappeared. For after all, what in the end is something like Marxism if not the pursuit of a type of governmentality which will certainly be pegged to a rationality, but to a rationality which is not the rationality of individual interests, but the rationality of history progressively manifesting itself as truth? (Foucault, 2008, p. 313)

   However, when considered with his arguments against historicism, this would not seem to be much of a mitigating observation vis-à-vis the previous claim. Furthermore, in the passage cited above, it is clear that Foucault relies on a clearly non-Marxian, socially-disembedded definition of capital (Foucault, 2008, p. 165).

5. As Marx elaborates in the *Grundrisse* (Marx, 1973 (1861)),

   > What distinguishes [the Proudhonists] from the bourgeois apologists is, on the one hand, their awareness of the contradictions inherent in the system and, on the other, their utopianism, manifest in their failure to grasp the inevitable difference between the real and the ideal shape of bourgeois society, and the consequent desire to undertake the superfluous task of changing the ideal expression itself back into reality, whereas it is in fact merely the photographic image [*Lichtbild*] of this reality. (cited in: Jameson, 1990, p. 96)

6. Indeed, Jameson suggests, broadly informed by Lukács' approach, that (contra Foucault's assessment) Marxism does follow a theory of 'governmentality'. As he frames it, the conventional charge that Marxism lacks 'any autonomous political reflection as such' is true, but represents a strength, not a weakness. Thus Marxism is not 'a political philosophy of the Weltanschauung variety', i.e. of the same type as categories such as liberalism, conservatism, populism, but in fact is focused on questions of economic

cooperation and organization, not organized around an abstracted political end per se. Thus, for Jameson, the true bourgeois 'homologue' to Marxism is not fascism, as is so often asserted, but neoliberalism: as both privilege questions of economic organization over political philosophy. As he formulates his proposition, 'we have much in common with the neo-liberals, indeed virtually everything – save the essentials!' (Jameson, 1990, pp. 99–100).

Disclosure statement

No potential conflict of interest was reported by the author.

References

Balibar, É. (2015). L'anti-Marx de Michel Foucault. In C. Laval, L. Paltrinieri, & F. Taylan (Eds.), *Marx and Foucault: Lectures, usages, confrontations* (pp. 84–104). Paris: La Découverte.

Bidet, J. (2016). *Foucault with Marx*. London: Zed Books.

Dale, G. (2010). *Karl Polanyi: The limits of the market*. London: Polity Press.

Foucault, M. (2003). Governmentality. In P. Rabinow, & N. Rose (Eds.), *The essential Foucault*. New York: New Press.

Foucault, M. (2007). *Security, territory, population: Lectures at the Collège de France, 1977-78*. London: Palgrave Macmillan.

Foucault, M. (2008). *"The birth of biopolitics": lectures at the Collège de France 1978-1979*. London: Palgrave Macmillan.

Hayek, F. A. (2001 (1944)). *The road to serfdom*. London: Routledge.

Jameson, F. (1990). 'Postmodernism and the market'. In R. Miliband, & L. Panitch (Eds.), *The socialist register 1990: The retreat of the intellectuals* (pp. 95–110). London: Merlin Press.

Keucheyan, R. (2016). Marx and Foucault: autour d'un livre récent. *Contretemps*.

Lemke, T. (2001). 'The birth of bio-politics': Michel Foucault's lecture at the Collège de France on neo-liberal governmentality. *Economy and Society, 30*(2), 190–207.

Lukács, G. (1967). *History and class consciousness: Studies in Marxist DIalectics* (R. Livingston, Trans.). London: Merlin Press.

Macherey, P. (2014). *Le sujet des normes*. Paris: Amsterdam.

Marx, K. (1973 (1861)). *Grundrisse: Foundations of the critique of political economy* (M. Nicolaus, Trans.). London: Penguin.

Marx, K. (1990 (1867)). *Capital*, Volume I, intro. E. Mandel, trans. B. Fowkes. London: Penguin.

Polanyi, K. (1957). *The great transformation: The political and economic origins of our time*. Boston: Beacon Press.

Selwyn, B., & Miyamura, S. (2013). Class struggle or embedded markets? Marx, Polanyi and the meanings and possibilities of social transformation. *New Political Economy, 19*(5), 639–661.

The great trasformismo: Antonio Gramsci and Karl Polanyi on the rise of Fascism

Adam David Morton 🆔

ABSTRACT

The purpose of this article is to explore the commonalities and differences between Karl Polanyi and Antonio Gramsci in their assessment of the origins of fascism as located within the rise of capitalism in the nineteenth century and its structural impasse in the twentieth century. Specifically, the aim is to trace a set of associations between Polanyi and Gramsci on the transformations wrought across the states-system of Europe prior to the crises that engulfed capitalism leading to the rise of fascism in the twentieth century. Focusing on the class structures that emerged out of the expansion of capitalism across Europe in the nineteenth century reveals that there was less a 'great transformation' in terms of a rupture with the past through the rise of liberal capitalism. Rather, there was more a slow and protracted process of class restoration known as passive revolution, or a 'Great Trasformismo', referring to the molecular absorption of class contradictions marking the consolidation and expansion of capitalist social relations. In sum, it is argued that *The Great Transformation* is understood better if read through the epoch of passive revolution, or The Great *Trasformismo*, which entailed the restoration and maintenance of class dominance through state power. This approach therefore opens up questions, rather than forecloses answers, about the historical geographies constituting the spaces and places of the political economy of modern capitalism.

What is fascism, observed on an international scale? It is the attempt to resolve the problems of production and exchange with machine-guns and pistol-shots. (Antonio Gramsci, 'Italy and Spain'. *L'Ordine Nuovo* [1921])

Fascism is that form of revolutionary solution which keeps capitalism untouched. (Karl Polanyi, 'Fascism and Marxian Terminology', *New Britain* [1934])

Picture Vienna, 1923. Within the group led by Ludwig von Mises, known as the Privatseminar, with close links to the Rockefeller Foundation, there existed of course Friedrich von Hayek who would later hone his analysis of socialism and fascism as common variants of the suppression of liberal individual freedom (Hayek, 1944/2011). Elsewhere across the city was Karl Polanyi working on the newspaper *Österreichische Volkswirt* in dialogue with currents of Marxism, including the Austro-Marxists of Otto Bauer and Rudolf Hilferding, practitioners of revolutionary humanism (see Dale, 2014). 'While Hayek looked back on the liberalism of the Belle Époque of pre-war Imperial Vienna', Kari Polanyi Levitt (2013, p. 24) tells us, 'Polanyi admired the Red Vienna of the 1920s as a remarkable achievement of the model of municipal socialism'.

Meanwhile, the same Vienna witnesses the arrival of Antonio Gramsci on 3 December 1923. The previous year Gramsci was in Moscow attending the Fourth Congress of the Communist International (5 November–5 December 1922) liaising, among others, with Leon Trotsky who would later recall that in Italy 'with the sole exception of Gramsci, the Communist Party wouldn't even allow of the possibility of the fascists' seizing power. Once the proletarian revolution had suffered defeat and capitalism had kept its ground, and the counter-revolution had triumphed, how could there be any further kind of counter-revolutionary upheaval?' (Trotsky, 1932/2004, p. 221). Working within the Comintern in Vienna alongside figures such as Victor Serge, prior to his return to Italy in May 1924, Gramsci completed articles for the *Correspondance Internationale* on the Italian domestic situation and fascism. Under the shadow of the 'March on Rome' (October 1922) with the fascists coming to power and Mussolini as Prime Minister, Gramsci clandestinely attended the Third National Congress of the Communist Party of Italy (PCd'I) in Lyons (20–26 January 1926), leading to the 'Lyons Theses' on the necessity of 'united front' tactics to combat fascism. After the days of Red Vienna, Karl Polanyi would write in *The Great Transformation* that 'to comprehend German fascism, we must revert to Ricardian England' (Polanyi, 1944/1957, p. 30). As Fred Block clarifies, the second 'great transformation' of the rise of fascism can only be understood in its relationship with the rise of market liberalism, as the first 'great transformation' (Block, 2002, p. xxii). Writing also in the days after Red Vienna in his *Prison Notebooks*, Antonio Gramsci would similarly question whether fascism is precisely a new liberalism under modern conditions. 'If liberalism was the form of "passive revolution" specific to the nineteenth century, wouldn't fascism be, precisely, the form of passive revolution specific to the twentieth century?' (Gramsci, 2007, p. 378, Q8§236).

The purpose of this article is to explore the commonalities and differences between Karl Polanyi and Antonio Gramsci in their assessment of the origins of fascism located within the rise of the 'new "liberalism"' of the nineteenth century and its structural impasse in the twentieth century. Specifically, the aim is to trace a set of associations between Polanyi and Gramsci on their analyses of the transformations wrought across the states-system of Europe prior to the crises that engulfed capitalism leading to the rise of fascism in the twentieth-century. As Sandra Halperin (2004, p. xvii) details in *War and Social Change in Modern Europe*:

> What if the change in the form of the state that occurred as part of the 'first transformation' represented not the rise to power of a 'new' and liberal industrial capitalist class but the means by which landed wealth consolidated its power over the state and, as a result, over the economy?

Focusing on the class structures that emerged out of the expansion of capitalism across Europe in the nineteenth century reveals that there was less a 'great transformation' in terms of a revolutionary break with the past through the rise of liberal capitalism. Rather, as will be argued, there was more of a slow process of class restoration or a 'great *trasformismo*', referring to the protracted molecular absorption of class contradictions marking the consolidation and expansion of capitalist social relations. The decomposition of these weak social formations of bourgeois rule, riven with surviving dynastic, aristocratic, and church interests within the states-system of the market economy, then enabled the conjunctural historical conditions of possibility that led to the emergence of fascism and the restoration of capitalism in the twentieth-century. In sum, it is argued that *The Great Transformation* is understood better if read through the great *trasformismo* of passive revolution, referring to the restoration and maintenance of class dominance through state intervention. The article proceeds in two main stages. The first section focuses on the account of the birth of the liberal creed, market economy, and the rise of fascism within *The Great Transformation* while attentive to Karl Polanyi's wider writings on the essence of fascism. Next, a reading of fascism is developed through a specific engagement with the writings of Antonio Gramsci to focus on the determinate market of capitalism and its transformation in the epoch of passive revolution. Anticipating some of the conclusions of the article, my argument should be regarded as a contribution to the intra- and inter-disciplinary endeavour of heterodox *comparative economy* (Peck, 2012, p. 114, 123). Here my contribution lies in considering the rise of fascism as a congenital bias for reaction within capitalism, which has a bearing on present circumstances of right-wing populism. In so doing, it will be possible to open up the socio-economic imagination to the complex affinities to Marxism within Polanyi and whether his writing 'can only be understood as a continuation of certain ideas within the Marxist tradition' (Block & Somers, 1984, p. 76); or whether he developed an original Marxist elaboration and analysis of capitalist dynamics (Burawoy, 2003, p. 255n.30); or if he was increasingly pulled out of the Marxist orbit (Dale, 2010, p. 384).

From the birth of the liberal creed to the essence of fascism

In a trilogy of contributions to the weekly *New Britain*, in 1934, Polanyi provides a brief but compelling sketch of fascism in dialogue with Marxist concepts and terminology. The term revolution within Marxist debates, he conjectures, has been too strictly confined to the sweeping changes within the economic realm. Instead, Polanyi wants to reveal a focus on a dialectic that structures fascism in terms of both its convulsive epochal implications *and* the continuations of capitalism it represents. In the first in this trilogy, he states, 'fascism is that form of revolutionary situation which keeps capitalism untouched' (Polanyi, 1934a, p. 128).[1] In clarifying, he means not literally 'untouched' but as an upheaval that provides 'the possibility of a capitalism "reformed", so as to make it comply with some measure of planning and security of employment as a contradiction in terms' (Polanyi, 1934a, p. 129). Like a thread left dangling, Polanyi remarks that, 'no society actually passes away before it has fully developed all its potentialities' (Polanyi, 1934b, p. 159), which is an unacknowledged but clear reference to Karl Marx's 'Preface' to *A Contribution to the Critique of Political Economy* commenting on the room for forward movement of a social order as long as further development of the productive forces is still possible. Echoing here Marx's statement that:

> No social order is ever destroyed before all the productive forces for which it is sufficient have been developed, and new superior relations of production never replace older ones before the material conditions for their existence have matured within the framework of the old society itself. Mankind thus inevitably sets itself only such tasks as it is able to solve, since closer examination will always show that the problem itself arises only when the material conditions for its solution are already present or at least in the course of formation. (Marx, 1859/1975, p. 426)

For Polanyi, in the third tranche of his restatement of Marxism, it is then concluded that fascism is the deadlock or impasse that is reached between capitalism and democracy when a class is unable to articulate leadership in defining a wider set of interests (Polanyi, 1934c, p. 188).

Written in the same conjuncture and with similar echoes is, of course, Otto Bauer's assessment of fascism as emblematic of a situation in which classes are in conflict but in provisional equilibrium, an unstable balance of forces, out of which the parasitic forms of capital come to constitute the ideology of fascism (Bauer, 1938/1978). With the embers of Red Vienna still glowing, Polanyi continues to elaborate on the 'essence' of fascism and its efforts to re-cast the structure of society both in terms of its philosophy and sociology. The formative principle, or essence, of fascism is the negation of society as a relationship of persons that defines its approach to history, science, morals, politics, economics and religion. 'This fascist philosophy is an effort to produce a vision of the world in which society is *not* a relationship of persons' (Polanyi, 1935, p. 370). In contrast to the philosophers of fascism of his day, Polanyi, therefore, elaborates a Marxist emphasis stating that 'the means of production must be controlled by the community. Then human society will be real, for it will be human: a relationship of persons' (Polanyi, 1935, p. 392), resonating again with Marx in this case thesis six from *Theses of Feuerbach*. Here it is detailed that the human essence is not an abstraction inherent in the individual but in the ensemble of social relations. It is this emphasis that Marx extends in the *loci classici* of *Capital* on the fetishism of the commodity-form when private labours appear not as direct social relations between persons at work but rather as material relations between persons and social relations between things (Marx, 1845/1975, p. 423; Marx, 1867/1990, p. 166). Finally fascism, for Polanyi, in terms of its sociological content, is linked to the liberalism of Ludwig von Mises, whereby 'fascism is condoned as the safeguard of liberal economics' (Polanyi, 1935, p. 392); or in von Mises' own words in those conditions where 'fascism and similar movements ... saved European civilisation', so 'the merit that fascism has thereby won itself will live on eternally in history' (1927/1962, p. 51).

These reflections reveal a fresh approach to the critique of political economy and fascism evident in Polanyi's early writings. Moving from these early rethinkings of Marxism, my argument is that these reflections can be productively connected to *The Great Transformation* in order to reveal Polanyi's relevance to understanding the slow transformation of capitalism in and through fascism. Missing from the extant literature on the rise and persistence of the far-right from a *longue durée* perspective is, precisely, the presence of Karl Polanyi (see Saull, Anievas, Davidson, & Fabry, 2014). Hence the importance of analysing how these early beginnings on the origins of fascism are rendered within the analysis of *The Great Transformation* in order to understand more fully the far-right as a path-dependent pathology within capitalism. In this respect, my assessment covers three dimensions. First, a focus on liberalism within the account of 'market economy' is developed. Here attention is granted to how, in noting the militant creed and the utopian springs of market economy, Polanyi assessed the dogma of *laissez-faire* liberalism that was enforced by the state and based on centrally organised and controlled interventionism. Second, this focus on liberalism is wedded to a theory of the 'survivals' of feudalism with Polanyi appreciating the great influence wielded by landed interests in Eastern Europe and the survival of feudal forms of property in Central and Western Europe during the nineteenth century that came to play a key role in the impasse of market economy leading to fascism. Finally, there is a focus on how, through a gearshift in the history of social change to break the institutional deadlock of liberalism, fascism emerged in Europe. 'The fascist solution of the impasse reached by liberal capitalism', argues Polanyi (1944/1957, p. 237), 'can be described as a reform of market economy achieved at the price of the extirpation of all democratic institutions'. So, in *The Great Transformation*, fascism is resolutely analysed as revitalising the economic system of market economy and therefore cannot be simply ascribed to local or aberrant causes, as no country is deemed to be immune to its emergence. These three strands on the liberal creed and the essence of fascism are then a platform from which to launch into an assessment of fascism as the passive revolution of the twentieth-century in the reflections of Antonio Gramsci in the second main section.

Liberalism and market economy

The militant creed and the utopian springs of the dogma of *laissez-faire* are at the centre of *The Great Transformation*. 'There was nothing natural about *laissez-faire*', Polanyi (1944/1957, p. 139) famously stated, 'free markets could never have come into being merely by allowing things to take their course'. State enforcement was rightly recognised as intrinsic to the constitution of *laissez-faire* to the extent that 'the road to the free market was opened by an enormous increase in continuous, centrally organised and controlled interventionism' (Polanyi, 1944/1957, p. 140). Almost at a meridional point in *The Great Transformation*, then, in the chapter on the birth of the liberal creed is a critique of liberalism, with Ludwig von Mises as a key target. Hence, Polanyi (1944/1957, p. 141) stated:

> even those who wished most ardently to free the state from all unneccesary duties, and whose whole philosophy demanded the restriction of state activities, could not but entrust the self-same state with the new powers, organs, and instruments for the establishment of *laissez-faire*.

It was Polanyi's hope – almost a wish-fulfillment – that the progress of the utopia of the 'self-regulating' market would be stopped by the double movement, a spontaneous countermovement reacting against economic liberalism to deliver the self-protection of society. However, primed to contest such an insurgent emergence in the form of the double movement were the anti-liberal means of interventionism through which the state could draw on the use of the force of law, especially violently, to establish the preconditions of the self-regulating market and sustain its maintenance (Polanyi, 1944/1957, p. 149). Alongside the famous maxim that '*laissez-faire* was planned; planning was not' (Polanyi, 1944/1957, p. 141), Polanyi offers a useful reminder to political economists that the use of anti-liberal means of state interventionism to establish liberal means of *laissez-faire* is a constant in the authoring of capitalism. As Polanyi states 'economic liberals must and will unhesitatingly call for the intervention of the state in order to establish it, and once established, in order to maintain it' (Polanyi, 1944/1957, p. 149), especially through recourse to authoritarian state power. The rise and fall of the market economy were then posited in *The Great Transformation* through the dominance of the crude commodity fictions of land, labour and money in their striving to become the sole director of the fate of human beings and the natural environment (Polanyi, 1944/1957, p. 73). The result of the 'self-regulating' mechanism of the market was then famously summarised as, 'instead of economy being embedded in social relations, social relations are embedded in the economic system', in circumstances when society runs as an adjunct to the market (Polanyi, 1944/1957, p. 57).

However, the social content of the market economy – meaning the tracking of the historically specific social relations that are constitutive of the economy – are unspecified. Statements such as 'the market mechanism became determinative for the life of the body social' are alluring but obscure more than they reveal (Polanyi, 1947/1968, p. 63). This is also an accurate assessment of Polanyi's rejection of a 'formal' meaning of the economic in preference for a 'substantive' meaning of the economic as an instituted process (see Polanyi, 1953/1959; Polanyi, 1957). With the formal meaning of the economic dismissed due to its narrowness defined by the logic of rational action, formal economics, and rules governed by the price mechanism in constituting a market system, Polanyi attempted to offer an alternative tool box in the form of a substantive meaning of the economic. This involved emphasising *activities* that may be called economic (fumbling towards a social relational appreciation); *institutions* that contain a concentration of such actions (muddling through to a recognition of structuring conditions); and economic *elements* encompassing ecological, technological and societal aspects of the economy relating the substantive process of production to the wider realms of the economy (twiddling around with the production conditions of capitalism and the capitalisation of nature) (Polanyi, 1953/1959, p. 167). This striving towards a more integral theory of the economy as an instituted process would then supposedly enable recognition of the *shifting place* occupied by the economy in society, referring to the manner in which the economic process is instituted at different times and places (Polanyi, 1953/1959, p. 168). However laudable the endeavour is to trace the trajectory of the shifting place of the economy in society through the instituted processes of embeddedness, Polanyi never comes to terms with the particularising aspects of the social foundations of modern capitalism. With Maurice Godelier (1986, p. 200–2001, 204), then, then is no theory of price formation, of profits, of the accumulation of capital so that Polanyi was:

> condemned in advance to being unable to do more than describe the shifting place of the economy in various societies, without ever really being able to pose the theoretical problem of its effect upon the functioning and evolution of societies, and therefore of its role in history.

The theory of the embeddedness of economic life espoused becomes wanting in delivering an explanation of the emergence of the market economy and the composition of the market as a social form (Wood, 1999, pp. 21–26). The consequence is that of a theoretical dualism – or the ontologically exterior treatment – of 'economy' and 'society': between an 'economy' embedded in social relations or social relations embedded in the 'economy' (see Morton, 2013 on the pitfalls of ontological exteriority). In concurrence with Kurtuluş Gemici (2007), viewing embeddedness as a gradational concept still means delineating 'spheres' of economy and society, as the market economy becomes the dominant economic system in history, which presupposes the economy as an autonomous sphere without social content and reifies the market economy in the way that mainstream economics conceptualises it. Hence there is a resurrection of the conceptualisation of the 'economic' and the 'social' as belonging to different social spheres (see Krippner, 2001). The implication is that there is still an assumption of separateness existing between the spaces of economic relations *and* social relations expressed in the market economy. That said, Polanyi's pursuit of a theory of the origins of fascism in the survivals of feudalism existing within market economy merits sustained attention. In *The Great Transformation*, argued Polanyi (1935, p. 392, 367), 'Liberals of the Mises school urge that the interference with the price system practiced by representative Democracy inevitably diminishes the sum total of goods produced; Fascism is condoned as the safeguard of Liberal economics' and thereafter capitalism 'continues its existence unscathed under a new alias'. Rather than an aberration, then, fascism is a product of capitalist transformation that has its origins entrenched in the class structures of modern state formation. It is to the conditions of the remnants and survivals of feudalism that attention is now cast to reveal the slow protracted character of the institution of capitalism, rather than the 'great transformation' entailed in the commodification of land, labour and money.

The survivals of feudalism

One of the most overlooked standpoints in *The Great Transformation* is Polanyi's honing in on feudal landed class interests embroiled in the system of continental European state formation in the nineteenth-century, which actually thwarted any process of radical 'great transformation'. The pivot of this analysis is what Polanyi calls his theory of 'survivals' or how the residues of pre-capitalist state and class formation became integrated into the emergence and institution of capitalism and what consequences emanated from such a protracted renovation. For Polanyi, then, 'the great influence wielded by landed interests in Western Europe and the survival of feudal forms of life in Central and Western Europe during the nineteenth century are readily explained by the vital protective function of these forces in retarding the mobilisation of the land' (Polanyi, 1944/1957, p. 183). The institutions and class interests of feudalism restricted the appropriation and commodification of land as ' … it had been forgotten by free traders that land formed part of the territory of the country, and that the territorial character of sovereignty was not merely a result of sentimental associations' (Polanyi, 1944/1957, pp. 183–184). The tumult of struggle and the blocked dynamic of capitalist transformation meaning that structures of power were retained within the new social order was captured thusly:

> The new system was first established alongside the old which it tried to assimilate and absorb, by securing a grip on such soil as was still bound up in precapitalistic ties . . . Some of this was achieved by individual force and violence, some by revolution from above or below, some by war and conquest, some by legislative action, some by administrative pressure, some by spontaneous small-scale action of private persons over long stretches of time. Whether the dislocation was swiftly healed or whether it caused an open wound in the body social depended primarily on the measures taken to regulate the process. Powerful factors of change and adjustment were introduced by the governments themselves. Secularisation of Church lands, for instance, was one of the fundaments of the modern state up to the time of the Italian *Risorgimento* and, incidentally, one of the chief means of the ordered transference of land into the hands of private individuals. (Polanyi, 1944/1957, pp. 179–180)

Harking back to his own analysis in the trilogy of *New Britain* articles Polanyi wrote a decade earlier – when fascism was surveyed as a temporary fix to the deadlock or *impasse* between capitalism and democracy – the restorative protection and projection of landed class interests comes to the fore once again in his account of state formation and capitalist changeover. In *The Great Transformation*, then, it is emphasised in more detail that:

> Opposition to mobilisation of the land was the sociological background of that struggle between liberalism and reaction that made up the political history of Continental Europe in the nineteenth century. In this struggle, the military and the higher clergy were allies of the landed classes, who had almost completely lost their more immediate functions in society. These classes were now available for any reactionary solution of the *impasse* to which market economy and its corollary, constitutional government, threatened to lead since they were not bound by tradition and ideology to public liberties and parliamentary rule. (Polanyi, 1944/1957, p. 185)

Most compellingly and stridently for the purposes of this article, the defining statement in *The Great Transformation* on the protracted passing of feudalism, the slow dissolution of agrarian landed classes, and the survival of state forms accommodating an emerging bourgeois class was Polanyi's grasp that 'economic liberalism was wedded to the liberal state, while landed interests were not – this was the source of their permanent political significance on the Continent ... *land and landed property were now credited with a congenital bias for reaction*' (Polanyi, 1944/1957, p. 185, emphasis added). This is why Halperin (2004, pp. 81–82) is right to emphasise that for continental European state formation and the rise of capitalism, 'the end of absolutism and the creation of the bourgeois state and bourgeois law did not bring about the separation of economic (class) power from political (state) power but, rather, a structure of power that fused both for the extraction of surplus, locally and abroad, by extra-economic compulsion'. It is for these reasons that Polanyi was minded to highlight that 'the rise of fascism is at the heart of the social wars and civil wars of our time', which eventually led to the collapse of ruling dynasties linked to empires such as the Hapsburg and Hollenzollern, the dispossession of feudal aristocracies by agrarian revolts, and the birth of new states in Central and Eastern Europe through processes of national and social renovation (Polanyi, 1937, p. 54). It is for that reason that fascism becomes in *The Great Transformation* part of history in the gear of social change, able to enforce market economy and ensure the *apparent* formal separation of the 'economic' from the 'political' sphere, so definitive of capitalist social property relations (Polanyi, 1944/1957, p. 223; Wood, 1995, pp. 29–31).

History in the gear of fascist social change

From the above delineation it would seem confounded to argue that 'Polanyi assigns no role to class in shaping the rise and spread of the market system' and that he ignores the class structures emerging alongside the introduction of capitalist forms of property ownership (Halperin, 2004, p. xiv). More precise would be to emphasise Polanyi's at times flawed perception of class formation posited, again, through an enforced separation between the 'economic' nature of class and the 'political' conditions of identity according to rank, status, social recognition and the 'culture contacts' of colonialism (Polanyi, 1944/1957, pp. 153–154; Burawoy, 2003, p. 223). Yet when it comes to ascertaining the violent attack of fascism – as a revitalisation and restoration of the market economy through a congenital bias towards reaction – the analysis is somewhat more class astute.

Alongside the pressures to institute market economy traced in *The Great Transformation* there arose two forces of dislocation that often combined as responses to the commodity fictions of capitalism. The first was a series of revolutions and counterrevolutions that swept across Central and Eastern Europe that were often reactions to military defeat as well as acts within the drama between liberal and constitutionalist actors. 'The Central and Eastern European upheavals and counter-upheavals of 1917-20 in spite of their scenario were merely roundabout ways of recasting the regimes that had succumbed on the battlefields', surveyed Polanyi (1944/157, p. 23). Following World War I and the counterrevolutions, the political regimes in Budapest, Vienna, Berlin, 'were found to be not very far different from what they had been before the War', something also true of Finland, the Baltic states, Poland, Austria, Hungary, Bulgaria, Italy and Germany up to the 1920s. 'The tendency of the times was simply to establish (or re-establish) the system commonly associated with the ideals of the English, the American, and the French revolutions. Not only Hindenburg and Wilson, but also Lenin and Trotsky were, in the broad sense, in the line of Western tradition' (Polanyi, 1944/1957, p. 23). Change was enacted in the 1930s with the abandonment of the gold standard in Britain, Five-Year Plans in Russia, the launching of the New Deal, National Socialist Revolution in Germany, and the collapse of the League of Nations in favour of autarchist empires. 'In Bulgaria, Greece, Finland, Latvia, Lithuania, Estonia, Poland, and Romania the restoration of the currency provided counter-revolution with a claim to power' (Polanyi, 1944/1957, p. 24).

The second response was the move (rather than the movement) of fascism to open up institutional deadlock between contending forces affected by the institution of market economy. Fascism revitalised the economic system of market economy and, to reiterate again, it was not ascribed to local causes as an aberrant or one-off development but was entrenched in the congenital bias for reaction within capitalism itself, meaning that no country was immune to its emergence. Hence Polanyi contends that 'fascist tactics were invariably those of a sham rebellion arranged with the tacit approval of the authorities who pretended to have been overwhelmed by force' (Polanyi, 1944/1957, p. 238). After the Great Depression, the true significance of fascism became clearer. 'The deadlock of the market system was evident … History was in the gear of social change' (Polanyi, 1944/1957, pp. 243–244). At this stage, the two forces of dislocation in the form of fascism and nationalist revisionism as counterrevolution became conflated. 'Counterrevolutions were the usual backswing of the political pendulum towards a state of affairs that had been violently disturbed' (Polanyi, 1944/1957, p. 240). Hence the collapse of more than a dozen thrones in Central and Eastern Europe were partly due to the backwash of defeat, not to the move toward democracy, with dispossessed classes and groups such as dynasties, aristocracies, churches, heavy industries, and the parties affiliated with them engineering such counterrevolutions. Bringing these two forces of dislocation together, Polanyi writes that 'By accident only … was European fascism in the twenties connected with national and counterrevolutionary tendencies. It was a case of symbiosis between movements of independent origin, which reinforced one another and created the impression of essential similarity, while being actually unrelated' (Polanyi, 1944/1957, p. 242). Overall, though, it was market economy that determined the structuring conditions for the radically different solutions of counterrevolution and fascist reaction, as *given alternatives* set within the international system (Polanyi, 1944/1957, p. 244, 248). Liberal market economy thus upheld a utopia that declared the self-regulating market as an essential freedom while occluding its own forms of compulsion, market dependence and unfreedom. For Polanyi, discarding that market utopia created a dividing line between liberalism on one hand with its extremity of fascism and socialism on the other hand (Polanyi, 1944/1957, p. 258). In a speech delivered to the Chamber of Deputies in the Parliament of Italy on 16 May 1925, Antonio Gramsci (1925/2007, p. 786), as leader of the Communist Party of Italy (PCd'I), asked: 'was the situation of capitalism in Italy after the war strengthened or weakened by the phenomenon of fascism?'. Rather than presenting it as a superficial and temporary phenomenon, we shall see how seriously Gramsci too understood the portent of fascism, in a way as a 'universal concept' and condition located in specific 'geographical' seats' such as Italy and elsewhere (Gramsci, 1971, p. 117, Q10II§61; Hesketh, 2017b). The political economy of fascism that unfolds in the next section on Gramsci thus covers three comparable domains to the above excursus, concerning (1) a focus on the market as a determinate historical form of economy; (2) an emphasis on how the determinate market of capitalism has to be situated within the historical nexus of state formation shaped by both the Italian *Risorgimento* and the international states-system; and (3) an endeavour to render fascism as a form of 'new' liberalism, a restoration-revolution in the twentieth-century referred to as a configuration of passive revolution.

Fascism as the passive revolution of the twentieth-century

Although largely neglected in commentaries on the *Prison Notebooks*, Antonio Gramsci advanced a conception of political economy that he referred to as 'Critical Economy' in order to distinguish it from the 'pure' or 'orthodox' economics of liberalism (see Bieler & Morton, 2003). Rather than seek to construct abstract hypotheses based on generalised, historically indeterminate conditions of a generic 'homo oeconomicus', the whole conception of 'Critical Economy' was historicist in the sense that categories should always be situated within historical circumstances and assessed within the particular context from which they derived, rather than assuming a universal 'homo oeconomicus' (Gramsci, 1995, pp. 166–167, Q10II§15; 171–173, Q10II§32; 176, Q15§45). As will be demonstrated shortly, the notion of *determinate market* was a key development across these writings. 'The "critique" of political economy starts', for Gramsci echoing Marx, 'from the concept of the historical character of the "determined market" and of its "automatism", whereas pure economists conceive of these elements as "eternal" and "natural"'. In the same note the critique of political economy then grasps 'the relations of force determining the market, it analyses in depth their contradictions, evaluates the possibilities of modification connected with the appearance and strengthening of new elements and puts forward the 'transitory' and 'replaceable' nature of the science being criticised' (Gramsci, 1971, p. 411, Q11§52; see also Gramsci, 2007, pp. 308–309, Q8§128). My argument here is that just as the *integral state* has been appropriately recognised as a guiding thread organising Gramsci's carceral research – organising the dialectical unity of the moments of civil society and political society concerning the capitalist state form (Thomas, 2009, pp. 136–137) – then so too should recognition be granted to a notion of the *integral economy* (see Jessop, 2006, pp. 350–355). Integral economics might then be regarded as a guiding thread dialectically mediating between 'classical' economics that retains a focus on the determinate market (drawing from David Ricardo) and historicist 'critical' economy (deriving from Karl Marx) as a rejection of 'pure' (neoclassical) economics (Gramsci, 2007, p. 191, Q7§42). This is important because in their combination the theory of the integral state and the integral economy potently offer a transcendence of liberal ideology across its pillars of state theory and political economy. It is worth recalling that free market liberalism is dismissed by Gramsci as holding to the belief that 'economic activity belongs to civil society, and that the state must not intervene to regulate it' (Gramsci, 1971, p. 160, Q13§18). However:

> In concrete historical life, political society and civil society are a single entity. Moreover, *laissez-faire* liberalism, too, must be introduced by law, through the intervention of political power: it is an act of will, not the spontaneous, automatic expression of economic facts. (Gramsci, 1996, pp. 182–183, Q4§38)

Within the theory of the *integral state*, the dismissal of *statolatry* – or the tendency to view the state as both a perpetual entity associated solely with direct governmental responsibilities within political society – should therefore be seen as of a piece with the theory of the *integral economy* and the discharge of *economism* – or the theoretical movement of free trade in which the market is regarded as an automatism and economic facts are commonly abstracted to produce the economy as a science of uniformities, regularities and choices based on rationality (Gramsci, 1971, pp. 268–269, Q8§130; Gramsci, 1995, pp. 174–175, Q15§43; Gramsci, 2007, pp. 310–311, Q8§130). Within Gramsci's critique of liberalism, then, there is a confluence of his theorisation of the integral state and the integral economy, when political thought and economic thought come together at the dawning of the determined market. It is to that epoch and its interpretation that attention now turns in more detail.

Liberalism and the determinate market

As introduced above, the determinate market is a rubric that refers not to the terms of a 'pure' market but the conditions of economic activity situated within determinate and historically limited 'relations of force' (Gramsci, 2007, p. 309, Q8§128). Hence there was recognition by Gramsci in his contributions on Critical Economy of the 'economy' as a determinate historical form, the content of which in terms of 'political-social milieu', assumed different types throughout history (Gramsci, 1995, pp. 171–173, Q10II§32). As Michael Krätke (2011, p. 75) usefully expounds in relation to market relations:

> the critical economist therefore strives to grasp them in their historical specificity; that is, instead of comprehending 'the market' as such, the critical economist seeks to comprehend the historically specific market (or the historically specific system of markets) in capitalism.

The historical materialist conception of the market is therefore based on a historicist methodology, meaning that it does not posit such relations as abstract universals outside of time and space (Gramsci, 1995, p. 178, Q10II§37ii; Gramsci, 2007, p. 335, Q8§174). Instead, 'abstraction will always be the abstraction of a historically determined category, seen in fact as a category and not as multiple individuality' (Gramsci, 1995, p. Q10II§32). The hallmark of historical materialism in this regard is the philosophy of internal relations that makes explicit a conception of capital through which connections are maintained and contained as aspects of a self-forming whole (Bieler & Morton, 2018a, pp. 3–11). Through this philosophy of internal relations, the dialectical method of historical materialism, therefore, focuses on internally related causes and conditions, rather than positing logically independent factors existing side-by-side one another (see Ollman, 1976, p. 48), as in arguments based on ontological exteriority discussed above. This philosophy of internal relations and the method of abstraction is strongly evident in

Gramsci's conception of the determinate market as a way of theorising the integral economy. Hence the market in this conception of the integral economy is:

> determined by the basic structure of the society in question and it is therefore this structure that one must analyse, identifying those of its 'relatively' constant elements which determine the market and so on, and the other 'variable and developing' ones which determine conjunctural crises up to the point when even its 'relatively' constant elements get modified and the crisis then becomes an organic one. (Gramsci, 1995, p. 180, Q10II§8)

As a key facet of the conception of an integral economy, then, the theorisation of the determinate market has to be situated within the philosophy of internal relations and dialectics. In a key note from 1930 entitled 'The unity in the component parts of Marxism' Gramsci outlines that the conception of unity comes from the dialectical contradictions connecting 'man' and 'nature' in three ways: 1) 'in economics, the centre of unity is value' – that is, the relation between producers and the forces of production; 2) 'in philosophy – praxis, that is, the relation between human will (superstructure) and the economic structure'; and 3) 'in politics – the relation between the state and civil society', that is the role of the state in constituting, regulating, and intervening in the general social milieu (Gramsci, 2007, p. 170, Q7§18). Dualisms are avoided, though, in the above conceptions. Witness, for example, Gramsci critiquing Georg Lukács, also in a note from 1930, as someone who 'presupposes a dualism between man and nature' and therefore 'is wrong because he falls into a conception of nature … that, in reality, fails to unify and relate man to nature'. As Gramsci asks, 'how can the dialectic be separated from nature?' (Gramsci, 1996, p. Q4§43). Instead, the dialectic is conceived as 'the concept of movement in history, of becoming' that internally relates as a unity elements of classical German philosophy, classical English economy, and French political practice to combine philosophy, economics, and politics or the theoretical, economic and political moments in a historicist form (Gramsci, 2007, p. 335, Q8§174; Gramsci, 1971, pp. 399–400, Q10II§9). As Peter Thomas (2009, p. 361, 382) has argued, these are not component parts but *moments* with each moment *internally related* to the other, they are immanent to each other because the social practices they sought to comprehend are recognised as determined by the same relations of force. A theory of integral economy is therefore linked to a broader integral state theory, which was regarded as intrinsic to historical materialism as itself an integral philosophy dialectically transcending traditional idealism and materialism (Gramsci, 2007, p. 179, Q7§29).

At the centre of this conception of the integral economy were, then, two further economic principles that also go on to constitute, in an internally related manner, the theory of the integral state. First, there was a strong value-theoretic component to critical economics and the theory of integral economy. As Gramsci (1995, p. 168, Q10II§23) stated, 'one must take as one's starting point the labour of all working people to arrive at definitions both of their role in economic production and of the abstract, scientific concept of value and surplus value' (Gramsci, 1995, p. 168, Q10II§23). The abstraction of *homo oeconomicus*, therefore, becomes 'operationalised' by demonstrating how 'use-value is potentially reduced to exchange value' within capitalism and how particular labour becomes crystallised in different commodities (Gramsci, 1995, pp. 171–173, Q10II§32; Gramsci, 1995, pp. 168–170, Q10II§23). Second, it is therefore also significant that Gramsci identified writings such as Henryk Grossman's *The Law of Accumulation and Breakdown of the Capitalist System* as 'very interesting' as well as *Capital*, Volume 3, as the 'object of fresh study' in order to establish the organic importance of contradictions at the centre of the law of the tendential rate of profit to fall (Gramsci, 2007, p. Q7§41; Gramsci, 1995, p. 431, Q10II§36; Gramsci, 1971, pp. 311–312, Q22§13).[2] It was here that the central significance of what Gramsci identified as 'Americanism and Fordism' took hold in constituting an effort by capital to overcome the tendency of the rate of profit to fall and offset, rather than avoid, crises (Gramsci, 2007, p. Q7§34; Gramsci, 1971, p. 280, Q22§1). Alongside his astute recognition of the reorganisation of social reproduction – wherein households and wider gender relations were being reshaped (also see Morton, 2007a, pp. 102–105) – Gramsci also stressed within 'Americanism and Fordism' how:

> it should be obvious that so-called high wages are a transitory form of remuneration. Adaptation to the new methods of work cannot come about solely through coercion: the apparatus of coercion needed to obtain such a result would certainly be more costly than high wages. Coercion is combined with persuasion in forms that are suitable to the society in question: money. However, if the new method takes hold, creating a new type of worker, if the material mechanical apparatus is perfected even further, and if excessive turnover is automatically restricted by widespread unemployment, then wages will decline as well. American industry is still exploiting the benefits of monopoly because it has had the initiative with the new methods and it can pay higher wages, but the monopoly will necessarily be limited over time and foreign competition on an equal level will make the high wages disappear along with the profits. Besides, it is well known that high wages are connected only with a labour aristocracy; they do not pertain to all American workers. (Gramsci, 1996, pp. 219–220, Q4§52)

Significantly, Krätke has surmised that 'Gramsci is not clear about what constitutes the specific difference between Marx's 'critical' economics and 'classical' economics' in these writings (Krätke, 2011, p. 80). But as Bob Jessop has astutely acknowledged in relation to Gramsci, 'although he made no major original contribution to Marxist economic analysis narrowly understood … Gramsci always accepted its fundamental principles and tendential laws as the starting point for his critique of political economy in its inclusive sense' (Jessop, 2006, p. 353). What is key here, though, is how this conception of integral economy is linked to the theorisation of the integral state as a rejection of liberal economics. 'Doesn't the study of the hypothesis of pure "economics"', questions Gramsci (2007, p. 191, Q7§42),

> … require that one set aside any consideration of "states" (I say "states" intentionally) and of the "legal" monopoly of property?' Hence within liberalism, 'it is asserted that economic activity belongs to civil society, and that the state must not intervene to regulate it. But since in actual reality civil society and state are one and the same, it must be made clear that *laissez-faire* too is a form of state."regulation", introduced and maintained by legislative and coercive means. (Gramsci, 1971, p. 160, Q13§18)

Here, as the previous main section evidenced, the resonance with Polanyi is tangible, for 'even those who wished most ardently to free the state from all unnecessary duties, and whose whole philosophy demanded the restriction of state activities, could not but entrust the self-same state with the new powers, organs, and instruments for the establishment of *laissez-faire*' (Polanyi, 1944/1957, p. 141). Now it remains to be shown how the consolidation and expansion of capitalism was enacted less through the 'great transformation' of liberalism and more through a 'great *trasformismo*' of slow and protracted molecular processes that marked the epoch of passive revolution in the consolidation and expansion of capitalist social relations, prior to situating the rise of fascism within that history.

The historical nexus of passive revolution

My own focus on passive revolution as a theory of state formation within the structuring conditions of uneven and combined development has attempted to place Antonio Gramsci firmly within a stream of classic social theory considering transformations in social property relations constitutive of capitalist modernity (see Morton, 2005, 2007a, 2007b, 2007c, 2010, 2011/2013, 2018a; and latterly Bieler & Morton, 2018a, 2018b).[3] From the outset, my purpose here has been to establish how a theory of state formation unfolds through the construal of the passive revolution that situates such social development within the causal conditioning of 'the international'. Through a focus on the Italian *Risorgimento*—the movement for Italian national liberation that culminated in the political unification of the country in 1860–1861—the condition of passive revolution was presented by Gramsci as a theory of the survival and reorganisation of state identity through which social property relations were instituted and/or reproduced in new forms. Lest we miss the causal conditioning of 'the international' in his account of Italian and wider European state formation, Gramsci spells it out for us very clearly.

> The *Risorgimento* is a complex and contradictory historical development that is made complete by all its antithetical elements, by its protagonists and antagonists, by their struggles and the reciprocal modifications that the struggles themselves determined, and also by the role of passive and latent forces, such as the great rural masses – in addition, to the very important function of international relations. (Gramsci, 2007, p. 256, Q8§33)

On the historical nexus of passive revolution, it is also clear that such transformations are not simply regarded as a reordering of social relations by state classes from above but can also encompass forms of social class agency from below. On the origins of the *Risorgimento*, there is:

> the historical fact popular initiative is missing from the development of Italian history, as well as the fact that 'progress' occurs as the reaction of the dominant classes to the sporadic and incoherent rebelliousness of the popular masses—a reaction consisting of 'restorations' that agree to some part of the popular demands and are therefore 'progressive restorations', or 'revolutions-restorations', or even 'passive revolutions'. (Gramsci, 2007, p. 252, Q8§25)

For reasons of brevity, I want here to hone in on the historical materialist methodological criteria that Gramsci deployed to understand concrete studies of passive revolution, which he stressed would have wider relevance beyond the case of Italy.

Across notes initially drafted in 1930, Gramsci unravelled a set of methodological criteria for understanding concrete historical instances of state formation. It is the 'Preface' to *A Contribution to the Critique of Political Economy* by Karl Marx that 'expounds the principles of historical materialism', he argued, and offers bearings in tracking the relation of forces shaping real history (Gramsci, 1996, p. Q4§19; Gramsci, 1996, pp. 177–188, Q4§38). In direct overlap with Polanyi, then, quoting from memory, Gramsci stated that the crucial problem for historical materialism was (Gramsci, 1996, p. 177, Q4§38; see Marx, 1859/1975, p. 426):

(1) the principle that 'no society sets itself tasks for the accomplishment of which the necessary and sufficient conditions do not already exist [or are not in the course of emerging and developing]' and
(2) that 'no society perishes until it has first developed all the forms of life implicit in its internal relations' (check the exact wording of these principles).

Equipped with the 'Preface' as a lodestar for historical materialism, Gramsci then expanded these methodological criteria in order to distinguish between transformations that may be fluctuating 'waves', or occasional conjunctural, movements and those that are more permanent, or organic, in modifying the relations of force linked to the state. In the case of Italy and the *Risorgimento* the notion of passive revolution was used to refer to the failure of the 'Jacobins' in the *Partito d'Azione* led by Giuseppe Mazzini and Giuseppe Garibaldi, among others, to establish a programme reflecting the demands of the popular masses and, significantly, the peasantry. Instead, challenges were thwarted and changes in property relations accommodated due to the 'Moderates', led by (Count) Camillo Benso Cavour, establishing alliances between big landowners in the Mezzogiorno and the northern bourgeoisie while absorbing opposition in parliament through continually assimilated change (or *trasformismo*) within the current social formation. According to Gramsci, after the French Revolution (1789), the emergent bourgeoisie there, 'was able to present itself as an integral 'state', with all the intellectual and moral forces that were necessary and adequate to the task of organising a complete and perfect society' (Gramsci, 2007, p. 9, Q6§10). In contrast to the instance of revolutionary rupture in France, other European countries went through a series of passive revolutions in which the old feudal classes were not destroyed but maintained a political role through state power. It was these survivals or feudal residues – referred to as 'forms of state based on city rather than territory' – that the forces of reaction would become established as reserves of fascism (Gramsci, 1971, p. 140, Q13§13). Consequently, such 'restorations are universally repressive' (Gramsci, 1996, p. 40, Q3§41). Therefore:

> [The] birth of the modern European states [proceeded] by successive waves of reform rather than by revolutionary explosions like the original French one. The 'successive waves' were made up of a combination of social struggles, interventions from above of the enlightened monarchy type, and national wars ... restoration becomes the first policy whereby social struggles find sufficiently elastic frameworks to allow the bourgeoisie to gain power without dramatic upheavals, without the French machinery of terror ... The old feudal classes are demoted from their dominant position to a 'governing' one, but are not eliminated, nor is there any attempt to liquidate them as an organic whole ... Can this 'model' for the creation of the modern states be repeated in other conditions? (Gramsci, 1971, p. 115 Q10II§61)

Gramsci's response to his own question was an affirmative one and he came to the conclusion, therefore, that:

> The important thing is to analyse more profoundly the significance of a 'Piedmont'-type function in passive revolutions—i.e. the fact that a state replaces the local social groups in leading a struggle of renewal. It is one of the cases in which these groups have the function of 'domination' without that of 'leadership': dictatorship without hegemony. (Gramsci, 1971, pp. 105–106, Q15§59)

In another resonance with his Austro-Hungarian contemporary peer, it is for this reason that, in relation to the *Risorgimento*, Gramsci singles out the 'congenital incapacity' prevalent within the relations of force constituting Italian state formation, denoting an unstable equilibrium of compromises between modernising state classes resulting in only a minimal hegemony maintaining the extant order (Gramsci, 1996, p. 181, Q4§38). Within these circumstances the politics of *trasformismo* comes to prevail, rather than genuine transformation, meaning the protracted absorption of class contradictions through 'molecular changes which in fact progressively modify the pre-existing composition of forces, and hence become the matrix of new changes' (Gramsci, 1971, p. 109, Q15§11). Crucially, within passive revolutionary conditions, the tactics of *trasformismo* become vital, referring to the manner in which recalcitrant elements of radicalism are displaced to restore or maintain class dominance and diffuse class contradictions through the state (see Hesketh & Morton, 2014). The class tactics of passive revolution are thus diffused through practices of *trasformismo* with the aim of establishing 'an ever more extensive ruling class' within the framework of the established order to eliminate the organising power of subaltern class movements (Gramsci, 1971, pp. 58–59, Q19§24). In bringing these themes together, the stress is on:

> *Trasformismo* as one of the historical forms of 'revolution-restoration' or 'passive revolution' ... in relation to the process of formation of the modern state in Italy. (Gramsci, 2007, p. 257, Q8§36)

In sum, *trasformismo* is extended not only so that it refers to processes of molecular transformation, or piecemeal absorption of opposition forces after Italian unification, but also in relation to the wholesale class offensive that unfolded in the twentieth-century, epitomised by fascism as its contemporary mode. Whereas, '"classic" *trasformismo* is the phenomenon that brought the parties together in the *Risorgimento*; this *trasformismo* brings into sharp relief the contrast between culture, ideology, etc. and class power' (Gramsci, 1996, p. 115, Q3§138). Akin to Polanyi, fascism was therefore congenitally linked to the survivals or residues of feudalism in the form of the Papacy, the declining aristocracy, agrarian landowners and rural producers, traditional intellectuals, weak political parties, the absolutist state, the city–country relation, and the territorial, class and spatial relations of social development in Italy encapsulated by the uneven development of the Mezzogiorno in the south and its complex relations with the north of Italy in terms of class stratification and racialised domination. It is these relations of force that are regarded to be in deadlock or an unstable equilibrium of compromises in the struggle for hegemony and the conquest of state power. It is for that reason that Gramsci questioned whether fascism was the most recent attempt in Italian history to further the expansion of capital: 'A new "liberalism" under modern conditions – wouldn't that be, precisely, fascism?' (Gramsci, 2007, p. 378, Q8§236).

Fascism as the 'new' liberalism

A year and a half before the 'March on Rome' and the fascist seizure of power in October 1922, it was Gramsci, writing in the newspaper *L'Ordine Nuovo*, who argued that 'fascism has presented itself as the anti-party':

> It has now become obvious that fascism can only be partially interpreted as a class phenomenon, as a movement of political forces conscious of a real aim. It has spread, it has broken every possible organisational framework … it has become an unchaining of elemental forces which cannot be restrained under the bourgeois system of economic and political government. Fascism is the name for the far-reaching decomposition of Italian society, which could not but accompany the decomposition of the state. (Gramsci, 1978, p. 38)

Consistent throughout his pre-prison writings and then across his output during confinement was Gramsci's tracing of the origins of fascism back to the historical weakness of the Italian state. 'Italian history is nothing but a compromise between the state and the landowners', Gramsci also wrote in 1921, presaging key themes also addressed in the 'Lyons Theses' where fascism was similarly regarded as modifying the social forces of reaction that had always dominated Italian state formation (Gramsci, 1978, p. 30, 340-75). Gramsci therefore develops a critique of the historical role (or lack of it) of Italian intellectuals in the formation of the state: condemning the enduring cosmopolitanism of the Italian intellectuals and their failure to assist in forging a national-popular unity; the absence in the Italian *Risorgimento* of the 'Jacobin moment' that distinguished the French Revolution; and a line of research on Italian history that understands the historical conditions of passive revolution leading to the emergence of fascism. With an emphasis on social struggle as the real dialectic of history, fascism was therefore viewed as the possible 'reaction that had always existed' (Gramsci, 1977, p. 353). Fascism was a restoration of the state *and* a reorganisation of capitalism through crisis shaping the history of Italy understood as an ongoing period in the history of passive revolution.

The form of appearance of fascism in Italy was also cast as an expression of Caesarism referring back to an unstable equilibrium of compromises or structural *impasse* when 'a situation in which the forces in conflict balance each other in a catastrophic manner' resulting in 'reciprocal destruction' (Gramsci, 1971, p. 219, Q13§27). Returning to his dialogue with Marx, now in relation to *The Eighteenth Brumaire of Louis Bonaparte* (Marx, 1852/1984, p. 102), Gramsci extends the focus on the situations of state crisis when a 'great personality' comes to play an arbitrating role in an attempt to balance the relations of force (Gramsci, 1971, p. 211, Q13§23). The fascist move was therefore regarded as a restoration of capitalism through the specific intervention of Caesarism that generally *could* be regarded as either 'progressive' or 'regressive'. A 'progressive' form of Caesarism (historically expressed in the cases of Caesar or Napoleon I) was identified as resulting in a change in the form of state. In contrast, a 'regressive' form of Caesarism (historically embodied in the instances of Napoleon III or Bismark) was reflected in a continuation of the form of state (Gramsci, 1971, pp. 219–222, Q13§27).

Allied with a social base in the urban and rural petty bourgeoisie, the ideology of fascism was, furthermore, recognised as an attempt by the ruling classes in Italy to develop the productive forces 'in competition with the more advanced industrial formations' (Gramsci, 1971, p. 120, Q10I§9). The political economy of fascism was, therefore, a response to 'the intervention of Anglo-American capital in Italy' that signified the growing predominance of finance capital over the state (Gramsci, 1978, p. 352, 403). Quite clearly that is why for Gramsci the representative of passive revolution 'both practical (for Italy) and ideological (for Europe)' was fascism (Gramsci, 1971, p. 120, Q10I§9; Gramsci, 1995, p. 350, Q10I§9). In the former, fascism was held to be a modification of conservative reaction that resulted in both colonial exploitation at home (in the form of exploiting the southern masses of the Mezzogiorno with the support of Catholic Action and the monarchy as the 'state form' of the fascist régime) and colonial exploitation abroad (in the form of expansion in Ethiopia) (Gramsci, 1978, p. 352, 371). These should be regarded as conjoined forms of colonial exploitation because 'capitalist Europe, rich in capital, exported it to the colonial empires it was then creating. But Italy not only had no capital to export, it had to resort to foreign capital for its own urgent needs' (Gramsci, 1992, p. 142, Q1§44). Following unification:

> The government of the Moderates from 1861 to 1876 had created solely and diffidently the external conditions for economic development – systematisation of the state apparatus, roads, railways, telegraph – and rectified the finances overwhelmed by the debts of the *Risorgimento*. (Gramsci, 1992, p. 141, Q1§44)

But specifically, the vigorous colonial expansion promoted by Francesco Crispi [1819-1901], Italian Prime Minister on various occasions between 1876 and 1896, was seen as crucial in offering the 'mirage of land' through 'castle-in-the-air-imperialism' to the Italian masses. In Crispi's mind, writes Gramsci, 'the Southern peasant wanted land … . [so] he presented him with the mirage of exploitable colonial lands' (Gramsci, 1992, p. 142, Q1§44). At the same time, the struggle over modernity in Italy was also linked in this same note to its own foreign domination. 'In Italy the struggle presented itself as a struggle against old treaties and against the foreign power, Austria, which represented and supported them in Italy with the force of arms, occupying Lombardy-Veneto and exercising control over the rest of the country' (Gramsci, 1992, p. 148, Q1§44). These factors of 'the international' circumscribing the specific conditions of Italian state formation—both in its own colonial relations as well as its own subjection to foreign domination—thus shaped the relative weakness of the Italian bourgeoisie leading to the scrutiny of fascism in Italy as a passive revolution.

Conclusion: the aura of the great *trasformismo*

Writing towards the end of the crucible of World War II, it was another veteran of the Red Vienna period in the form of Victor Serge – also in the city in 1923 in the direct social milieu of Antonio Gramsci although indirectly in relation to Karl Polanyi – who wrote that, 'Great wars (like great revolutions, with which they are often linked) are accompanied by great social transformations. . . The Second World War, the most vast, most destructive and therefore most dangerous known to history, brought societies to transformations that certainly exceeded all predictions' (Serge, 1944/1994, p. 177).[4] While pointing to the importance of class struggle in forming planned economies within modern capitalism in order to reconstruct a new and democratic Europe, this essay – written in the same year as *The Great Transformation* – also portends that new totalitarian and despotic movements may also take hold. Just a few years later, intellectually shadowboxing with his *bête noire*, it was Polanyi himself who stated that 'There are those who argue, like Hayek, that since free institutions were a product of market-economy, they must give place to serfdom once that economy disappears', rather than understanding that some new form of serfdom might arise out of capitalism (Polanyi, 1947/1968, p. 75). But rather than a 'great transformation' leading to the institution of liberalism and the utopia of market economy, I have argued that what was inaugurated throughout the nineteenth century and into the twentieth century across continental Europe was a 'great *trasformismo*' – the molecular process of the restoration of class and state power in line with bourgeois interests – that was subsequently deepened by fascism. While a cautionary note should be cast towards the attempt to view Speenhamland as an earlier species of passive revolution (Burawoy, 2003, pp. 219–220), it is important to draw attention to the relevance of passive revolution in assisting our understanding of the processes of European state formation and the expansion of capitalism across the nineteenth and into the twentieth century. My argument has established that through a shared engagement with Marx, both Polanyi and Gramsci were similarly preoccupied with the survivals or residues of feudalism, the congenital bias for the reaction that always exists within capitalism, subject to specific contingencies, and how the militant creed of *laissez-faire* liberalism was and is always enforced by the state. However, my position is that in Polanyi the wadding of the market economy is missing in *The Great Transformation*, leaving unspoken or unexplained the constituent elements of the economy as an instituted process. Hence the problematic confusing and switching between the dis-embedded and re-embedded conditions of economic expansion within accounts of capitalism, which is due to the lack of convincing intermediate concepts to back fill market economy as an instituted process. In contrast, the constituent elements of a theory of integral economy are present in *The Prison Notebooks*. In the latter, a fulsome emphasis on the 'decisive nucleus of economic activity' is unmistakable within a wider theory of the integral state (Gramsci, 1971, p. 161, Q13§18). The accent on the determinate market precludes a de-socialised conception of the market economy as it historicises economic activity internally related to a theory of the integral state. For sure, a theory of primitive accumulation is assumed and not explained in the *Prison Notebooks* but, that said, further work can still be done to unravel Gramsci's approach to integral economy and the presence of absolute and relative surplus value, the study of the dynamic of socially necessary labour time, the observations on the law of the tendency of the rate of profit to fall within 'Americanism and Fordism', and thus the conception of value and surplus value, within his attention to uneven development (Morton, 2007a, p. 206). Finally, though, my position here does not support the rather numbing assessment that sentences Karl Polanyi's *The Great Transformation* to an inability to surpass the strengths of Marx(ism) and transcend capitalism (Selwyn & Miyamura, 2013). Rather, at one with Jamie Peck (2013, pp. 1562–1563), a more constructive 'Polanyi-plus' approach is endorsed that is capable of opening up questions, rather than foreclosing answers, about the historical geographies constituting the spaces and places of the political economy of modern capitalism. This entails reading Polanyi alongside other texts and placing his work in dialogue with complementary theories to reveal horizons beyond the germinal concepts of embeddedness, the double movement, and the fictitious commodities of the market economy. As a consequence, my argument should be regarded as a contribution to heterodox and open-ended conversations within *comparative economy* across intradisciplinary and interdisciplinary debate in economic geography, economic and historical sociology, feminist economics, political economy and international studies (Peck, 2013). Concurrent with Gareth Dale (2016, pp. 33–54), Polanyi *was* clearly pulled out of the Marxist orbit but this should not be taken as a dismissal of his contributions. Reading Polanyi and Gramsci on the origins of fascism today is just one theme that can open up new questions for a comparative economy about the crisis conditions in tomorrow's spaces and places of modern capitalism.

For the present, it was liberal capitalism in the form of *Pax Americana* that for Polanyi implied 'a universality which commits those who believe in it to reconquer the globe on its behalf' (Polanyi 1943, p. 87). It was the retrenchment of liberal capitalism in the guise of 'Americanism and Fordism' that for Gramsci was consolidated on a global scale through the conditions of passive revolution. Today, as the hegemony of liberal capitalism increasingly fades, there remains the dangerous rise of the congenital bias for a reaction towards fascism, or at the very least right-wing populist reaction. That is the aura of authoritarianism within capitalism that needs to be recognised, not as some continuation of a 'great transformation', but as the slow and protracted deliverance of class restoration known as a passive revolution or a great *trasformismo*.

Notes

1. These are now collected in the anthology Karl Polanyi, *Economy and Society: Selected Writings*, edited by Claus Thomasberger and Michele Cangiani (see Polanyi, 2018).
2. See Henryk Grossman, *The Law of Accumulation and the Breakdown of the Capitalist System*, trans. Jairus Banaji. London: Pluto Press, 1992. This was first published in 1929 and although it came to his attention in a review of 1931 it seems that Gramsci was never able to obtain a copy of the book.
3. Elsewhere significant strides have been made to affirm the production of space in the constitution of state power and passive revolution across different scales. Also drawing from Henri Lefebvre, the important contribution from Chris Hesketh, for example, is to emphasise that space is not a passive locus of social relations in the constitution of state power and conditions of passive revolution (see Hesketh, 2017a, p. 22; Lefebvre 1974/1991, p. 11).
4. An enhanced focus on the relevance of Victor Serge in understanding the struggle for space, the spatial logistics of the state, and how the modern state organises space is available in Morton (2018b).

Acknowledgements

This article was presented at the international workshop 'Questioning the Utopian Springs of Market Economy', University of Sydney (15–16 August 2014); the 5th International Conference on Gramscian Studies, Benemérita Universidad Autónoma de Puebla (BUAP), Puebla/México (1–4 December 2014); the Centre for the Study of Social and Global Justice (CSSGJ) Seminar Series, University of Nottingham/UK (23 March 2015); the Annual Political Studies Association (PSA) Conference, Sheffield/UK (30 March–1 April 2015); and the 9th Australian International Political Economy Network (AIPEN) conference, Monash University, Melbourne/Australia (8–9 February 2018). I would like to thank all the participants in these events and, especially, Andreas Bieler, Gareth Bryant, Damien Cahill, and Chris Hesketh for their constructive feedback as well as members of the Marxism Reading Group at the Centre for the Study of Social and Global Justice (CSSGJ) for our shared reading of Karl Polanyi, although they may not thank me in return for our subsequent shared reading of Friedrich Hayek!

Disclosure statement

No potential conflict of interest was reported by the author.

ORCID

Adam David Morton ⓘ http://orcid.org/0000-0003-1003-8101

References

Bauer, O. (1938/1978). Fascism. In T. Bottomore, & P. Goode (Eds.), *Austro-Marxism* (pp. 167–186) (intro. Tom Bottomore, Trans. Tom Bottomore and Patrick Goods, Trans). Oxford: Clarendon Press.

Bieler, A., & Morton, A. D. (2003). Globalisation, the state and class struggle: A "critical economy" engagement with open marxism. *British Journal of Politics and International Relations, 5*(4), 467–499.

Bieler, A., & Morton, A. D. (2018a). *Global capitalism, global War, global crisis.* Cambridge: Cambridge University Press.

Bieler, A., & Morton, A. D. (2018b). Interlocutions with passive revolution. *Thesis Eleven, 147*(1), 9–28.

Block, F. (2002). 'Introduction' to Karl Polanyi, *The Great Transformation: The Political and Economic Origins of Our Time,* foreword by Joseph E. Stiglitz. Boston: Beacon Press.

Block, F., & Somers, M. R. (1984). *'Beyond the economistic fallacy: The holistic social science of Karl Polanyi', in Theda Skocpol (ed.) vision and method in historical sociology.* Cambridge: Cambridge University Press.

Burawoy, M. (2003). For a sociological marxism: The complementary convergence of Antonio Gramsci and Karl Polanyi. *Politics & Society, 31*(2), 193–261.

Dale, G. (2010). Social democracy, embeddedness and decommodification: On the conceptual innovations and intellectual affiliations of Karl Polanyi. *New Political Economy, 15*(3), 369–393.

Dale, G. (2014). 'Karl polanyi in Vienna: Guild socialism, austro-marxism and Duczynka's alternative'. *Historical Materialism, 22*(1), 34–66.

Dale, G. (2016). *Reconstructing karl polanyi: Excavation and critique.* London: Pluto Press.

Gemici, K. (2007). Karl Polanyi and the antinomies of embeddedness. *Socio-Economic Review, 6,* 5–33.

Godelier, M. (1986). *The mental and the material: Thought economy and society.* London: Verso.

Gramsci, A. (1925/2007). 'Speech delivered to the Italian chamber of deputies' [16 May 1925]. *Cultural Studies, 21*(4/5), 779–795.

Gramsci, A. (1971). *Selections from the prison notebooks* (Quintin Hoare and Geoffrey Nowell-Smith, Ed. and Trans). London: Lawrence and Wishart.

Gramsci, A. (1977). *Selections from political writings 1910-1920.* (John Matthews, Ed. and Trans.). London: Lawrence and Wishart.

Gramsci, A. (1978). *Selections from political writings 1921-1926.* (Quintin Hoare, Ed. and Trans). London: Lawrence and Wishart.

Gramsci, A. (1992). *Prison notebooks, Vol. 1.* (Joseph A. Buttigieg & Antonio Callari, Ed. and Trans). New York: Columbia University Press.

Gramsci, A. (1995). *Further selections from the prison notebooks.* (Derek Boothman, Ed. and Trans). London: Lawrence and Wishart.

Gramsci, A. (1996). *Prison notebooks, Vol. 2.* (Joseph A. Buttigieg, Ed. and Trans). New York: Columbia University Press.

Gramsci, A. (2007). *Prison notebooks, Vol. 3,* ed. and trans. Joseph A. Buttigieg. New York: Columbia University Press.

Halperin, S. (2004). *War and social change in modern Europe: The great transformation revisited.* Cambridge: Cambridge University Press.

Hayek, F. A. (1944/2001). *The road to serfdom.* London: Routledge.

Hesketh, C. (2017a). *Spaces of capital/spaces of resistance: Mexico and the global political economy.* Athens, GA: University of Georgia Press.

Hesketh, C. (2017b). Passive revolution: A universal concept with geographical seats. *Review of International Studies, 43*(3), 389–408.

Hesketh, C., & Morton, A. D. (2014). Spaces of uneven development and class struggle in Bolivia: Transformation or *trasformismo*? *Antipode, 46*(1), 149–169.

Jessop, B. (2006). Gramsci as a proto- and post regulation theorist. In B. Jessop & N.-L. Sum (Eds.), *Beyond the regulation approach: Putting capitalist economies in their place* (pp. 348–373). Cheltenham: Edward Elgar.

Krätke, M. (2011). Antonio gramsci's contribution to a critical economics. *Historical Materialism, 19*(3), 63–105.

Krippner, G. R. (2001). The elusive market: Embeddedness and the paradigm of economic sociology. *Theory and Society, 30*, 775–810.

Lefebvre, H. (1974/1991). *The production of space.* (Donald Nicholson-Smith, Trans). Oxford: Blackwell Publishing.

Mark, K. (1859/1975). *Preface to A contribution to the critique of political economy.* (intro. Lucio Colletti, Trans. Rodney Livingstone and Gregor Benton, Trans). London: Penguin.

Marx, K. (1845/1975). *Theses on feuerbach.* (intro. Lucio Colletti, Trans. Rodney Livingstone and Gregor Benton, Trans). London: Penguin.

Marx, K. (1852/1984). *The eighteenth brumaire of louis bonaparte.* London: Lawrence and Wishart.

Marx, K. (1867/1990). *Capital: A critique of political economy, volume 1.* (intro. Ernest Mandel, Trans. Ben Fowkes, Trans). London: Penguin.

Morton, A. D. (2005). The Age of absolutism: Capitalism, the modern states-system and international relations. *Review of International Studies, 31*(3), 495–517.

Morton, A. D. (2007a). *Unravelling Gramsci: Hegemony and passive revolution in the global political economy.* London: Pluto Press.

Morton, A. D. (2007b). Waiting for gramsci: State formation, passive revolution and the international. *Millennium: Journal of International Studies, 35*(3), 597–621.

Morton, A. D. (2007c). Disputing the geopolitics of the states system and global capitalism. *Cambridge Review of International Affairs, 20*(4), 599–617.

Morton, A. D. (2010). The continuum of passive revolution. *Capital & Class, 34*(3), 315–342.

Morton, A. D. (2011/2013). *Revolution and state in modern Mexico: The political economy of uneven development* (Updated edition). Lanham, MD: Rowman & Littlefield.

Morton, A. D. (2013). The limits of sociological marxism? *Historical Materialism, 21*(1), 129–158.

Morton, A. D. (2018a). The architecture of "passive revolution": society, state and space in modern Mexico. *Journal of Latin American Studies, 50*(1), 117–152.

Morton, A. D. (2018b). The urban revolution in victor serge. *Annals of the American Association of Geographers.* doi: 10.1080/24694452.2018.1471387

Ollman, B. (1976). *Alienation: Marx's conception of Man in capitalist society* (2nd ed.). Cambridge: Cambridge University Press.

Peck, J. (2012). Economic geography: Island life. *Dialogues in Human Geography, 2*(2), 113–133.

Peck, J. (2013). For polanyian economic geographies. *Environment and Planning A, 45*(7), 1545–1568.

Polanyi, K. (1934a). Fascism and marxian terminology. *New Britain: A Weekly Organ of National Renaissance, 3*(57), 128–129. 20 June.

Polanyi, K. (1934b, June 27). Marxism Re-stated I. *New Britain: A Weekly Organ of National Renaissance, 3* (58), 159.

Polanyi, K. (1934c, July 14). Marxism Re-stated II. *New Britain: A Weekly Organ of National Renaissance, 3* (59), 187–188.

Polanyi, K. (1935). The essence of fascism. In J. Lewis, K. Polanyi, & D. K. Kitchin (Eds.), *Christianity and the social revolution* (pp. 359–394). London: Victor Gollancz.

Polanyi, K. (1937). *Europe today, preface G.D.H. Cole.* London: Workers' Educational Trade Union Committee.

Polanyi, K. (1943). Universal capitalism or regional planning? *The London Quarterly of World Affairs, IX*(I), 86–91.

Polanyi, K. (1944/1957). *The great transformation: The political and economic origins of Our time.* Boston, MA: Beacon Press.

Polanyi, K. (1947/1968). *'Our obsolete market mentality', in karl polanyi, primitive, archaic and modern economies, ed. George dalton* (pp. 59–77). New York, MA: Anchor Books.

Polanyi, K. (1953/1959). Anthropology and economic theory. In M. H. Fried (Ed.), *Readings in anthripology, volume II: Readings in cultural anthropology* (pp. 161–184). New York, NY: Thomas Y. Cromwell.

Polanyi, K. (1957). The economy as instituted process. In K. Polanyi, C. M. Arensberg, & H. W. Pearson (Eds.), *Trade and market in the early empires: Economics in history and theory* (pp. 243–270). Glencoe: The Free Press.

Polanyi, K. (2018). *Economy and society: Selected writings.* In Claus Thomasberger and Michele Cangiani (Ed.), Cambridge: Polity Press.

Polanyi Levitt, K. (2013). *From the great transformation to the great financialisation: On karl polanyi and other essays.* London: Zed Books.

Saull, R., Anievas, A., Davidson, N., & Fabry, A. (eds.). (2014). *Longue durée of the Far-right: An international historical sociology.* London: Routledge.

Selwyn, B., & Miyamura, S. (2013). Class struggle or embedded markets? Marx, polanyi and the meanings and possibilities of social transformation. *New Political Economy, 19*(5), 639–661.

Serge, V. (1944-45/1994). Planned economies and democracy. *Revolutionary History, 5*(3), 177–198.

Thomas, P. (2009). *The gramscian moment: Philosophy, hegemony and marxism.* Leiden: Brill.

Trotsky, L. (1932/2004). What next? Vital questions for the German proletariat. In L. Trotsky (Ed.), *The struggle against fascism in Germany* (pp. 164–297). New York, NY: Pathfinder Press.

von Mises, L. (1927/1962). *The free and prosperous commonwealth: An exposition of the ideas of classical liberalism.* Princeton, NY: D. Van Norstrand.

Wood, E. M. (1995). *Democracy against capitalism: Renewing historical materialism.* London: Verso.

Wood, E. M. (1999). *The origin of capitalism: A longer view.* London: Verso.

Polanyi, Hayek and embedded neoliberalism

Damien Cahill

ABSTRACT

Written originally on the seventieth anniversary of the publication of Friedrich von Hayek's *The Road to Serfdom* and Karl Polanyi's *The Great Transformation*, this article critically analyses how the ideas of Hayek and Polanyi have been deployed to understand neoliberalism. It argues that dominant scholarly interpretations tend to miss the significance of each thinker to an understanding of neoliberalism, as well as some of the key dynamics of neoliberal forms of capitalist regulation. Drawing upon the work of Polanyi, the article advances the concept of embedded neoliberalism. From the 1970s neoliberal regulations became deeply embedded in a series of institutions, class relations and ideological norms. This helps to explain both the durability of neoliberalism, and the onset of crisis in 2008. In this context, Hayek's ideas are best understood as providing a malleable set of concepts underpinning neoliberal ideology, rather than the chief causal agent in the neoliberal transformation of states and economies.

The political economic principles articulated by Friedrich von Hayek and Karl Polanyi in their best known works, *The Great Transformation* and *The Road to Serfdom*, both published in 1944 as the Second World War was heading to its tragic conclusion, are often seen as emblematic of the two modes of organizing capitalist economic relations which followed. Polanyi is typically seen as emblematic of the Bretton Woods international architecture of the post-war period that lasted from roughly 1945–1973. Here Polanyi's concept of the socially embedded economy is viewed as synonymous with social protections and market regulations which underpinned the prosperity and relative political stability within the core economies during the 'golden age' of capitalism.

In contrast the neoliberal era, which reshaped states and the way they regulated the capitalist economy from the early 1980s and is now in crisis, is typically viewed as the age of Hayek as well as embodying Polanyi's warnings about the perils of the self-regulating market and the disembedding of the economy from its social support structures. Hayek's broadsides against what he viewed as the collectivist impulses at the heart of the post-war economic order, his advocacy of an alternative competitive market-based order as the only guarantee of individual freedom, and his key role in forming, and leadership of, the Mont Pèlerin Society, which came to form the epicentre of a global intellectual movement dedicated to proselytizing such ideas, have been interpreted by numerous scholars as underpinning the neoliberal policy revolution that swept across capitalist states in the latter decades of the twentieth century.

This article argues that such commonplace assumptions may lead us to miss the central dynamics of these two distinct periods of capitalist regulation, and the significance of the thought of both

Hayek and Polanyi to each period. An alternative reading of the analytical utility of Polanyi's and Hayek's intellectual output in relation to the neoliberal order, in particular, is therefore offered. The argument developed here is that Polanyi's concept of the socially embedded economy is most useful for illuminating the constitutive features of capitalism when it is interpreted as what Gemici (2008) calls a 'methodological principle' rather than as a 'historical variable'. This means understanding economies as 'always embedded' in institutions that provide order, cohesion and an overarching logic to economic processes. It is argued that this perspective prompts consideration of the institutions, class relations and ideological frameworks in which neoliberal forms of regulation became embedded. This socially embedded nature of neoliberalism, it is contended, provides neoliberalism with significant durability in the face of crisis, but also contains immanent contradictions that are presently unravelling.

With respect to Hayek, it is argued that his thought is less useful as a guide to understanding the central dynamics of neoliberalism, but rather more useful when understood as providing a key anchor point for the ways in which the neoliberal order has often been presented. More specifically, it is argued that Hayek's *oeuvre* provides a palette of concepts that underpin the ideological framework in which neoliberalism is embedded and which offer a justification for the neoliberal order.

Polanyi and the concept of the socially embedded economy

The 'socially embedded economy' is one of the most enduring concepts from Polanyi's *The Great Transformation* to have been appropriated by scholars. One of the most influential of such appropriations is Ruggie's concept of 'embedded liberalism' which sees in the combination of global currency regulations and domestic commitments to welfare capitalism a re-embedding of markets in society and their subordination to social goals, as advocated by Polanyi in opposition to the devastation caused by the 'self-regulating market' through which the economy had previously been disembedded from its social support structure (Ruggie, 1982). Within this interpretation 'embeddedness' is understood as being synonymous with social protection and market regulation.

More recently this interpretation and the associated concept of the double movement, has been deployed to understand the processes at the heart of neoliberalism. According to such an interpretation the processes of deregulation and privatization pursued by states from the 1970s, by removing the regulations and social support structures that quarantined people and nations from market disciplines, 'disembedded' markets from their social support structures, with predictably deleterious consequences (e.g. Altvater, 2009; Best, 2003; Ruggie, 2008).

This understanding conforms to the interpretation of Polanyi's embeddedness concept as a 'historical variable' (Gemici, 2008). Under such an interpretation, economies or markets are more or less embedded to the extent that they are regulated or constrain markets through social protections – the more regulated or socially protected the economy, the more embedded it is.

Certainly, there are elements of Polanyi's argument in *The Great Transformation* which support the 'embeddedness-as-a-historical variable' interpretation. In pre-capitalist economies, argues Polanyi (2001, p. 71), markets were 'never … more than accessories of life. As a rule, the economic system was absorbed in the social system'. According to Polanyi, prior to the rise of capitalism, markets were subordinated to social norms, regulations, customs and goals. However, integration was rent asunder by the attempts to realize what Polanyi views as the utopian goal of the 'self-regulating market'. Inspired by the political economic doctrines of Bentham, Smith and Ricardo, policy makers attempted to realize in practice the vision of *laissez-faire*. For Polanyi, this entailed 'the institutional separation of society into an economic and a political sphere'. This creates a historically unprecedented situation in which the human economy becomes disembedded from society:

> normally the economic order is merely a function of the social order. Neither under tribal nor under feudal nor under mercantile conditions was there, as we saw, a separate economic system in society. Nineteenth century society, in which economic activity was isolated and imputed with a distinctive economic motive, was a singular departure. (Polanyi, 2001, p. 74)

Thus, Polanyi seems to take the view that prior to the rise of the 'self-regulating market', the economy and society were fused, and entangled, whereas the rise of capitalism entailed breaking this fusion. As Dale (2010) notes, there is more than a hint of naturalism in his depiction of the organic unity of pre-capitalist society, and the 'extreme artificiality' of the market economy and certainly it supports an interpretation of Polanyi as adhering to the 'embeddedness as historical variable' view of markets. In pre-capitalist society, markets were highly embedded in so far as they were subordinate to the dictates of society, whereas under nineteenth century capitalism markets came to be disembedded, subordinating society to their logic.

Nonetheless, this sits rather uncomfortably against other passages from *The Great Transformation*. Polanyi argues that 'the road to the free market was opened and kept open by an enormous increase in continuous, centrally organized and controlled interventionism' (Polanyi, 2001, p. 146). Polanyi's point is that the state provided the necessary underpinnings for the development and expansion of the market economy. For Polanyi (2001, p. 145), 'free markets could never have come into being merely by allowing things to take their course', because markets are generally poor at providing the pre-requisites for their own reproduction, including the rules and norms that govern and facilitate market conduct. Such recognition, however, seems to be at odds with Polanyi's argument that the rise of the 'self-regulating market' disembedded the economy from its social context, as Polanyi's historical narrative implicitly posits the self-regulating market as dependent upon, and hence embedded within, an enlarged state regulatory apparatus.

To Polanyi's mind, such an increase in state activity seems to be distinct from the protective regulations enacted by the state designed to quarantine labour, land and money from the full force of market dependence. Yet here too, there seems to be a clear contradiction between his 'embeddedness as historical variable' assumptions, and his more detailed description of the course of nineteenth century history. This is articulated most clearly through Polanyi's concepts of 'fictitious commodities' and 'the double movement'. In *The Great Transformation*, Polanyi distinguishes between 'fictitious commodities' and 'genuine commodities' The latter have a price, are traded in markets, are produced for sale and comprise most commodities available in a market economy. The former however, while sharing with 'genuine commodities' the qualities of being priced and traded in markets, are not produced for sale. Land, labour and money are all examples of such 'fictitious commodities' according to Polanyi for, although not produced for sale, the self-regulating market demands that they be treated 'as if' they are genuine commodities – hence they are regulated according to a 'fiction'. This distinction between genuine and fictitious commodities is central to Polanyi's interpretation of 'the political and economic origins of our time'. To treat fictitious commodities as if they were genuine commodities and to subject them to the full force of market imperatives, argues Polanyi, would have devastating consequences, undermining the social, natural and monetary basis of the market economy: 'no society could stand the effects of such a system of crude fictions even for the shortest stretch of time unless its human and natural substance as well as its business organization was protected against this satanic mill' (Polanyi, 2001, pp. 76–77). The effect, Polanyi argues, was to produce a 'socially protective counter-movement' – a set of regulations effectively shielding land, labour and money (by which

Polanyi seems to mean *fiat* money) from the vagaries of the 'self-regulating market'. Therefore, Polanyi (2001, p. 79) argues that '[s]ocial history in the nineteenth century was thus the result of a double movement: the extension of the market organization with respect to genuine commodities was accompanied by its restriction with respect to fictitious ones'. Despite the utopian aspirations of those elites who attempted to disembed markets from their social foundations, Polanyi seems to suggest that in practice markets came to be re-embedded through the state regulations that protected society from the full force of the self-regulating market.

How can such a contradiction within Polanyi's best known work be understood, and is it possible to rescue anything of value? A useful way forward is offered by Block and Somers (2014). They argue that Polanyi's understanding of the capitalist economy was in a process of transition whilst writing the book. Yet, this process was incomplete. Polanyi was time-constrained in writing the book – he wished to see it published before the end of world war two so that it could shape debates regarding social reconstruction in the post-war period (Block & Somers, 2014, pp. 81–82). Consequently, Polanyi was unable to revise the work as he may have wished and 'the resulting manuscript was left with a number of contradictions and conflicts' (Block & Somers, 2014, p. 73).

The key concept that is immanent within the book, but which is not specifically articulated and incorporated consistently throughout, Block and Somers contend, is that of the 'always-embedded market economy': that the state is necessary for the development and expanded reproduction of the capitalist economy by providing both the 'non-contractual bases of contract, the set of legal rules and institutions required to formalize property rights and contractual obligations' and for the commodification of land, labour and money (Block & Somers, 2014, p. 93). They (2014, pp. 73–74) argue that 'Polanyi glimpsed the idea of the *always-embedded market economy*, but he was not able to give that idea a name or to develop it theoretically because it represented too great a divergence from his initial theoretical starting point'. Thus, Polanyi's analysis remains incomplete, nonetheless, '[h]e provides us with some extremely important suggestions about how to carry out an analysis of the always-embedded market economy' (Block & Somers, 2014, p. 95). This is consistent with those who argue that Polanyi was heavily influenced (and hence constrained) in his thinking by concepts inherited from neoclassical economics (e.g. Gemici, 2015). It was simply too great a conceptual leap to transition from his ingrained neoclassical modes of thinking to a more heterodox view of the economy.

The 'always embedded market economy' interpretation of the direction of Polanyi's thought is even more compelling when read in the context of his later essay, 'The Economy as Instituted Process' (Polanyi, 1957). Here Polanyi argues that 'the human economy is always and everywhere embedded in institutions, economic and non-economic' (Polanyi, 1957, p. 250). According to Polanyi, an examination of historically existing economies, whether capitalist, feudal or tribal, reveals that they are always 'instituted' – by which he means given regularity, cohesion and stability by an institutional architecture. Such architecture includes both formally constituted institutions such as states and corporations, as well as informal institutions such as beliefs, customs and culture. Clearly this maps quite neatly onto the 'always embedded market economy' concept. Rather than there being 'a hard core of market behaviour existing outside of social life (and hence that needed to be embedded)', markets are more usefully understood as 'fully social institutions' (Krippner, 2001, pp. 778, 782).

This understanding of economies as being always institutionally embedded accords much better with the history of actual human economies than does the embedded/disembedded dualism. Whereas Polanyi's distinction between fictitious and genuine commodities in *The Great Transformation* seems to fall into the trap of commodity fetishism by ignoring the social relations that underpin all commodity production in a capitalist economy (Dale, 2010, p. 77), if we instead take his nascent concept of the 'always embedded economy' as a master-frame, then the social relations at the heart of capitalism become more legible. Thus, the utility of the 'always embedded economy' concept is that it quickly cuts through the fetishism at the heart of common presentations of the economy. Such presentations tend to view states and markets or economy and society as separate and antithetical spheres of human activity. They are underpinned by a 'diachronic' (Radice, 2010) form of analysis, in which more of one means less of the other. In contrast, the 'always embedded economy' concept prompts consideration that beneath the ubiquity of markets and prices – perhaps the most visible signs of the dominance of capitalism in people's everyday lives – lies a host of social relations, regulations and norms that facilitate their functioning.

Polanyi and neoliberalism

As noted earlier, there is a tendency within literature on neoliberalism to understand it as a process of disembedding markets, in contrast to the post-war economy, which, following Ruggie, is viewed as a system of 'embedded liberalism'. According to such a view, neoliberal processes of privatization, deregulation and marketization dismantled the regulatory architecture of the post-war economy, removing the constraints that had subordinated markets to society. Scholars who take such a view typically also focus on efforts to re-embed the economy in society through socially protective counter-movements stemming from an appreciation of the socially and economically destructive effects of neoliberalism (e.g. Ruggie, 2008).

However, such an interpretation sits uncomfortably alongside the 'always embedded market economy' framework. Indeed, this framework suggests that just as the post-war economy was institutionally embedded, so too is the neoliberal economy embedded within, and crucially dependent upon, a matrix of institutions (see Cahill, 2014). In order to elaborate this perspective, the following discussion first examines the formal institutions that underpin the neoliberal order. Discussion then turns to the social relations that have been crucial to the development and reproduction of the neoliberal order and, finally, the ideational frameworks that buttress neoliberalism will be examined. Each of these, it is argued, forms part of the neoliberal institutional ensemble that facilitated a revival of capital accumulation in the wake of the crisis that beset the capitalist world economy in the 1970s but which also contained immanent contradictions and weaknesses.

This is quite distinct from other concepts of embedded neoliberalism that have variously been proposed. Moreover, it overcomes their significant limitations, is consistent with a view of capitalist economies more generally as being 'always embedded', and does not assume a neat coherence between neoliberal ideas and neoliberal policies and economic processes.

Cerny (2008), for example, proposes a concept of 'embedded neoliberalism' that is conceived primarily in ideational terms. For Cerny, neoliberalism is in the first instance 'a relatively closed doctrine', which was transformed 'into a hegemonic concept that is seeping into and co-opting the whole spectrum of political life' (Cerny, 2008, p. 3). Cerny (2008, p. 2) argues that neoliberal discourse 'has become deeply embedded in twenty-first century institutional behaviour, political processes and understandings of socio-economic "realities"'. For Cerny then, causal priority is accorded to neoliberal ideas. Neoliberalism, as a discourse, or set of ideas, becomes institutionally embedded and normalized, and thus structures the behaviour of policy makers and other elites.

Cerny gives causal priority to neoliberal ideas but encounters problems when accounting for variation in neoliberal practices and in explaining why these practices diverge from doctrinal neoliberalism. Cerny (2008, p. 40) admits such a wide variety of neoliberal ideas and such flexibility within neoliberal discourse that it is not at all clear what neoliberalism might mean. For example, according to Cerny (2008, p. 40), '[n]eoliberalism is increasingly what actors make of it'. Cerny (2008, pp. 28–39) also argues that embedded neoliberalism is mediated by other material factors – interests, institutions and other economic processes – however this prompts the question of what has causal priority in political economic change and how useful is the embedded neoliberalism concept if *other* (non-ideational) social forces are actually driving such changes? Ultimately, then, Cerny's concept of embedded neoliberalism has limited analytical utility. This is not to dismiss the argument that a neoliberal commonsense has developed among policy makers. Rather it is to recognize that, in order to understand the embedded nature of neoliberalism, and the dynamics of neoliberalism, an understanding is required of the relationship between the ideological and other mechanisms through which neoliberalism is embedded.

Bastiaan van Apeldoorn (2009) also offers a concept of embedded neoliberalism as it pertains to the European Union. He views 'embedded neoliberalism' as a 'hegemonic project', undertaken by states and 'reflecting as well as mediating the interests of social and political forces bound up with transnational European capital' (van Apeldoorn, 2009, p. 22). He understands European neoliberalism as embedded to the extent that it is combined with socially protective policies and institutions at the national level. He also identifies a contradiction between, on one hand, such policies which contribute to the embedded nature of neoliberalism, and, on the other hand, the 'disembedding' (van Apeldoorn, 2009, p. 24) dynamic at the heart of neoliberalism, which is evident primarily at the supra national European level. This concept of embedded neoliberalism relies upon a particular interpretation of Polanyi – that Polanyi conceived of socially protective economic processes as contributing to a dynamic of social embeddedness, and an antithetical set of liberal economic processes which serve to disembed the economy from its social foundations.

> Drawing on Polanyi, embeddedness here refers to the role of the state in sustaining and reproducing markets by in effect protecting society from the destructive effects of the self-regulating market ... The term 'embedded' in embedded neoliberalism thus refers to what Polanyi called the *principle of social protection*. (van Apeldoorn, 2009, pp. 24–25)

However, it is not clear why only socially protective regulations contribute to embeddedness and not other forms of state regulation of economic activity. Surely these latter regulations are also fundamentally social in nature? The strength of van Apeldoorn's conception, though, is that it points towards a concept of neoliberalism as constituted by state practices and embedded class relations (van Apeldoorn, 2009, pp. 31–38). While the analytical utility of the conceptions of 'embedded neoliberalism' as put forward by Cerny and van Apeldoorn are therefore limited, each does nonetheless point towards elements of a more fruitful analysis of neoliberalism. Cerny's conception draws attention to the ways in which neoliberal practices are embedded in 'shared mental model[s]' (Cerny, 2008, p. 2) and the formation of a neoliberal 'common sense' (Cerny, 2008, p. 2) among political and economic elites. Alternatively, van Apeldoorn draws attention to the ways in which neoliberal policy practices are embedded within a distinct configuration of class relations, but also prompts consideration of the existence of contradictions between different elements of neoliberalism.

If we are to take seriously the concept of the 'always embedded economy', and infer from this that neoliberalism is an inherently socially embedded economic form, then any account of 'embedded neoliberalism' must identify the distinct mechanisms through which neoliberalism is socially embedded, but also resist the temptation to counterpose this against elements of neoliberalism which supposedly entail disembedding of the economy from its social foundations.

Neoliberalism, as a distinct and historically specific state project (Jessop, 2002) emerged unevenly from the 1970s, as the outcome of conflict, compromise and policy experimentation by and between state elites, employers, major owners of capital, union leaders and workers. It entailed the reconfiguration of the ways in which states regulated capitalist economic processes and facilitated processes of social reproduction. In general (but also stressing its temporal and geographical unevenness) neoliberalism entailed a greater engagement of private capital and markets, or market-like arrangements, in the provision of public services, a removal of many of the restrictions and transaction costs pertaining to firms during the post-war period, a reorientation of fiscal policy in favour of lower rates of corporate and personal income tax and a slowing of the rate of public expenditure and income growth, as well a shift to a more rules-based inflation targeting monetary policy, alongside workfare programmes and the rise of greater managerial prerogatives in the employment relationship.

Polanyi's concept of the always embedded economy is useful here in prompting an investigation of the social factors underpinning this state project and thereby to understand its considerable durability. Three mechanisms through which the neoliberal state project became institutionally (in the broadest, Polanyian sense) embedded seem especially important. First, neoliberal forms of regulation and modes of service provision have become embedded at the formal institutional level, especially within the state. Contrary to much popular (and some scholarly) discourse, the process of neoliberalisation did not entail a withdrawal of the state from economic regulation nor, in most cases, did it entail a diminution of the state. While there was certainly a process of 'rolling back' a host of the regulations that had governed the operation of firms during the post-war decades, there was also a process of 'rolling out' new neoliberal state institutions and regulations (Levi-Faur, 2005; Peck & Tickell, 2002). Thus, the state was reconfigured rather than retrenched, and part of this reconfiguration was the establishment of a series of formal rules and regulations that are 'structurally biased' (van Apeldoorn, 2009, p. 26) towards neoliberalism, effectively pre-committing states to maintain or extend neoliberal forms of governance. Such rules and regulations have bequeathed a particular stickiness to neoliberal state transformations. Examples include the fiscal and monetary policy constraints of the European Union, various forms of competition policy, the articles of the World Trade Organisation, as well as numerous free trade agreements, all of which commit states to neoliberal forms of governance. As several authors have observed, the structural bias towards neoliberal policies gives them a constitutional element (Gill, 2001; Nicol, 2010). The neoliberal bias is institutionally embedded in such a way as to make neoliberal policy norms part of the rules, principles and precedents by which nation states are governed, thus effectively constitutionalizing neoliberalism. Nicol (2010, p. 46) therefore calls such measures a 'constitutional law protection of neoliberal capitalism', which draws attention to the ways in which such regulations limit the policy freedom of states to move in non-neoliberal directions, irrespective of the ideology or policy preferences of state elites.

The second key mechanism through which the neoliberal state project has become socially embedded is the transformation that has occurred within capitalist social relations since the 1980s. At a general level, and expressed to various degress within different national and regional contexts, there has been a shift in the balance of class forces brought about by the weakening of labour and the strengthening of capital. Labour market deregulations granted management greater flexibility and discretion over the deployment and dismissal of labour within the production process, enabled the rise of precarious forms of employment, and inhibited the ability of trade unions to organize. Direct attacks upon organized labour by states, or by capital supported by states, also played a part in shifting the balance of class forces. This is not to suggest that class struggle was absent during the neoliberal period, nor to ignore those instances where such struggles stymied the advance of specific neoliberal initiatives (Bailey, Clua-Losada, Huke, & Ribera-Almandoz,

2017). Nonetheless, in general terms, Glyn (2006, p. 127) is surely right to conclude that 'it seems impossible to depict all of this as signaling anything other than a major retreat for labour.'

All of these changes occurred alongside the development of greater political organization and coherence among the capitalist class (Hacker & Pierson, 2010, pp. 175–177; Phillips-Fein, 2009). This, in conjunction with the declining organizational strength of labour, meant that there was a diminished counter-veiling force against the interests of business. As Hacker and Pierson (2010, pp. 179–180) argue:

> Strong labour unions are closely associated with low levels of inequality and more generous social programs … The decline of organised labour has greatly diminished the pressure on policymakers to sustain or refurbish commitments to social provision made in the middle decades of the last century.

The changing balance of class forces from the 1970s onwards therefore facilitated a roll-out of neoliberalism, both with respect to industrial relations and to social and economic policy more broadly.

The third mechanism through which the neoliberal state project came to be socially embedded was a general ideological shift during the neoliberal era. Over time, the neoliberal state project developed 'bipartisan' support from both conservative and social democratic parties (Belloc & Nicita, 2011, p. 123). Part of this broad policy convergence was the solidification of neoliberal discursive frames as a policy 'common sense' or 'rationality' (Beeson & Firth, 1998) among political elites across the capitalist world. The practices of neoliberalism have become the default approach to policy across the capitalist world, and neoliberal theories came to operate as justifications for such policies, as well as ways of explaining observed reality, guiding thinking about the desirable course, nature and scope of policy making in capitalist economies. Within such discursive frames, the neoliberal policy revolution is understood as a rational, and almost inevitable response to the logic of market forces, and alternatives to neoliberalism are cast as unrealistic or romantic anachronisms, with opponents viewed as motivated by ideology or narrow self-interest.

Together these mechanisms of institutional, class-relational and ideological embedding formed something akin to a social structure of accumulation or mode of regulation (Kotz, 2015). Together, and in their complex inter-relations, they lent significant inertia to the neoliberal state project and facilitated capital accumulation on a global scale from the 1980s until the onset of crisis in 2008. Yet, the institutional ensemble that afforded neoliberalism such inertia also contained immanent contradictions, which helps explain the political and economic crises that have become characteristic of contemporary capitalism. In the USA, for example, financial deregulation facilitated much greater access by working class households to credit, thus boosting effective demand in the context of wage stagnation. Yet it also led to the integration of workers much more directly (even though this was only faintly perceived by many at the time) into global financial markets through the securitization of their debt repayments (Krippner, 2011; Soederberg, 2010). While boosting profits, it also ultimately provided the pre-conditions for the collapse of the sub-prime mortgage market in 2007, which quickly ballooned into a global economic crisis.

The roots of the ensuing political crisis can also be usefully located within the contradictory institutional underpinnings of embedded neoliberalism. As Ayers and Saad-Filho (2015, p. 603) highlight, 'formal democracy has come to constitute the political form of neoliberalism' yet this has entailed simultaneously a process of depoliticization, whereby major economic policy settings, such as monetary policy for example, are quarantined from popular deliberation. This contradictory political form, combined with the spread of economic crisis and austerity across the globe since 2008, has provided the context for the significant decline in support for traditional social democratic parties (who had become part of the neoliberal consensus) across the advanced capitalist economies, the

THE UTOPIAN SPRINGS OF MARKET ECONOMY

concurrent rise of authoritarian and racist parties and leaders, and the surge in support for more left-wing leaders within traditional centre-Left parties where disaffection with neoliberal democracy has been leveraged to great effect.

Hayek and neoliberalism

And what of Hayek? His work is often taken as providing the inspiration, blueprint and/or intellectual driving force for the neoliberal transformation of states and economies. The rise of neoliberalism is often viewed as the culmination of a concerted campaign by Hayek and his followers to wind back the collectivist impulses and policies championed by the likes of Polanyi and to realize a liberal utopia. Indeed, there is a tendency among scholars to read neoliberal forms of regulation through the work of Hayek as if the two phenomena were essentially synonymous. Echoing Polanyi's analysis of the rise of *laissez-faire* in nineteenth century England, which attributed this phenomenon to the influence the utopian 'liberal creed' exercised over political elites through the intellectual founders of political economy, there is a propensity to understand the rise of neoliberal forms of economic regulation as the result of policy makers coming under the sway of neoliberal ideas, through the influence of neoliberal intellectuals such as Hayek and the think tanks, such as the Institute of Economic Affairs, that proselytized his ideas. In one of the more influential recent examples of this propensity Mirowski (2009, 2013) argues that Hayek was crucial to the articulation of the neoliberal thought collective's central strategy of the 'double truth' doctrine:

> Hayek hit upon the brilliant notion of developing the 'double truth' doctrine of neoliberalism – namely, an elite would be tutored to understand the deliciously Schmittian necessity of repressing democracy, while the masses would be regaled with ripping tales of 'rolling back the nanny state' and being set 'free to choose' – by convening a closed Leninist organization of counter-intellectuals. (Mirowski, 2013, p. 86)

He contends it is mistaken to understand neoliberalism as entailing advocacy of small states and free markets. Rather, according to Mirowski, this is simply the neoliberal thought collective's own 'exoteric' propaganda about themselves. While fundamentalist neoliberal intellectuals might publically advocate a withering away of the state, in private and among themselves within the secretive confines of the Mont Pèlerin Society and other invitation-only meetings of the thought collective, they develop quite a different 'esoteric' doctrine – that the state should be used to enforce competition and market rule even if this entails suppressing democracy or expanding the size and scope of government. This strategy, argues Mirowski, was highly successful in shaping the course of state transformations along the lines set out by Hayek and his fellow travelling neoliberal intellectuals.

Examples of this form of ideas-centric reasoning abound and prompt consideration of the ways in which Hayek might properly be understood as relevant for an appreciation of the dynamics of neoliberalism. It will be argued here that just as the utility of Polanyi's work for understanding neoliberalism has been widely misinterpreted, so has Hayek's contribution to neoliberalism been largely misunderstood. The article will first consider Hayek's contribution to the development of neoliberalism through the 'neoliberal thought collective' (Mirowski & Plehwe, 2009) before analysing how the contribution of Hayek's ideas to embedded neoliberalism should properly be understood.

Hayek and the neoliberal thought collective

One of the ways in which Hayek is relevant to an understanding of the neoliberal policy revolution concerns his role as an activist. Hayek was a key figure in the formation of the Mont Pèlerin Society which became the nucleus of the 'neoliberal thought collective' – an intellectual movement with the aim of effecting a neoliberal reconstruction of the state and whose organizational backbone was a network of think tanks, which, although small in number until the early 1980s, thereafter grew into a global phenomenon, numbering approximately 400 think tanks across 80 countries by the early twenty-first century (Stone, 2013, p. 72).

Hayek's project was to reconstruct the foundations of a free society, which he viewed as threatened by the rise of 'collectivism'. This argument was articulated most forcefully and famously in *The Road to Serfdom*. Dedicated 'To the socialists of all parties', it argued that a collectivist consensus had come to dominate politics in the West, leading to the mistaken and dangerous belief that rational economic planning could secure economic prosperity and was compatible with human flourishing. He contended that economic planning inevitably led society down the 'road to serfdom' as it entailed particular conceptions of the good to be imposed on society, thus infringing individual liberties: 'The exigencies of planning', Hayek (1944, p. 97) wrote, 'consists essentially in depriving us of choice, in order to give us whatever best fits into the plan and that at a time determined by the plan'. In contrast, Hayek (1944, pp. 20–21) advocated a return to the principles of individualism: 'the respect for the individual man *qua* man, that is the recognition of his own views and tastes as supreme in his own sphere'.

The chief novelty of Hayek's book was his argument that social democracy, socialism and Nazism were essentially synonymous due to their shared commitment to collectivism. Moreover, in Hayek's view, even mild forms of social democratic planning regimes would inevitably lead to totalitarianism. Collectivism, for Hayek, was fundamentally an ideational phenomenon. It is an argument made frequently throughout *The Road to Serfdom*. He elaborates and returns often to this theme, arguing for example that collectivism was a manifestation of a particular 'trend of ideas', beginning in Germany, and spreading throughout Europe and England, such that

> students of the currents of ideas can hardly fail to see that there is more than a superficial similarity between the trend of thought in Germany during and after the last war and the present current of ideas in this country. (Hayek, 1944, p. 10)

Contra Polanyi, Nazism did not come to power due to the failings of capitalism, but due to the power of collectivist ideas.

This analysis of the source of collectivism also shaped the strategy Hayek advocated to combat it. Hayek would come to argue that neoliberals should replicate the successful tactics of socialists, which, he thought, consisted in targeting opinion formers – 'second-hand dealers in ideas' – and trying to win them over to an alternative philosophy. One glimpses this in *The Road to Serfdom*:

> It is at least doubtful whether at this stage a detailed blueprint of a desirable internal order of society would be of much use – or whether anyone is competent to furnish it. The important thing now is that we come to agree on certain principles and free ourselves from some of the errors which have governed us in the recent past. (Hayek, 1944, p. 220)

Yet the strategy is outlined much more clearly in his later (1949) essay 'The Intellectuals and Socialism'. Impressed by what he saw as the success of the British Fabians in converting a generation of opinion formers into socialists, Hayek argued that liberals should replicate such tactics. Moreover, for such an endeavour it would not be sufficient merely to put forward proposals for piecemeal change, nor simply to subject current policy to critique. Rather, Hayek called for liberals to articulate a more utopian conception of the good society based upon first principles which, even if not realizable in its totality, nonetheless demonstrated the values, ideals and rationale upon which a free society must be based, and which would provide both a goal to strive towards, and a benchmark against which current arrangements could be evaluated:

> What we lack is a liberal Utopia, a program which seems neither a mere defense of things as they are nor a diluted kind of socialism, but a truly liberal radicalism … and which does not confine itself to what appears today as politically possible. (Hayek, 1949, p. 432)

Hayek returned to this point in his later work. For example, in his Preface to *The Constitution of Liberty* he stated,

> I am not concerned here exclusively with facts, nor do I confine myself to statements of cause and effect. My main aim is to picture an ideal, to show how it can be achieved, and to explain what its realization would mean in practice. (Hayek, 2006, p. ix)

He continues this argument in the Introduction: 'If we are to succeed in the great struggle of ideas that is under way, we must first of all know what we believe' (Hayek, 2006, p. 2). This theme was also elaborated by Hayek in *Law Legislation and Liberty*:

> an ideal picture of a society which may not be wholly achievable, or a guiding conception of the overall order to be aimed at, is nevertheless not only the indispensible precondition for any rational policy, but also the chief contribution that science can make to the solution to the problems of practical policy. (Hayek, 1973, p. 65, v1)

The themes articulated by Hayek provided much of the impetus for the inaugural meeting of what became known as the Mont Pèlerin Society on April 1–10, 1947 in Switzerland at the Hôtel du Parc, on the slopes of Mont Pèlerin, overlooking Lake Geneva. Hayek was the driving force behind the gathering, to which he invited a small group of those he considered like-minded intellectuals, mainly economists, although with a smattering of philosophers and journalists. Thirty-nine attended the gathering (Burgin, 2012, p. 102) with the purpose, as outlined by Hayek in a note circulated to invitees 'to work out in continuous effort, a philosophy of freedom which can claim to provide an alternative to the political views now so widely held' (in Cockett, 1995, p. 104). Although composed of intellectuals, the conference had a clear activist character: 'We must train an army of fighters for freedom' wrote Hayek in a briefing note for the Conference (Hayek in Cockett, 1995, p. 104).

During the next several decades, a series of think tanks such as the Institute of Economic Affairs, and the American Enterprise Institute heeded Hayek's call and unflinchingly promoted the neoliberal agenda. Funded largely through corporate support, these think tanks, and their activist leaders were, as Stedman Jones (2012, p. 136) argues, 'exceptionally talented at bridging the gap between the technical and academic work of neoliberal scholars and the wider political and public debate'. They distilled the central propositions of key neoliberal intellectuals such as Hayek into forms more legible for a broader audience and, followed his advice in primarily targeting opinion formers. As DeMuth (2007), former head of the American Enterprise Institute attests, there was a certain utility in having a fundamentalist approach to policy: 'It is a great advantage, when working on practical problems, not to be constantly doubling back to first principals. We know our foundations and concentrate on the specifics of the problem at hand'.

Hayek remained a key source of inspiration for the movement, even as he became less central to its organizational leadership from the 1960s onwards (Burgin, 2012, pp. 152–154). Moreover, his intellectual output provides a useful guide to the tactics adopted by the movement. In this sense, it is proper to credit Hayek as an influential figure in the rise of neoliberalism.

In contrast, there is rather less good reason to follow so many other scholars of neoliberalism down the path of ascribing either to Hayek or to his thought the status of chief causal agent in the neoliberal policy revolution itself. This is not simply for the reason that the neoliberal thought collective was somewhat plural in its intellectual composition and Hayek was but one of several intellectual leaders. More importantly it is due to the character of Hayek's *oeuvre* itself, the forms in which Hayek's ideas have circulated, the ways in which ideas articulate with other social forces to produce political economic change and the many key elements of the neoliberal policy revolution that seem to have departed from the Hayekian script or have proceeded without any direct influence from Hayek or, indeed, other key figures from the neoliberal thought collective.

Staying with Hayek's ideas for the moment, Hayek's aspiration to utopian analysis accurately captures the normative character of much of his intellectual output. It is unlikely, as Hayek implicitly admitted, that his political economic vision was 'wholly achievable'. His was a liberal ideal with little concern for the compromises and constraints acting upon policy-makers. This gives cause for scepticism of attempts to reduce neoliberal policy to the influence of Hayek's ideas.

Yet, not only the character, but equally, the content of Hayek's normative ideas suggests against the thesis of a Hayek-led process of ideational causation. This is particularly true with respect to his view of the proper role of the state. On this point Hayek is highly ambiguous. As noted, the target of Hayek's critique was collectivism and economic planning whereby the state substituted particular conceptions of the good, for the outcomes that would otherwise spontaneously emerge through the voluntary interaction of free individuals pursuing their subjective preferences through market exchanges.

Hayek (1944, pp. 20–21) advocated a return to the principles of individualism. He was clear, however, that this should not be conflated with support for *laissez-faire*: 'Probably nothing has done so much harm to the liberal cause as the wooden insistence of some liberals on certain rough rules of thumb, above all the principle of *laissez-faire*' (Hayek, 1944, p. 24). Rather, he saw a positive role for the state in creating the conditions under which a market order could operate, yet he was equally clear that it was the spontaneous forces of markets that should primarily be relied upon for the satisfaction of human needs and desires and, indeed, that this provided the only basis for the flourishing of the individual and of human civilization more generally.

For Hayek, the good society is one measured against a negative conception of liberty 'in which coercion of some by others is reduced as much as is possible' (Hayek, 2006, p. 11). The best way of achieving this state of liberty, according to Hayek, is by allowing humans to interact voluntarily. Because markets enable people to secure their interests through voluntary interaction, Hayek argues that markets are the most appropriate way of arranging human affairs. In general, the role for the state in such a liberal order is to provide the rule of law which protects 'the known private spheres of the individuals against interference by others and delimiting these private spheres' (Hayek, 2006, p. 20). The rule of law also provides legal frameworks to underpin the operation of markets, such as the enforcement of contracts and the ability to 'own and acquire property' (Hayek, 2006, p. 19). Hayek admits that state coercion of individuals is inevitable, but argues that this should be limited 'to instances where it is required to prevent coercion by private persons' (Hayek, 2006, p. 20).

However, Hayek also allows for a potentially much greater role for the state than is suggested by the 'freedom from coercion' principle. He argues that so long as state coercive rules are 'known general rules', widely understood and not applicable to particular classes of individuals, then they are permissible. In this case, coercion is justified because the individual is able to predict that certain types of action will lead to coercive responses by the state and therefore 'the individual never need be coerced unless he has placed himself in a position where he knows that he will be coerced' (Hayek, 2006, p. 20). Yet, one can imagine many types of state regulation that might constitute 'known rules' and yet would contravene an indivudual's 'free action', which 'presupposes the existence of a known sphere in which the circumstances cannot be so shaped by another person so as to leave one only that choice prescribed by the other' (Hayek, 2006, p. 19). Thus begins the process whereby *The Constitution of Liberty* legitimates a host of seemingly illiberal state activities. Indeed, Hayek (2006, p. 190) allows that '[e]ven the most fundamental principles of a free society, however, may have to be temporarily sacrificed when, but only when, it is a question of preserving liberty in the long run, as in the case of war'.

As noted, Hayek (2006, p. 202) argues against the principle of *laissez-faire* as a guiding doctrine of government. Because markets are the best mechanisms for allowing individuals to pursue their own interests, a host of government measures might be appropriate to provide an environment in which markets and, hence, liberty, can flourish. While he is opposed to 'all controls of prices and quantities' (Hayek, 2006, p. 200), as well as government monopolies (Hayek, 2006, p. 196), he concludes that 'it is the character, rather than the volume of government activity that is important' (Hayek, 2006, p. 194).

This points to a significant obstacle in ascribing causation to Hayek's ideas over the neoliberal policy revolution. Hayek's writing on the proper role of the state allows for significant variation. Precisely what role Hayek thinks the state should play is far from clear. Keynes highlighted this in a letter to Hayek about *The Road to Serfdom*: 'You agree that the line has to be drawn somewhere [regarding the scope of the state], and that the logical extreme is not possible. But you give us no guidance whatsoever as to where to draw it' (Keynes in Peck, 2010, p. 48). As Shearmur (2006, p. 149) argues much of Hayek's subsequent work can be read as an attempt to address Keynes' critique, yet, contradictions and a lack of clarity regarding Hayek's views of the proper role of the state are evident throughout his work. Indeed, a host of otherwise collectivist regimes could, potentially be defended on Hayekian grounds. Consider for example the many welfare capitalist regimes that prevailed across western Europe in the decades after World War II. Whilst 'collectivist' in their orientation and part of the consensus against which Hayek aimed *The Road to Serfdom*, viewed from another perspective they were functional to the reproduction of capitalist social relations and a market-based order (Lacher, 1999; Cahill and Konings, 2017). Thus, state forms against which Hayek and other neoliberals defined themselves are potentially justifiable using their own normative frameworks, and the Hayekian conception of the proper role of the state is so broad as to make inferences about causation all but impossible. That Hayek's work is therefore contradictory should hardly be surprising. Contradictions can be identified within most social theory, and, as Hunt and Lautzenheiser (2015, p. 408) argue, 'give the best insight into the thinker's ideological orientation'.

A further problem concerns the public circulation of Hayek's ideas. An author has little control over how their ideas are received or interpreted. Given this, there would seem to be little merit in the expectation that any particular text should be interpreted or acted upon as intended by the author. This is true of Hayek's texts and ideas just as much as any other author. Yet, this mistaken view of authorial intent is precisely the assumption underpinning arguments, such as Mirowski's, that the neoliberal policy revolution can be read through the intellectual output of Hayek. The example of the public reception of *The Road to Serfdom* illustrates this point. After the initial publication of the *The Road to Serfdom* in 1944, Hayek travelled to the USA in 1945 for a lecture tour to promote the book. Chicago University Press was the publisher in the USA, but the book had also been abridged by *Readers Digest*, and this abridged version was also subsequently available through the Book-of-the-Month-Club, through which over one-million copies were sold (Burgin, 2012, pp. 87–89). Whilst this significantly boosted publicity for Hayek's tour and for *The Road to Serfdom* itself, it also fostered a public interpretation of Hayek's ideas that in some respects was radically different to what he outlined in his original work. As Burgin (2012, p. 88) argues:

> From the beginning, he [Hayek] found the textual life of *The Road to Serfdom* difficult to control. As he repeatedly observed, his message did not always align with its depiction in the hands of its advocates. In particular, he grew frustrated at a tendency among his more reactionary readers to disregard all his caveats and qualifications in order to represent the text as a call for a return to laissez-faire.

Hayek (in Burgin, 2012, p. 92) himself lamented that during his tour he observed 'far too many people talking about what I am represented to have said rather than about the argument that I have actually used'. This is relevant for an assessment of Hayek's contribution to the development of the neoliberal sate project for it suggests that we should be attentive to the variegated forms in which Hayek's ideas have circulated and the manifold ways in which they have been received.

A further problem with attempts to explain the neoliberal policy revolution with reference to Hayek, or indeed, with reference to the neoliberal thought collective more generally, is that several early-movers down the neoliberal policy path had few, if any, direct relationships with the neoliberal thought collective, nor do they seem to have been particularly sympathetic to them. For example, before Margaret Thatcher came to power in Britain, the Labour Government in 1977 sold a 17 per cent stake in the government-owned British Petroleum company, thus taking the government's share of the company down to 51 per cent – 'the starting point of modern-day privatisations' (Wolf & Pollitt, 2008, p. 3). There is, as yet, no credible evidence to suggest that this was the result of Prime Minister Callaghan coming under the influence of Hayek, or the Institute of Economic Affairs, which was closely aligned to the conservative side of politics. Indeed, the Energy Minister at the time, Tony Benn, was from the radical left-wing of the Party, and would go on to become one of the fiercest critics of the Thatcher government's privatization programme.

Yet, the actions of devotees of Hayek, such as British Prime Minister Margaret Thatcher, also pose a problem for those who wish to ascribe to Hayek the status of chief casual agent of the neoliberal policy revolution. Thatcher was an admirer of Hayek and was close to the neoliberal think tanks such as the Institute of Economic Affairs. Soon after becoming Prime Minister in 1979 she wrote to Hayek: 'I am very proud to have learnt so much from you over the past few years. I hope that some of those ideas will be put into practice by my Government' (Thatcher, 1979). Thatcher's public speeches were often infused with the discourse of Hayek and of radical neoliberalism more generally, particularly her focus on the virtues of the individual, and the corrosive effects of the welfare state and 'big government'.

In practice, however, such rhetoric wasn't always matched by political reality. In the early years of Thatcher's prime-ministership, her government pumped money into state-owned industries to make them more attractive for the market in the lead up to privatization, which, as Gamble (1988, p. 104) notes, 'meant that the Government was forced to authorize more public spending on precisely those programmes it most wanted to see cut' – precisely the sort of politicization of public budgeting decried by Hayek decades earlier. Moreover, due to the 'automatic stabiliser' nature of welfare payments, the Thatcher government's expenditure on unemployment assistance actually increased during the early 1980s. Of course, each of these could presumably also be defended on Hayekian grounds – such as that apparent deviations from the Hayekian critique of collectivism were justified on the grounds that they were necessary to secure a free society in the longer term – yet this merely highlights the absurdity of seeing Hayek as a blueprint for 'actually existing neoliberalism' (Brenner & Theodore, 2002; Cahill, 2014). Moreover, it prompts the question of why some of Hayek's proposals were adopted, and not others. As Beggs (2015, p. 10) asks with respect to the outcomes of neoliberal monetary policy, 'Why the independent, inflation-targeting central bank and not the free banking Hayek once championed?' If only *some* of Hayek's proposals were adopted over others, then this begs the question of why? In turn, this inevitably prompts consideration of the role played by other social forces in creating the environment in which some ideas and not others would appeal. When considered together these points suggest that there are good grounds for scepticism that neo-liberal policy makers were taking their cues from a Hayekian script. If instead the claim made by many scholars of neoliberalism were merely that Hayek influenced the climate of opinion, then this might be unobjectionable. Yet this is also a very weak claim, and the argument put by such scholars is often much stronger and emphatically ideas-centric than this.

If it would therefore be a mistaken strategy to read actually existing neoliberalism through the lens of Hayek's published work, it need not be concluded that Hayek's work is irrelevant for an understanding of this phenomenon, or that it did not contribute to its construction. Outside of his influence over the character of the neoliberal thought collective, the chief contribution of Hayek's ideas is to the contours of the pervasive ideological framework (discussed earlier) in which neoliberal forms of regulation and service provision are embedded.

Hayek produced a body of work that 'represents the relations of modern capitalist society one-sidedly' (Foley, 2004, p. 340) by ignoring issues of power and compulsion and focusing instead on freedom and voluntarism in market exchanges. While congruent with certain elements of capitalist society, it misses and obscures others. For example, market exchanges, while formally free, are also underpinned by asymmetrical power relations. Whether it be decisions about what to produce, or on what terms labour power will be hired, the institutionalized form of capital generally occupies a privileged position. Similarly, while market exchanges are formally voluntary, the extension of such exchanges to more and more areas of social life generally arises from people losing access to non-market forms of provisioning, thereby leading to market relations becoming essentially compulsory. Moreover, while formally free to choose, people's actual ability to exercise such market choices is significantly dependent upon their location within the unequal distribution of economic resources that is a feature of actually existing neoliberalism, thus excluding some from access to commodified goods and services. Hayek's ideas thus form the basis of an ideology that both explains and misrepresents the world. The broadness and ambiguity of Hayek's views on the proper role of the state are also relevant here. It lends Hayek's ideas a malleability that is amenable to selective appropriation to justify, explain or critique a range of state policies and has contributed to their ideological role.

None of this is to suggest that those for whom neoliberal discursive frames constitute part of their common sense conception of the world have necessarily read, imbibed nor fully understood Hayek's key texts. Indeed, it is not necessary for someone to have read Hayek (or Friedman, Buchanan or Becker for that matter) for them nonetheless to interpret the economy and economic policy through the neoliberal discursive frame. Such frames are circulated, through neoliberal think tanks, significant sections of the mainstream media, as well as being privileged by the institutional architecture through which neoliberal policy practices are embedded. Hayek's ideas have circulated in ways that have variously served as inspiration, justification and interpretive lens. His work has bequeathed a pastiche of discursive tools for thinking through a series of contextually specific problems to which particular solutions are justified. Hayek and his ideas are thus best understood as emblematic rather than causal of the neoliberal policy revolution. While Hayek may have contributed to the expanded reproduction of neoliberalism, he was not its author.

Conclusion

Interest in the work of Karl Polanyi and Friedrich Hayek has only grown as the contradictions inherent within neoliberal forms of regulation generate crises that continue to reverberate across the capitalist world. Typically, Hayek's work is viewed as crucial to deciphering the ways in which states and economies have been transformed through neoliberalism. Such ideas-centric analyses see Hayek as one of the chief authors of the neoliberal policy revolution through which the world came to resemble Hayek's utopian visions of market order. Polanyi on the other hand is typically seen as offering prescient warnings about the dangers of disembedding markets from their social foundations, a warning that neoliberals, it is often assumed, failed to heed and that is now being exposed through crisis.

This article has critically examined each of these intepretations by evaluating them against the development and constitution of actually existing neoliberalism. The conception of embedded and disembedded markets as expressed by Polanyi in *The Great Transformation* was shown to be deeply ambiguous. Moreover, in so far as it has led scholars to adopt the view of social embeddedness as a 'historical variable', it was shown to be a poor guide to understanding the economy-society relationship under capitalism. Drawing upon the work of Block and Somers, an alternative reading of Polanyi's concept was put forward – that of the 'always embedded economy'. Applying this to neoliberalism it was argued that 'actually existing neoliberalism' can usefully be understood as embedded within a particular set of formal institutional rules, transformed social relations, and ideological norms. This, it was argued, sheds light both on the durability of neoliberalism and its contradictory nature.

With respect to Hayek, the article highlighted the implausibility of interpretations that attribute a strong causal role to his work in the development of actually existing neoliberalism. Evidence for this was found in the nature of his ideas – both the utopianism and their lack of clarity with respect to the proper role of the state – the forms in which they circulated, the structural context of governing within capitalist states, and the fact that some early neoliberal governments had little contact with and/or sympathy for Hayek or his ideas. Nonetheless, it was argued that Hayek's ideas made an important contribution to the development of the ideological norms within which neoliberal forms of regulation became embedded. The very imprecision of his conception of the proper role of the state and his starkly utopian conception of markets and their virtues allowed Hayek's ideas to serve as a malleable set of tools that could be selectively appropriated as interpretive frames for a sympathetic reading of actually existing neoliberalism. While this analysis has focused on the work of Hayek, it nonetheless points to the limitations of scholarship that attempts to understand neoliberalism primarily as a realization of the normative doctrines of leading neoliberal intellectuals including Friedman, Buchanan, Becker or the think tanks that proselytized their ideas. This analysis therefore suggests that ideas form but one of the types of institutions in which economic processes are embedded, including neoliberalism. Thus it contributes to an understanding of how ideas matter within processes of political economic transformation and suggests that ideas should be properly understood as having influence within the context of the institutional ensemble that underpins the capitalist economy.

Disclosure statement

No potential conflict of interest was reported by the author.

References

Altvater, E. (2009). Postneoliberalism or postcapitalism? The failure of neoliberalism in the financial market crisis. *Development Dialogue, 51*, 73–86.

Ayers, A., & Saad-Filho, A. (2015). Democracy against neoliberalism: Paradoxes, limitations, transcendance. *Critical Sociology, 41*(4–5), 597–618.

Bailey, D., Clua-Losada, M., Huke, N., & Ribera-Almandoz, O. (2017). *Beyond defeat and austerity: Disrupting (the critical political economy of) neoliberal Europe*. London: Routledge.

Beeson, M., & Firth, A. (1998). Neoliberalism as a political rationality: Australian public policy since the 1980s. *Journal of Sociology, 34*(3), 215–231.

Beggs, M. (2015). *Inflation and the making of Australian macroeconomic policy, 1945–1985*. Basingstoke: Palgrave.

Belloc, F., & Nicita, A. (2011). The political determinants of liberalization: Do ideological cleavages still matter? *International Review of Economics, 58*(2), 121–145.

Best, J. (2003). From the top-down: The new financial architecture and the re-embedding of global finance. *New Political Economy, 8*(3), 363–384.

Block, F., & Somers, M. (2014). *The power of market fundamentalism: Karl Polanyi's critique*. Cambridge, MA: Harvard University Press.

Brenner, N., & Theodore, N. (2002). Cities and the geographies of "actually existing neoliberalism". *Antipode, 34*(3), 349–379.

Burgin, A. (2012). *The great persuasion: Reinventing free markets since the depression*. Cambridge, MA: Harvard University Press.

Cahill, D. (2014). *The End of Laissez-Faire? On the durability of embedded neoliberalism*. Cheltenham: Edward Elgar.

Cahill, D., & Konings, M. (2017). *Neoliberalism*. Cambridge: Polity.

Cerny, P. (2008). Embedding neoliberalism: The evolution of a hegemonic paradigm. *The Journal of International Trade and Diplomacy, 2*(1), 1–46.

Cockett, R. (1995). *Thinking the unthinkable: Think tanks and the economic counter-revolution 1931–1983*. London: Harper Collins.

Dale, G. (2010). *Karl Polanyi*. Cambridge: Polity.

DeMuth, C. (2007, October 11). Think tank confidential. *Wall Street Journal*. Retrieved from https://www.wsj.com/articles/SB119206742349355601

Foley, D. (2004). Rationality and ideology in economics. *Social Research, 71*(2), 329–342.

Gamble, A. (1988). *The free economy and the strong state: The politics of Thatcherism*. Durham: Duke University Press.

Gemici, K. (2008). Karl Polanyi and the antinomies of embeddedness. *Socio-Economic Review, 6*, 5–33.

Gemici, K. (2015). The neoclassical origins of Polanyi's self-regulating market. *Sociological Theory, 33*(2), 125–147.

Gill, S. (2001). Constitutionalising capital: EMU and disciplinary neoliberalism. In A. Bieler, & A. Morton (Eds.), *Social forces in the making of New Europe* (pp. 47–69). New York: Palgrave.

Glyn, A. (2006). *Capitalism unleashed: Finance, globalisation, and welfare*. Oxford: Oxford University Press.

Hacker, J., & Pierson, P. (2010). Winner-Take-All politics: Public policy, political organization, and the precipitous rise of top incomes in the United States. *Politics and Society, 38*(2), 152–204.

Hayek, F. A. (1944). *The road to serfdom*. Sydney: Dymock's Book Arcade.

Hayek, F. A. (1949). The intellectuals and socialism. *The University of Chicago Law Review, 16*(3), 417–433.

Hayek, F. A. (1973). *Law legislation and liberty, volume 1: Rules and order*. Chicago: University of Chicago Press.

Hayek, F. A. (2006). *The constitution of liberty*. London: Routledge.

Hunt, E. K., & Lautzenheiser, M. (2015). *History of economic thought: A critical perspective* (4th ed.). London: M. E. Sharpe.

Jessop, B. (2002). *The future of the capitalist state*. Cambridge: Polity.

Kotz, D. (2015). *The rise and fall of neoliberal capitalism*. Cambridge, MA: Harvard University Press.

Krippner, G. (2001). The elusive market: Embeddedness and the paradigm of economic sociology. *Theory and Society, 30*(6), 775–810.

Krippner, G. (2011). *Capitalizing on crisis: The political origins of the rise of finance*. Cambridge, MA: Harvard University Press.

Lacher, H. (1999). Embedded liberalism, disembedded markets: Reconceptualising the Pax Americana. *New Political Economy, 4*(3), 343–360.

Levi-Faur, D. (2005). The global diffusion of regulatory capitalism. *The ANNALS of the American Academy of Political Science, 598*, 12–32.

Mirowski, P. (2009). Postface: Defining neoliberalism. In P. Mirowski, & D. Plehwe (Eds.), *The road from Mont Pelerin: The making of the neoliberal thought collective* (pp. 417–455). Cambridge: Harvard University Press.

Mirowski, P. (2013). *Never let a serious crisis go to waste: How neoliberalism survived the financial meltdown*. London: Verso.

Mirowski, P., & Plehwe, D. (Eds.). (2009). *The road from Mont Pèlerin: The making of the neoliberal thought collective*. Cambridge, MA: Harvard University Press.

Nicol, D. (2010). *The constitutional protection of capitalism*. Oxford: Hart Publishing.

Peck, J. (2010). *Constructions of neoliberal reason*. Oxford: Oxford University Press.

Peck, J., & Tickell, A. (2002). 'Neoliberalizing space'. *Antipode, 34*(3), 380–404.

Phillips-Fein, K. (2009). *Invisible hands: The businessmen's Crusade against the new deal*. New York: W. W. Norton.

Polanyi, K. (1957). The economy as instituted process. In K. Polanyi, C. Arensberg, & H. Pearson (Eds.), *Trade and market in early empires: Economics in history and theory* (pp. 243–270). Glencoe: Free Press.

Polanyi, K. (2001). *The great transformation: The political and economic origins of our time*. Boston: Beacon Press.

Radice, H. (2010). Confronting the crisis: A class analysis. In L. Panitch, G. Albo, & V. Chibber (Eds.), *The crisis this time: Socialist register 2011* (pp. 21–43). London: The Merlin Press.

Ruggie, J. (1982). International regimes, transactions, and change: Embedded liberalism and the postwar economic order. *International Organization, 36*(2), 379–415.

Ruggie, J. (Ed.) (2008). *Embedding global markets: An enduring challenge*. Aldershot: Ashgate.

Shearmur, J. (2006). Hayek's politics. In E. Feser (Ed.), *The Cambridge companion to Hayek* (pp. 148–170). Cambridge: Cambridge University Press.

Soederberg, S. (2010). Cannibalistic capitalism: The Pradoxes of neoliberal pension securitization. In L. Panitch, G. Albo, & V. Chibber (Eds.), *The crisis this time: Socialist register 2011* (pp. 224–241). London: The Merlin Press.

Stedman Jones, D. (2012). *Masters of the universe: Hayek, Friedman, and the birth of neoliberal politics*. Princeton: Princeton University Press.

Stone, D. (2013). *Knowledge actors and transnational governance: The private-public policy Nexus in the global Agora*. Basingstoke: Palgrave.

Thatcher, M. (1979, May 18). Letter to Friedrich Hayek: thanks for congratulations. Retrieved from https://www.margaretthatcher.org/document/112178

van Apeldoorn, B. (2009). The contradictions of 'embedded neoliberalism' and Europe's multi-level legitimacy crisis: The European project and its limits. In B. van Apeldoorn, J. Drahokoupil, & L. Horn (Eds.), *Contradictions and limits of neoliberal European governance: From Lisbon to Lisbon* (pp. 21–43). New York: Palgrave Macmillan.

Wolf, C., & Pollitt, M. G. (2008). 'Privatising national oil companies: Assessing the impact on firm performance', *judge business school working papers*. Cambridge: Cambridge University.

Karl Polanyi as a spatial theorist

Philip Roberts

ABSTRACT

The 'spatial' turn in political economy has re-invigorated Marxian analysis, allowing for new research programmes into urbanization, geopolitics, and social movement activity amongst other topics. This tendency emerged through a critical re-reading of Marx and Gramsci, amongst others, uncovering spatial analyses embedded in the logic of their arguments. Conversely, Karl Polanyi's interlocutors have tended to add geographical analysis as an additional layer of theory, reading space 'in' to the text. However, a close reading reveals that a concern with space permeates Polanyi's analysis. As such, it is possible to read space 'out' of Polanyi, adding a level of theoretical rigour and logical consistency when applying his insights to geographic topics. This article carries out an exegesis of Karl Polanyi's work, uncovering a theoretical framework that deals with space, place, scale, fixity, and motion. From this vantage point, the article considers the potential implications of this new geographical reading of Polanyi.

Karl Polanyi's work finds a way into the toolbox of virtually every heterodox political economist. Though far from prolific compared to Marx, Keynes, or Weber, ideas from Polanyi's writings permeate fields from economic anthropology to global sociology. Concepts such as the 'embeddedness' of the economy within social institutions, the 'fictitious' character of commodities that are not inherently produced for exchange, and a 'double movement' as political movements naturally seek to curb the excesses of a shift towards market society have all found their niche. At a global level, Polanyi's concepts have been adopted by actors with contradictory political projects. For example, John Gerrard Ruggie's valorization of the Bretton Woods capitalist world order as 'embedded liberalism' (Ruggie, 1982), and Ronaldo Munck's call for a Polanyian 'counter-movement' that would abolish global capitalism altogether (Munck, 2006). However, less attention is paid to reading Polanyi systematically, in order to explore how less explicit concepts are woven through his analysis (exceptions include Block & Summers, 2014; Blyth, 2002; Dale, 2010).

By contrast, historical materialist scholars often engage with the work of Karl Marx and subsequent figures by drawing out new analytical frameworks via rigorous exegesis. Most notable of these is the 'spatial' turn in Marxian analysis. Lefebvre (1991), and later Harvey (1982) and Smith (1984) are amongst those who have perceived an essentially spatial logic in the thought of Karl Marx. More recently, a second wave of Marxian theorists identified a geographical dimension in the work of Antonio Gramsci (See, *inter alia*, Jessop, 2005; Morton, 2013; Said, 1994, p. 49). The new analyses arising out of this exegesis have been fundamental to understanding key political issues. These include how passive revolution connects the uneven spatial development of the international system to geopolitics (Hesketh, 2017), how urban-redevelopment conditions class hegemony (Jessop, 1997), and how social movements develop counter-hegemonic projects through conquering space (Karriem, 2013). As social theorists have often stressed the compatibility between Polanyian analysis and historical materialism (Block, 2003; Burawoy, 2003; Dale, 2010; though see Silver, 2003, for a contrasting view), it suggests that a similar exegesis of Polanyi's work might bear equally useful insights.

The purpose of this article is to explore spatial themes in Polanyi's work. My inquiry will focus on *The Great Transformation* ([1944] 2001), whilst drawing in insights from secondary texts. Through this exegesis, I will examine the implicitly spatial framework on which a systemically Polanyian analysis rests. The purpose of the exercise is to read Polanyi sympathetically, in search of new insights. I will therefore focus less on the empirical validity of Polanyi's propositions, and more on the internal logic and narrative of the texts. In this sense, I follow a similar approach to Lacher (1999a, 1999b). Lacher's articles addressed the dubious appropriation of Polanyi's concept of 'embeddedness' as an explanation for the Bretton Woods regime of liberal global capitalism. By highlighting the centrality of decommodification to Polanyi's thought, Lacher exposed the theoretical inconsistency of this appropriation, and the political limitations of analyses that valorized 'embedded liberalism' as an alternative to neoliberal globalization (Lacher, 1999b, p. 357). This article therefore addresses how Polanyi's spatial analysis is interwoven through his core theoretical concepts. In so doing, it explores the implications for appropriating his work in a logically consistent manner.

This article proceeds through three stages. In the first, I will examine Karl Polanyi's encounters with space in the work of subsequent appropriators. The purpose of this section is to show how Polanyian concepts have been spatialized by attaching geographical frameworks to his ideas, reading space 'into' Polanyi. The second section then explores how spatial concepts are already implicit in Polanyi's work. In this way I read space 'out' of Polanyi, with a focus on space, place, scale, fixity, and motion. The purpose of this section is twofold, demonstrating the inherent spatiality of Polanyian analysis, and identifying how reading space 'into' Polanyi may not be logically consistent with his overall framework. The third and final section examines the limitations to space in Polanyi's work. The goal of this section is to problematize specific aspects of Polanyi's spatial theory, in order to identify the problems that contemporary theorists must resolve in order to integrate Polanyi's considerable contributions into a critical theory of political economy.

Reading space 'into' Polanyi

As suggested above, this paper is not the first time that Polanyi's thought has encountered geography. Authors from a variety of disciplines have sought to use Polanyian concepts in a spatial framework. Most visible amongst these is Hess (2004; see also Oinas, 1997). However, rather than excavating a spatial theory from *The Great Transformation*, Hess aims to apply spatial insights in order to renovate existing theory. Indeed, Hess is openly critical of Polanyi's work as lacking geographical elements, in that 'His framework is essentially non-spatial, i.e. geographical (pre)conditions do not have any explanatory power.' (Hess, 2004, p. 169). Hess focuses on the concept of embeddedness, particularly as developed by Granovetter (1985). The intention behind Hess's appropriation of Polanyi, he states, is to ' … go back to the origins of the embeddedness concept and rethink its applicability and appropriateness at different geographical as well as analytical levels.' (Hess, 2004, p. 166). This development is couched as a response to critics who malign the concept of embeddedness as being too loose (Martin & Sunley, 2001, p. 153). Hess's solution is to situate Polanyi's contributions to political economy within a spatial framework derived from the work of Deleuze and Guattari

(1988). By appropriating the concept of the rhizome from Deleuze and Guattari, Hess attempts to show how actors are geographically embedded in territorial networks, defined both by historical legacies and a continual process of flux (Hess, 2004, pp. 176–179). Notably, this post-structural concept functions as a geographical *metaphor*, including notions of cartography and connectivity (p. 180). However, Polanyi's analysis is concerned with uncovering and exploring essential changes to society via historical and anthropological inquiry, rather than constructing anti-foundational narratives via metaphor. This framework is therefore at odds even with the basic ontological and epistemological approach deployed by Polanyi in *The Great Transformation*.

Philip Cerny (1994, 1995) has also engaged with Karl Polanyi as a means of understanding spatial transformations in the global economy. Notably, he identifies *The Great Transformation* as responding to a 'scale shift' in economic life, derived from the interstate economic competition of the early twentieh-century that gave rise to fascism, Stalinism, and the New Deal (Cerny, 1995, p. 605). Equally, Cerny notes that Polanyi relates the rise of *haute finance* – more commonly international finance – with the attempt to establish an international market that was also self-regulating (Cerny, 1994, pp. 319–320). However, Cerny stops short of suggesting that any spatial framework can be read out of the text. The problem of self-regulating markets is taken as a point of departure for discussing financial globalization, and for exploring various responses thereto derived from other theoretical traditions (pp. 322–324). The implicit claim, therefore, is that new approaches need to be layered on top of Polanyi's work in order to grasp the spatial dynamics of financial globalization.

Other authors have invoked the need to add geography to Polanyi's thought in service of the counter-globalization movement (Evans, 2000, 2008; Munck, 2002, 2004, 2006, 2010). Following on from Burawoy (2003), Ronaldo Munck attempts a synthesis of Karl Polanyi and Antonio Gramsci, in an endeavour to theorize the potential for resistance against neoliberal globalization (Munck, 2004, 2010). However, Munck is emphatic concerning the need to 'globalize' Polanyi, whom he identifies as essentially confined within the parameters of the nation-state (Munck, 2004, p. 253). In order to provide a suitable challenge to twenty-first century capitalism, according to Munck, Polanyi needs to be 'scaled up' to the global level (Munck, 2010, p. 241, 2004, p. 255). In a similar line, Evans (2000, 2008) appeals to Polanyi's concept of a 'double-movement' or 'counter-movement' against the socially deleterious effects of globalization. However, like Munck, Evans focuses on the lack of a strategy for transnational social organization in *The Great Transformation*, rather than exploring the specific spatial logics that could be read out of Polanyi's work (Evans, 2000, pp. 273–274). Thus, these thinkers maintain the view that Polanyi's thought must be spatialized before it can function as a framework for international political economy.

Finally, Peck (2013) has sounded a call for a sustained engagement with Polanyi's thought by the discipline of economic geography. As Peck (2013, p. 1546) notes, the encounters of economic geography with Polanyi's thought have usually been via contact with analyses from sociology and anthropology, rather than sustained engagement with his works and legacy. Unlike the authors reviewed above, Peck (2013, p. 1546) does observe that Polanyi's analysis contains integral geographical relevance, because it requires local economic practices be understood in the context of extra-local processes. That is, the relational character of Polanyi's thought makes it a geographical framework. The drive of the article makes clear that Polanyi's work has a natural sympathy to economic geography, particularly the study of variegation (p. 1555). However, Peck does not attempt to read specifically geographical categories out of Polanyi. Instead, he suggests that the framework and broader philosophy present in Polanyi is amenable to a spatial development by economic geographers, embracing holism, institutionalism, and comparative methods (p. 1545).

To summarize this section, it is clear that a variety of thinkers have identified sympathies between Karl Polanyi's theory of political economy and a geographical framework of analysis. Those interested in analysing business networks, organizing anti-capitalist movements, or renovating economic geography have all drawn inspiration from Polanyi's work. However, crucially it is not the geographical elements that have inspired them. Indeed, only consulting the sources above, one could be forgiven for thinking that Polanyi's thought contained no spatial logic at all. My aim in the remainder of this article is to argue the reverse. First, that Polanyi's thought contains an inherent spatial logic. Second, that this logic tells us something meaningful about the uses and limitations of Polanyian analysis.

Reading space 'out of' Polanyi

Contrary to the claims arranged above, I argue that Polanyi's work is permeated by a concern for space, and that his analytical framework rests on foundations that are clearly geographical. Whilst *The Great Transformation* works at a set of different registers, including historical anthropology, international relations, and the history of ideas, a geographical mode of thought is employed at key junctures. This includes observations concerning place, space, fixity and motion, circulation and barriers, the urban and the rural, and the role of scale in social, economic, and political conflict.

At the most general level, Polanyi's method is suffused with a concern for geographical factors. This commitment is made clear in his most directly methodological work 'The Economy as Instituted Process.' (Polanyi, 1957). It is in this essay that Polanyi introduces the two major approaches to economic analysis as he sees it. On the one hand, 'formalism', which is concerned with how actors make choices concerning resource allocation under conditions of scarcity, in other words examining how prices are formed within a market society (p. 246); on the other, 'substantivism', which is concerned with examining the whole range of activities and constraints that are bound up in the satisfaction of human needs, and in doing so through historically grounded empirical examination (pp. 243–244). Contrary to the abstract rationality emphasized by formalism, this substantive exploration of empirical factors that shape economic life is inherently geographical, as Polanyi clarifies:

> Preoccupation with the market thus makes for good economic theory, rather than for good economic history. Eventually, we will find that trade routes, too, as well as means of transportation may be of no less incisive importance for the institutional forms of trade than the types of good carried. For in all these cases the geographical and technical conditions interpenetrate with the social structure. (Polanyi, 1957, p. 261)

In discussing the economy as an 'instituted process', Polanyi further observes how reciprocity is imposed upon communities through geographical factors of soil and climate, as opposed to a strictly intentional political project (Polanyi, 1957, p. 254). Across the two previous references, Polanyi describes to two distinct ways in which space and the economy structure each other. On the one hand, the geographical distribution of resources and the natural features of terrain set natural boundaries and meeting points. On the other, the costs of transportation, embodied in the form of trade, give a social structuration of space and the geographical intertwining of different societies. Therefore, Polanyi's criticism of economic formalism, that 'What nature made distinct, the market makes homogeneous.' (Polanyi, 1957, p. 261), applies not only to institutions but to the geography that underpins them, and which economic rationalism obscures from view. Thus, the forms of economic activity that underpin non-market societies can be understood through the substantive analysis of geographical factors. In this sense, space is not only a descriptive category for Polanyi, but also an explanatory tool.

Leading from this commitment to substantivism, one of the key elements to understanding the role of the spatial in Polanyi's thought is the relationship between natural and intentional elements of social life. Contrary to Krippner's (2002, p. 778) critique of the failure of Polanyi's heirs in economic sociology to examine the nature of markets, Polanyi gives a clear exposition that markets are a specific kind of place. In chapter five of *The Great Transformation*, where he traces the 'Evolution of the Market Pattern' (Polanyi, 2001, p. 59), Polanyi clearly relates institutional development to existing spatial constraints. This is illustrated through an examination not just of how markets function on a technical level, but of where they arise, in that:

> Markets developed naturally out of it where the carriers had to halt as at fords, seaports, riverheads, or where the routes of two land expeditions met. "Ports" developed at the places of transshipment. (Polanyi, 2001, p. 63)

Extending this line of analysis, Polanyi effectively turns the classical argument for the establishment of markets and the expansion of trade on its head, arguing that:

> The orthodox teaching started from the individual's propensity to barter, deduced from it the necessity of markets, and inferred finally the necessity of trade, eventually of foreign trade, including even long distance trade ... the true starting point is long distance trade, a result of the geographical location of goods, and of the "division of labour" given by location. Long distance trade often engenders markets. (Polanyi, 2001, pp. 61–62)

Accordingly, Polanyi sees geography playing a primary role in structuring institutional growth and activity. This point is given greater empirical weight in his later work, particularly the essay 'Ports of Trade in Early Societies', which examined the relationship between long distance trade and prices from Mexico, Africa, and India, to Babylon. (Polanyi, 1963, pp. 32–33). This places his thought in a relationship with other geographical thinkers, including Mackinder (1904) and Diamond (1999), and counterpoises his analysis to thinkers such as Acemoglu and Robinson (2011), who have more recently argued for the primacy of institutions over geography. Therefore, a theoretical framework which reads geography out of Polanyi would necessarily be based upon the geographical distribution of resources, at least within the analysis of how markets develop.

Counterpoised to this concern with the natural origins of economic geographies, that is space as a natural feature of social life, is an examination of the transformations of space that arise out of intentional activity. This is particularly clear in Polanyi's analysis of the shift from societies containing markets to the 'market society' in which all other institutions are subjected to the dictates of economic rationality. As Polanyi outlines, this requires both the constitution of new scales of economic activity, and the reshaping of particular spaces. This dimension of Polanyi's theoretical framework brings another set of categories into play, in the form of circulation and barriers, and the urban and rural spaces along with the relationship between them. The way that markets develop within Polanyi's analysis also tells us about the role of another place, and particularly how this role is transformed through direct, i.e. intentional, state intervention. The space that is most obviously transformed in Polanyi's analysis of the Great Transformation is the urban environment.

> The most significant result of markets - the birth of towns and urban civilization - was, in effect, the outcome of a paradoxical development. Towns, insofar as they sprang from markets, were not only the protectors of those markets, but also the means of preventing them from expanding into the countryside and thus encroaching on the prevailing economic organization of society. (Polanyi, 2001, p. 65)

In this analysis, the sub-national space of economic life is restricted to the towns, to urban places, and local trade and long-distance trade were sharply divided and their ingress into the countryside was strictly limited (Polanyi, 2001, p. 66). Fundamentally, Polanyi viewed the urban environment of pre-market society in England, that of the medieval town, as a bulwark against the development of the national market economy that was a necessary element of the rise of market society (Polanyi, 2001, pp. 67–68). This was achieved through the strict partitioning of space through creating barriers to the circulation of goods from long-distance trade, denying merchant capitalists influence over the institutions attached to rural life (Polanyi, 2001, p. 68). Similarly, social institutions were initially defended against the logic of market society through legislation that created barriers to the circulation of labour (Polanyi, 2001, p. 92). Thus, Polanyi observes that

> Internal trade in Western Europe was actually created by the intervention of the state. Right up to the time of the Commercial Revolution, what may appear to us as national trade was not national, but municipal. (Polanyi, 2001, p. 66)

Continuing the analysis outlined above, Polanyi maintains that the national market could never arise simply out of economic rationality and the impulse to truck and barter. Instead, it required state intervention to intentionally create an internal national market by breaking down the barriers between external and internal trade, and between urban and rural commerce (Polanyi, 2001, p. 67). This creation of the national scale of economic activity (Polanyi, 2001, p. 69) cuts against the earlier claims that Polanyi takes the national scale as a kind of given. The actual picture is rather more complex, in that Polanyi effectively counterpoises a 'natural' scale of the national society to an 'intentional' scale of the state-instituted national market. Further evidence of this relationship exists in the analysis of money and national currency, as Polanyi observes that 'Currency has become the pivot of national politics' (Polanyi, 2001, p. 25), in view of its role in ' … establishing the nation as the decisive economic and political unit of the time' (Polanyi, 2001, p. 212). The role of national money linked to national markets, that is money 'stamped with a national die' (Polanyi, 2001, p. 211), thereby formed the basis of the interplay between national and international scales.

Thus, Polanyi's analysis of the construction of national markets, and the market society more generally, fits within the much later debate over the social construction of scale (Marston, 2000). Polanyi's view of the role of scale particularly is noteworthy in that the household is posited as the primary scale of one type of non-market society (Polanyi, 2001, p. 50, 1957, p. 254), implying that this 'natural' scale of social reproduction could be counterpoised to the 'utopian' scale of the market society that emerged later on at a national level. Accordingly, for Polanyi the study of societies, markets, and economies is necessarily a study of the emergence of different scales. Initially these are given naturally, by territorial borders defined by natural features, or by the boundaries of the family unit. Subsequently, scale emerges out of intention, particularly the intentions of states in creating national economies, marked by a national currency.

More profoundly, Polanyi grasps at the relationship between the market and the structuration of space. This is not to suggest that society breaks down as the market becomes 'disembedded' from space, to revisit an old debate from a new angle (Block, 2003). Rather, it reflects the transformations of place that are established when the market institution comes to dominate, as social relations take their logic from market imperatives (Polanyi, 2001, p. 60). The structuring of space therefore no longer takes place with reference to natural boundaries and imperatives, as was the case of the establishment of markets at specific sites dictated by geographical features such as rivers. Rather, the structuring of space goes from being concrete to virtual, as places are remade according to the imperatives of the price mechanism. In this sense, Polanyi's work is a critique of the market society as a utopian project, in the literal translation of a 'good place that is nowhere' (Polanyi, 2001, p. 3) Under market society, activity is directed by the price mechanism (Polanyi, 2001, p. 71), and therefore space becomes partitioned by the price system. The spatial effects for societies under the market system of economic rationalism are described by Polanyi in vivid detail, as ' ... the commodity fiction disregarded the fact that leaving the fate of soil and people to the market would be tantamount to annihilating them.' (Polanyi, 2001, p. 137) In particular, his examination of the relationship between market and nature, describes how the latter, ' ... would be reduced to its elements, neighbourhoods and landscapes defiled, rivers polluted ... ' (Polanyi, 2001, p. 76). However, the picture is not as simple as a straightforward destruction of geography. Notably, the removal of barriers to trade and the creation of a national market as described above is not a kind of smoothing out of space by market society, leaving it featureless. Instead, the barriers to trade and the circulation of labour are replaced by a new barrier, that of the enclosures system (Polanyi, 2001, pp. 73 &189). Thus, just as markets are not simply disembedded from institutions under the market society, so space is not destroyed but rather reshaped. In this sense, Polanyi's writing parallels that of Marx, as explored by Smith ([1984] 2010). Particularly, Smith's exegesis of nature within Marx's thought showed how the natural environment was remade under capitalism in a comparable sense to the refashioning of the built environment (p. 65). The interlinking of these two analyses is at the core of Marxian contributions to geography, establishing a theoretical bridge between society, space, and nature. Accordingly, a closer reading of Polanyi's framework allows for an equivalent linking of these issues.

As reviewed above, the two-sided analysis of space, split into the natural and the intentional, is woven throughout Polanyi's analysis in *The Great Transformation*. However, Polanyi also explores the interaction between different kinds of space from another angle. From the outset, *The Great Transformation* contains an implicit notion of conflicts between different scales of social activity. In the first two chapters, Polanyi examines the international system from an essentially nationalist perspective, seeing different nation states effectively as containers for discrete social projects, or as 'power units' in the international system (Polanyi, 2001, pp. 3, 5–6, 30). Each chapter explores the relationship between the national scale and the transnational, concretized as the world market and particularly the gold standard (Polanyi, 2001, pp. 26, 28–29, 23). As Polanyi observed, the national politics of the post-World War I era were increasingly defined by attempts to salvage the international system (Polanyi, 2001, p. 28). However, at the most basic level Polanyi's theoretical framework remains rooted in the national scale, as only developments at this level could be sufficient to explain the global transformation heralded by the collapse of the international gold standard (Polanyi, 2001, p. 29). Accordingly, the ontological scales of the 'international' and the 'national' and particularly their interplay and interaction are central to the broader perspective of Polanyi's analysis. The scalar logic of his thought relies heavily on this interaction for its explanatory power, in particular the reconciliation of warlike states through the pacifying influence of international finance (Polanyi, 2001, pp. 11–16). This is perhaps ironic, in that the literature on global production networks which draws so much inspiration from Polanyi tends to bypass this relationship, focusing instead on the interaction between the global and the local or regional scales. Similarly, as noted above, Peck (2013, p. 1546) neatly skips over the national-international system scalar relationship which is so central to Polanyi's analysis, opting for a more general view of the relationship between local and extra-local forces. Contrary to these appropriations, Polanyi is particularly emphatic concerning the centrality of the national, noting that even international finance relied upon national attachments (Polanyi, 2001, p. 12). Therefore, a spatial Polanyian framework would draw its explanatory structure from the relationship between nation-states and international system when examining global capitalism and emphasize the importance of the national far more than has been the case with Polanyi's appropriators to date.

In summary, far from requiring space to be integrated into it, the substantivist analysis developed in *The Great Transformation* relies upon geographical categories at key stages in the argument. These range from the structuring of space through territorial features which give rise to specific institutions, to the intentional re-scaling of economic activity, the conflict between scales of social agency, and the re-making of space through the dominance of the market mechanism. The question is therefore not how do we make Polanyi's thought geographical, but what are the consequences of Polanyi's spatial theorizing? The final section of the article addresses this issue.

Spatial limitations of *The Great Transformation*

Though there is a rich geographical theme woven throughout Polanyi's thought, when we examine the spatial categories, analyses, and descriptions in *The Great Transformation* it throws up at least two key limitations. The first is the relationship between different regions of the global economy, and the second is the constraint on theorizing agency imposed by Polanyi's appeals to scale. These are explored in turn below.

Polanyi's geographical scope is notably broad, encompassing Europe but also Oceania in *The Great Transformation*, and elsewhere stretching to include Africa, India, Latin America, and the Near East (Polanyi, 1957, 1963). However, the core of his argument on market society remains firmly rooted in the study of Europe. In the first chapter of *The Great Transformation*, entitled 'The Hundred Years Peace', Polanyi leads with the assertion that nineteenth-century civilization has collapsed (Polanyi, 2001, p. 3), whilst the remainder of the text examines only European and American society. The implication is that for Polanyi, nineteenth-century civilization is a Western project, and the different trajectories of market society development occurring elsewhere are skipped over entirely. In effect, Polanyi subscribes to a diffusionist analysis of capitalism, seeing capitalist development as an event which takes place in Europe and is then spread throughout the world via colonialism and seafaring trade (Polanyi, 2001, pp. 29, 31–32, 171 and 188). This forms part of the descriptive mode of Polanyi's spatial analysis, which describes the spatial dispersion of the 'great transformation' of traditional societies into market societies. However, that is not to say that description of this type is neutral or without political consequences. Indeed, Polanyi later went to some lengths to repudiate arguments which located the first development of market society in Babylonia, instead insisting that ancient Greece had been the first site where all the elements of a market-organized economy had appeared (Polanyi, 1963, p. 38). In this way, a framework which seeks to be faithful to Polanyi's analysis would be inherently Eurocentric. Particularly, parallels can be drawn between Polanyi's view of the spatial expansion of capitalism, and the Political Marxist school which saw capitalist development occurring in Europe before being transmitted elsewhere (See Brenner, 1977, 1982; Teschke, 2003, for examples). This opens up the possibility of expanding Polanyian analysis, not only through critique, but by application of the spatial logics outlined in the previous section to the study of non-Western contexts in order to grasp the actual geographical dispersion of capitalist development.

Returning to the themes raised in the previous section, the logic of Polanyi's counterpoising of the two moments of the 'double-movement' outlined in *The Great Transformation* (2001, p. 138) may in fact undermine his overall argument. In essence, discussion of the double-movement is grounded upon the two-sided relationship that animates the whole of Polanyi's geographical thought, that of the interplay between the natural and the intentional. As the above discussion shows, Polanyi considered the construction of market society as dependent upon intentional action, particularly by nation states. States were central to the construction of economic scales for the action and functioning of market society. Conversely, the social counter-movement against the depredations of the market society was essentially unconscious, spontaneous, natural, and pragmatic (Polanyi, 2001, pp. 81 and 147). Indeed, as Polanyi is at pains to point out, the sheer diversity of responses to the failure of market society precluded any possibility that they were a concerted action (Polanyi, 2001, p. 152). Crucially, this spontaneous action is not framed through class interest, as might be the case in Marxist analysis, but through an appeal to the self-interest of society at large (Polanyi, 2001, pp. 169). Chapter 20 of *The Great Transformation* makes this framing clearer, in a return to the panoramic view of European society employed in the earlier chapters. Surveying the diversity of responses to the collapse of nineteenth-century civilization, from socialism to fascism, Polanyi outlines a scale of social action that stretches beyond national borders. Though particular solutions are processed nationally, the impulse for change is essentially transnational, occurring at the level of the species which instinctively protects itself from the calamitous logic of market rationality. The rhetorical function of this move is clear. By positioning the intentional and socially destructive force of market society against the natural, unconscious, and self-preserving action of the international counter-movement, Polanyi legitimates the natural scales of social co-ordination which typify non-market societies. However, in doing so he effectively empties out his theoretical framework of any set of principles for how social resistance against the re-emergence of market societies could take place.

The problem, therefore, is not of adding a global scale of social action to Polanyian analysis, as suggested by commentators above. A closer reading of the text makes clear that such a scale already exists, and that it plays a crucial role in Polanyi's argument, bound by the interplay between the natural and intentional aspects of social existence. The problem instead, for those who wish to use Polanyi consistently, is to grasp the limitations placed by this treatment of space. For, if the response to the intentional construction of the national and international scales of market society, through national markets and the gold standard, is one of spontaneous reaction, this cannot form a guide to organizing agency on either level. I contend that if there is something that does need adding to Polanyi's work, it is not space, but rather a more elaborated theory of agency.

Conclusions: unwinding the spaces of *The Great Transformation*

In summary, it appears that the literature that adds spatial concepts to Polanyi may be quite mistaken. Spatial concepts are clearly a part of Polanyi's argument, particularly in developing the counterposition of natural and intentional elements of social life. As demonstrated above, this adds to the richness of his analysis within *The Great Transformation*, in that the substantivist approach to economic analysis incorporates geographical elements into the constitution of social life, rather than obscuring them as does economic formalism. This leads to a detailed discussion of space, place, and scale that suffuses the whole of *The Great Transformation*, and bears the weight of its argument at key moments. However, the ways in which geography is incorporated into Polanyi's theoretical framework lend themselves to determinism.

In contradiction of globalization theorists, it seems that we do not need to add a 'global' scale of action to Polanyi's work. Rather, it is already present. However, the appeal to 'natural' scales of coordination at the national and global levels effectively obscures the play of agency. It is a barrier to enquiries into how movements against the market were organized intentionally, and how they should be put together in the future. Polanyi assumes that this activity was spontaneous, and for the purposes of political organization this is inadequate. Instead of the addition of spatial concepts to Polanyi's work, it may be that what it really requires is an exploration of how the scales of the counter-movement against the dominance of the market society were also socially constructed. Though there is not sufficient space here to elaborate a solution to this issue, the problems in Polanyi's spatial thought may not be insoluble. Philip McMichael's work on 'incorporated comparison' offers a Marxian analysis of how historical comparisons on the national level can be used to build a global picture, without assuming an ontological prior international scale (McMichael, 1990). A similar method could in principle be built out of Polanyi's work on the national scale. This might offer a middle path between reading 'in' a global scale of agency that might be inconsistent, and reading the global 'out' of Polanyi in the ways described above.

Finally, if we are to use *The Great Transformation* today, the place to which it refers must be broken up. For Polanyi, Europe was presented as the future towards which all other societies were headed through the incorporation of land, labour, and money into the market mechanism. The West as the representative space of all civilization, whose past other spaces will later repeat, needs to be unwound in order to demonstrate how a shift away from market society in one place may entail a shift toward it in another. However, this is not an exhortation to dispense with Polanyi. Though much of *The Great Transformation* is clearly Eurocentric, as outlined above, Polanyi's method offers possibilities for conducting non-Eurocentric research. Polanyi recognized that investigation of non-Western civilizations yielded insights about contemporary societies. This is clear in how the early analysis of *The Great Transformation* contrasts the smooth organization of of Trobriand economic reciprocity with the comparative chaos of the market society (Polanyi, 2001, pp. 52–53). Comparison between different spaces in the global economy in this manner could yield meaningful research on how market societies may be contested, re-embedded, and decommodified. Once again, we may get more from reading 'out' of Polanyi than reading new material 'in'.

Disclosure statement

No potential conflict of interest was reported by the author.

References

Acemoglu, D., & Robinson, J. A. (2011). *Why nations fail: The origins of power, prosperity, and poverty.* London: Profile Books.

Block, F. (2003). Karl Polanyi and the writing of The Great Transformation. *Theory and Society, 32*(3), 275–306.

Block, F., & Summers, M. R. (2014). *The power of market fundamentalism: Karl Polanyi's critique.* London: Harvard University Press.

Blyth, M. (2002). *Great transformations: Economic ideas and institutional change in the twentieth century.* Cambridge: University Press.

Brenner, R. (1977). The origins of capitalist development: A critique of neo-Smithian Marxism. *New Left Review (I), 104,* 25–92.

Brenner, R. (1982). Agrarian class structure and economic development in pre-industrial Europe: The agrarian roots of European capitalism. *Past and Present, 97*, 16–113.

Burawoy, M. (2003). For a sociological Marxism: The complementary convergence of Antonio Gramsci and Karl Polanyi. *Politics & Society, 31*(2), 193–261.

Cerny, P. G. (1994). The dynamics of financial globalization: Technology, market structure, and policy response. *Policy Sciences, 27*(4), 319–342.

Cerny, P. G. (1995). Globalization and the changing logic of collective action. *International Organization, 49* (4), 595–625.

Dale, G. (2010). *Karl Polanyi: The limits of the market.* Cambridge: Polity Press.

Deleuze, G., & Guattari, F. (1988). *A thousand plateaus: Capitalism and schizophrenia.* London: Athlone.

Diamond, J. (1999). *Guns, germs, and steel: The fates of human societies.* London: Vintage Books.

Evans, P. B. (2000). Fighting marginalization with transnational networks: Counter-hegemonic globalization. *Contemporary Sociology, 29*(1), 230–241.

Evans, P. B. (2008). Is an alternative globalization possible? *Politics & Society, 36*(2), 271–305.

Granovetter, M. (1985). Economic action and social structure: The problem of embeddedness. *American Journal of Sociology, 91*(3), 481–510.

Harvey, D. (1982). *The limits to capital.* Oxford: Blackwell.

Hesketh, C. (2017). Passive revolution: A universal concept with geographical seats. *Review of International Studies, 43*(3), 1–20.

Hess, M. (2004). "Spatial" relationships? Towards a reconceptualization of embeddedness. *Progress in Human Geography, 28*(2), 165–186.

Jessop, B. (1997). A Neo-Gramscian approach to the regulation of urban regimes: Accumulation strategies, hegemonic projects, and governance. In M. Lauria (Ed.), *Reconstructing urban regime theory: Regulating urban politics in a global economy* (pp. 51–74). London: Sage.

Jessop, B. (2005). Gramsci as a spatial theorist. *Critical Review of International Social and Political Philosophy, 8* (4), 421–437.

Karriem, A. (2013). Space, ecology, and politics in the praxis of the Brazilian landless movement. In M. Ekers, G. Hart., S. Kipfer & A. Loftus (Eds.), *Gramsci: Space, nature, politics* (pp. 142–160). Oxford: John Wiley & Sons.

Krippner, G. R. (2002). The elusive market: Embeddedness and the paradigm of economic sociology. *Theory and Society, 30*(6), 775–810.

Lacher, H. (1999a). The politics of the market: Re-reading Karl Polanyi. *Global Society, 13*(3), 313–326.

Lacher, H. (1999b). Embedded liberalism, disembedded markets: Reconceptualising the Pax Americana. *New Political Economy, 4*(3), 343–360.

Lefebvre, H. (1991). *The production of space.* Oxford: Blackwell.

Mackinder, H. (1904). The geographical pivot of history. *The Geographical Journal, 23*(4), 421–437.

Marston, S. A. (2000). The social construction of scale. *Progress in Human Geography, 24*(2), 219–242.

Martin, R., & Sunley, P. (2001). Rethinking the "economic" in economic geography: Broadening our vision or losing our focus? *Antipode, 33*, 148–161.

McMichael, P. (1990). Incorporating comparison within a world-historical perspective: An alternative comparative method. *American Sociological Review, 55*, 385–397.

Morton, A. D. (2013). Travelling with gramsci: The spatiality of passive revolution. In M. Ekers, G. Hart., S. Kipfer & A. Loftus (Eds.), *Gramsci: Space, nature, politics* (pp. 47–64). Oxford: John Wiley & Sons.

Munck, R. (2002). *Globalization and labour: The New 'great transformation'.* London: Zed Books.

Munck, R. (2004). Globalization, labor and the "Polanyi problem". *Labor History, 45*(3), 251–269.

Munck, R. (2006). Globalization and contestation: A Polanyian problematic. *Globalizations, 3*(2), 175–186.

Munck, R. (2010). Globalization, crisis and social transformation: A view from the south. *Globalizations, 7*(1-2), 235–246.

Oinas, P. (1997). On the socio-spatial embeddedness of business firms. *Erdkunde, 51*, 23–32.

Peck, J. (2013). Disembedding Polanyi: exploring Polanyian economic geographies. *Environment and Planning A, 45*(7), 1536–1544.

Polanyi, K. (1957). The economy as instituted process. In K. Polanyi, C. M. Arnesberg, & H. W. Pearson (Eds.), *Trade and market in the early empires: Economies in history and theory* (pp. 242–270). Glencoe: The Free Press & The Falcon's Wing Press.

Polanyi, K. (1963). Ports of trade in early societies. *The Journal of Economic History, 23*(01), 30–45.

Polanyi, K. ([1944] 2001). *The great transformation: The economic and political origins of our time.* Boston: Beacon Press.

Ruggie, J. G. (1982). International regimes, transactions, and change: Embedded liberalism in the postwar economic order. *International Organization, 36*(02), 379–415.

Said, E. W. (1994). *Culture and imperialism.* New York, NY: Vintage Books.

Silver, B. J. (2003). *Forces of labor: Workers' movements and globalization since 1870.* Cambridge: Cambridge University Press.

Smith, N. ([1984] 2010). *Uneven development: Nature, capital, and the production of space.* Athens: University of Georgia Press.

Teschke, B. (2003). *The myth of 1648: Class, geopolitics and the making of modern international relations.* London: Verso.

Against exceptionalism: the legitimacy of the neoliberal age

Martijn Konings

ABSTRACT

After the financial crisis of 2007–08, many commentators, adopting a broadly Polanyian logic of reasoning, expected a departure from neoliberalism. The failure of this shift to materialize has typically been accounted for in 'exceptionalist' terms: the persistence of neoliberalism is understood not as a function of a specific legitimacy it has itself engendered, but in terms of external interventions by elites who manage to 'capture' executive and regulatory institutions and so to bypass democratic pressures. This paper argues that such an approach underestimates the endogenous sources of legitimacy and resilience that neoliberal governance commands. It criticizes the idea that neoliberalism is at its core dependent on a Schmittian exceptionalism and suggests a perspective on Hayek's articulation of neoliberalism that dissociates it from such an exceptionalist approach. The article proceeds to interrogate the rationality of neoliberalism by examining its distinctively secular temporal logic, rooted in speculation, preemption and reaction.

In the immediate aftermath of the financial crisis of 2007–08, progressive commentary was pervaded by intense optimism about the return of social-democratic or progressive-liberal forms of politics and policy as the pillars of a new social compromise. Many declared the end of neoliberalism and its replacement with a regime committed to the re-regulation of financial capital. The crisis was viewed as a turning point in the 'Polanyian' logic of double movements, a model of the dynamics of capitalist society that has found tremendous traction among critical scholars in recent decades (Block & Somers, 2014; Fraser, 2013; Streeck, 2012). According to the Polanyian conceptual schema, periodic 'disembedding' movements, when the speculative logic of the market becomes unmoored from its foundations, will be followed by 're-embedding' movements, when society regroups and intervenes to re-subordinate markets and restore foundations.

The Polanyian model is relevant not just in its own right but also because it formalizes some of the key assumptions of contemporary progressive thought and the terms that it has adopted to confront neoliberalism. It sees the capitalist economy and the democratic polity as governed by logics that are different but in principle compatible (as evidenced by the combination of political stability and economic prosperity that characterized the early postwar period). But it insists that we cannot take this harmony for granted: with a certain cyclical regularity, the expansionary logic of the market will rear its head to upset the balance between economic freedom and political community. At such moments, imperatives of economic growth and accumulation come into conflict with the sovereignty and community organized through public and civic institutions.

As we now know all too well, the re-embedding movement did not occur, and political optimism turned to gloom before too long. And yet, this has not done much to prompt a significant intellectual reorientation of the progressive critique of contemporary capitalism. Discerning out-of-control market dynamics above all else, it denounces the irrationality of neoliberalism's naïve faith in market self-regulation and its inability to appreciate the importance of democratic deliberation and consensus for social order and stability. The resilience of neoliberalism is seen to be 'exceptional' – not grounded in an organically functioning support system of norms and practices but dependent on ad hoc tricks and nefarious political schemes. Many explanations for the failure of neoliberalism to disappear centre on the idea of institutional capture, according to which politicians and policy-makers have been unable to pursue reforms because of the ways in which public institutions and discourses have been captured by financial capital.

Such explanations are incomplete and at times misleading. Of course, the role of elites has been an important factor in preventing popular grievances from translating into politically effective messages, and in preventing any change at the level of institutional politics from translating into durable policy changes. But the idea of institutional capture cannot stand on its own as an explanation for the failure of neoliberalism to expire. The power of elites is itself a function of the continued viability of neoliberal institutions and discourses, and to simply say that their power prevented the demise of neoliberalism therefore runs the risk of being somewhat tautological or uninformative. It does not account for the structural conditions that have permitted neoliberalism to escape what appeared to be an inevitable fate. The question that needs answering is precisely how elites could continue to access such tremendous material, institutional and symbolic resources even in a context where discontent with key neoliberal institutions was at an all-time high and the political air was thick with contempt and distrust towards bankers (cf. Kiersey, 2011, p. 25). Capture explanations do not so much explain what happened, but rather provide a more or less plausible reason for something that was expected to occur yet has not.

The progressive-liberal model of what constitutes a coherent social order very quickly gives rise to exceptionalist modes of explanation: developments are not explained in their own right but rather as deviations from a normative logic that dictates the need for judicious combinations of capitalism and democracy. Progressive capture accounts are in this way part of a wider trend of explanation that follows a 'Schmittian' logic. According to Schmitt's political theory, secularized societies are incapable of generating their own mechanisms of legitimation, and their sources of order and authority are always derived from pre-modern models of religious or monarchical authority. This is why Schmitt's political theory is a political theology: as he famously put it, 'All significant concepts of the modern theory of the state are secularized theological concepts.' (Schmitt, 1922/1985, p. 36). The operative mechanism here is that of the 'state of exception' and the way it opens up a space for authority as pure decision that does not require legitimation through ordinary mechanisms of public accountability (cf. Agamben, 2005). Whereas the Polanyian schema sees the uncertainty of a crisis as something that democratic forces can use to their advantage, Schmittian explanations follow the opposite logic, viewing moments of systemic instability as occasions when the normal rules of liberal democracy are rendered inoperative and developments come to be governed by unaccountable elite decisions. In this way, the Schmittian line of argument has become the excuse story for the failure of the Polanyian line of argument.

Schmitt's political theology was most powerfully challenged in Blumenberg's book *The Legitimacy of the Modern Age* (1966/1983), on which the subtitle of this essay is a variation. Blumenberg rejected the idea that modern institutions' claims to legitimacy were derivative of pre-modern models of transcendent sovereign power. Instead, he argued, modern reason 're-occupied' traditional problematics, producing ways of thinking and doing that were characterized by their own, endogenously produced sources of legitimacy. Blumenberg's conviction that the secularism of the modern era is marked by a qualitative break with the theologies of the pre-modern era would seem to eliminate many routes for critique, as it rules out the possibility of identifying the irrational aspect in a putatively rational world. This concern is perhaps not misplaced in relation to Blumenberg's own work, which often seemed more concerned to advance a pragmatic defence of the Enlightenment project than with opening up *new* ways to critically analyze the structures of secular legitimacy. This paper takes up the latter task, i.e. to develop a critique of neoliberalism that does not start by assuming that the legitimacy problems of the present are caused by the absence of traditional structures of authority and community. Instead, drawing on Foucault and analyzing Hayek, it focuses on the paradoxical temporality that is fostered by modern capitalism and that should be seen as fully endogenous to secular life. Those paradoxes are not external intrusions for which theological models provide adequate explanations, but rather problematic aspects of a social experience that we construct in real, secular time (Konings, 2018).

Although Polanyi did not think of his own theory as a political theology, the terms on which he understood the problem of capitalist order are closely aligned with Schmitt's. Those terms make it difficult to understand the organic sources of contemporary neoliberal order. In particular, they do not allow us to make sense of what is an increasingly visible feature of contemporary political life, i.e. the fact that authoritarian impulses often do not work by sidelining the populace but by mobilizing its energies and sentiments. Of course, authoritarianism and populism combine in different ways in different countries, and it is certainly the case that the balance varies considerably across different incarnations of neoliberalism; but a Polanyian perspective nonetheless simply does not render comprehensible the ways in which resurgent forms of democratic engagement have boosted not just the left but equally often the right. Treatments of, for instance, Tea Party populism and its demand for fiscal austerity have had a highly dismissive tone: it is treated as an irrational, fringe phenomenon that is at odds with the real values of American democracy (e.g. Skocpol & Williamson, 2012). Nor have progressive perspectives been able to offer penetrating readings of the ways in which authoritarian tendencies have fed off the revival of popular engagement with questions of finance and debt (Golumbia, 2016). Defining democratic and popular impulses in opposition to neoliberalism, progressive approaches turn a blind eye to their increasingly visible symbiosis.

This paper proceeds as follows. It begins by situating neoliberalism conceptually, arguing that prevailing perspectives have tended to understand neoliberalism primarily as a return to classic liberalism, understood as a naïve and untenable assertion of the primacy of markets vis-à-vis states. It is this assumption that underlies the embrace of Polanyi, who was a critic of *liberalism*, as a critic of *neoliberalism*. As a result, the Polanyian critique of neoliberalism does not engage the important ways in which that contemporary paradigm differs from its predecessor. The assumption that neoliberalism is an unnatural project of market disembedding makes it difficult to understand the organic sources of its staying-power and leads to Schmittian assumptions about its emergence and persistence. The next section pursues Foucault's intuitions about the character of neoliberalism as a specific rationality of secular governance. In particular, it picks up on Foucault's relatively undeveloped interest in Hayek's thought and suggests that this provides a helpful perspective on the specific character of neoliberal reason. The structure of neoliberal reason as articulated by Hayek operates at a level that is not effectively discerned by the Polanyian critique; the former's practical operation eludes the latter's conceptual schema. The third section critically interrogates the rationality of neoliberalism and the way it fosters particular patterns of legitimacy. It does so by highlighting the paradoxes embedded in the patterns of secular time that neoliberal practices engender. In this way, it provides one possible answer to the question of how we might be able to develop a critical perspective on neoliberalism without resorting to exceptionalist lines of critique. The article concludes with some reflections on the implications of the analysis for how we should view the present state of neoliberalism.

Situating neoliberalism conceptually

The Polanyian schema relies on a fairly literal interpretation of the 'neo' in 'neoliberal': it sees neoliberalism as a simple revival of or return to classic laissez-faire liberalism, marked above all by the subordination of public institutions to the market. As a result, it is often unclear in what qualitative respects liberalism can be seen to be 'new' – it seems we are just dealing with a re-run of classic liberalism. Neoliberalism is accordingly criticized as representing a naïve faith in market self-regulation that is oblivious to the ways in which speculative dynamics undermine the foundations of social order.

Debates in recent years have paid more attention to the specific ideological and institutional sources of the rise of neoliberalism. One prominent line of thinking (Harvey, 2005; Klein, 2008; Mirowski, 2013) has tended to conceive of it as a discrete project brought to prominence by specific elites, actors and ideas who seek to bypass the ordinary mechanisms of political decision-making to impose neoliberal policy templates. But in this way they have tended to reproduce some of the problems discussed in the above. In Mirowski's account, neoliberalism is an exceptionalist, Schmittian project: a form of government that works by paralyzing or bypassing the normal rules of democracy. Others have pursued this path of enquiry by turning to the concept of authoritarian neoliberalism (Bruff, 2014).

Although shock, awe and capture have at times been key modalities of neoliberalism, it is not clear that such an emphasis is useful for understanding all aspects of neoliberalism. This is the case especially in the Western world, where neoliberal programmes have often come to power by mobilizing a great deal of political support. The power of neoliberalism does not just involve the top-down imposition of a pro-capital regime, but is rooted in a broader field of beliefs, practices and institutions. Along such lines, recent contributions have relied on Foucault's lectures on neoliberalism in the *Birth of Biopolitics* (1979/2008) to reflect on the contours of a distinctive 'neoliberal rationality', so steering the analysis of neoliberalism away from exaggerated concern with the actions of small circles of elites (e.g. Brown, 2015; Dardot & Laval, 2013). To view neoliberalism through this lens is to argue that it is not simply a naïve faith in the virtues of utilitarian logics but instead a more or less coherent governance philosophy and that its practical operations are sustained by governmentalities, i.e. subjectively rooted dispositions, inclinations and affinities.

Foucault cautions against the tendency to view neoliberalism simply as a return to classical liberalism. Whereas classic liberalism had always made strong claims about the natural legitimacy or self-evident efficiency of the market in managing risk, neoliberalism was driven by an awareness that this solution was too simple and that the continued viability of capitalism required more than faith in the natural efficiency of markets. Whereas classic liberalism saw its task as removing institutional obstacles to the utilitarian logic of the market, neoliberalism is characterized by an awareness that the order it envisages needs to be actively constructed, institutionally, discursively and politically. For Foucault, then, neoliberalism needs to be understood as an engagement with the limitations of classic liberalism as these had manifested themselves amidst the social and economic instability of the early twentieth century.

THE UTOPIAN SPRINGS OF MARKET ECONOMY

Neoliberal ideas originated during the interwar period, when capitalism experienced a crisis that precipitated the collapse of the international liberal order and the turn to economic nationalism. Under these circumstances, capitalism had lost much of its legitimacy, and capitalist elites' fear of the power of labour movements and the danger of Communism can hardly be overestimated. As Plehwe (2009, p. 10) reports, the word neoliberalism was used first in the 1920s by authors who were specifically minded to rescue liberal principles in the face of advancing socialist forces. He (2009, p. 11) also observes that interwar Vienna served as something of an intellectual training ground for the neoliberal movement: there, Ludwig von Mises and Friedrich Hayek entered into debates with proponents of socialist policies that would eventually take the form of the socialist calculation debate (see Hayek, 1949). Both realized acutely that, if neoclassical economics was correct, the case for capitalism and against socialism was on shaky grounds. Their defense of capitalism was less concerned with the ideal efficiency of markets and rather emphasized the practical limitations of human knowledge about the future and the way this undermines socialist ambitions for the transparent shaping of secular life in line with collectivist principles.

Neoliberal thought can thus be viewed as an attempt to reformulate the principles of classic liberalism in a context where the latter had lost much of their legitimacy (Cahill & Konings, 2017). This involved a recognition of the limits of liberalism and an awareness that a revitalization of capitalism could not simply be a reactionary project seeking a return to earlier times. In that sense, neoliberalism has always been rooted in an appreciation of the problems associated with the liberal market utopia that Polanyi was so critical of. The contemporary Polanyian critique of neoliberalism as a critique of disembedding fails to acknowledge that neoliberals themselves already grappled with very similar issues and proposed particular solutions to make capitalism viable again. Polanyi was a critic of liberalism, and in that sense enlisting him in the critique of neoliberalism is an anachronistic move. To say that neoliberalism involved a reflexive engagement with the limits of classic liberalism, rather than simply being an attempt to restore that dystopia, means that we need to recognize the ways in which the neoliberal project has been minded to produce its own sources of legitimacy.

Neoliberalism as a rationality

As Dean and Villadsen (2016, pp. 133–5) have noted, Foucault's work (at least in the parts that are relevant to our purposes here) can be read as adopting a theory of secularization that is close to Blumenberg's: it analyzed liberalism and neoliberalism as rationalities of governance by engaging the question of how order, norms and authority are constructed in a historical context where metaphysical certainties and theological justifications of authority have lost their traditional force. Unlike Blumenberg's, however, Foucault's approach is characterized by an appreciation of the important role of discourses of political economy in the making of modernity.

Central here was the way in which conceptions of money and economics began to change in the context of the Scottish Enlightenment. Premodern forms of authority had always prominently included a critique of commerce and other money-making activities as subverting the natural order instituted by God (Le Goff, 1988). But as it became increasingly difficult to believe that human history was literally orchestrated by an outside force, the mechanisms that produce order were increasingly viewed as situated at the level of the secular itself. What became thinkable was the idea of secular self-organization, as expressed in Smith's notion of the 'invisible hand' (Sheehan & Wahrman, 2015).

Money now appeared no longer as an irrational, corrupting force but rather as a harmless facilitator of economic interaction – it was 'neutral', as Hume (1752/1985) was the first to argue, a mere means of coordination. In neoclassical economics the neutrality tenet has come to refer specifically to allocative efficiency, but in the context of the Scottish Enlightenment it was deeply embedded in a republican mode of thought that viewed the self-organizing rationality of the market as a bulwark against illegitimate concentrations of authority and monarchical tyranny. The neutrality postulate therefore had a clear political dimension: far from being differentiated in the way that they are nowadays in political theory, republican and liberal discourses were closely intertwined. The liberal-republican image of the market is imbued with a moral and political significance that contemporary critics of unbridled capitalism tend to miss (Kalyvas & Katznelson, 2008).

To say that the idea of market neutrality is central to the modern economic imaginary is to underscore that at the very same time as the modern subject begins to recognize the absence of metaphysical guarantees and the inevitability of secular risk, it becomes deeply invested in the prospect of security: as it becomes aware that the future is not determined by an outside authority, it becomes invested in the possibility of controlling that future and rendering it predictable. Foucault (1978/2007, 1979/2008) observed that discourses of political economy emerged alongside discourses of security. He viewed modernity as engendering a distinctive 'security dispositif': together with the emerging legitimacy of secular time arises the idea that the future can be rationally controlled. The imaginary of liberal governance is thus shaped by the tension between the ever-present need to engage risk on the one hand and the prospect of achieving immunity from the downsides of secular contingency on the other. The notion of market neutrality is an image of the economic that modulates the politics of capitalism – i.e. a regulative fantasy.

Neoclassical economics sanitized this liberal imaginary: conceptualizing money as a technical one-off solution to the problem of coordination, it took time and uncertainty out of risk and so obscured the paradoxical affective structure embedded in the liberal conception of the market. Hayek understood well that in this way it had abandoned important political ground – evident in the ease with which the methods of neoclassical economics could be adopted by the enemies of liberalism. In the socialist calculation debate, he took on the ways in which neoclassical assumptions regarding knowledge and the future had made socialist planning seem like a viable option of social organization. And he viewed progressivism and social democracy as premised on a very similar epistemological naivety.

Even though he was not able to pursue this connection in much detail, Foucault considered Hayek's work as holding important clues to the logic of neoliberalism (Gane, 2014). Whereas neoclassical theory suppresses the role of uncertainty and speculation in economic life, Hayek's work highlights and thematizes it. He was deeply indebted to Smith's understanding of spontaneous economic ordering but went further in dissociating this idea from the theological connotations it still had in Smith (Petsoulas, 2001). Hayek's work categorically denies the possibility of outside interventions or steering and views the emergence of economic order as driven by nothing but trial and error in the here-and-now, uncertainty and discovery. Smith had advanced the 'invisible hand' metaphor in order to address the question of how order might still be possible in a secularizing world that can no longer easily see itself as governed by a divine mind. Hayek (1988), however, proposed his understanding of spontaneous self-organization not to address a concern about the limitations of secular reason but precisely in response to its 'conceit': the faith in rationalist constructivism that he saw as the defining characteristic of twentieth-century socialism and progressivism. His claim was not just that acting without certainty was acceptable but that it was necessary and imperative.

Whereas classic liberalism was primarily concerned to discount the uncertainty of the future, neoliberalism is interested in the outer edges of calculability, the incalculable and unpredictable (Cooper, 2011). In a Hayekian logic, failure is itself a productive event, an indispensable aspect of the discovery processes that generates order. This means that neoliberal reason is characterized by a concern with time and the future that remains suppressed in classic economic liberalism (and is entirely absent in neoclassical economics). It is accordingly more interested in financialization than commodification (Cooper, 2008, p. 10), more taken with the promises and prospects of investment than the immediate utility of consumption, more engaged with the generative role of speculation than the stasis of general equilibrium (cf. Vogl, 2015, p. 57).

Crucially, however, these insights only ever served as a renewal of commitment to the tenet of market neutrality. Even as Hayek's understanding of self-organization incorporated influences from twentieth-century systems theory, it often seems as it his work was written at a time before it became customary to distinguish republicanism from liberalism, imagining the market above all as a source of protection against cumulative inequalities (Vatter, 2014). In Hayek's work market neutrality comes to serve more and more as a regulatory horizon, permanently out of reach, forever receding and demanding an intensified commitment to the uncertainties of the market. The fact that risk and uncertainty never result in equilibrium conditions only serves to heighten the importance of the active engagement of the uncertainty that is the only possible source of order. Neoliberal reason thus recovers the liberal-republican imaginary of market neutrality while recharging the productive tensions of the risk-security axis.

This affective forcefield is sustained by a willingness to attribute the non-neutrality of real-world capitalism to external sources of corruption. The fact that capitalist life is often so patently at odds with the republican image of the market never becomes the occasion for a revision of that image but only heightens the importance of ensuring its realization. The progressive understanding of neoliberalism's persistence in terms of its affiliation with Schmittian exceptionalism is therefore not simply misleading but also suffers from a serious blind spot: it fails to see that neoliberal reason *itself* already contains a critique of exceptionalism and institutional capture, and that the way in which it has directed that critique precisely at the progressive political project has been central to its rhetorical traction and political success. The unreflexive moment here is thrown into even sharper relief when one recalls that capture theory is *literally* a neoliberal theory, pioneered by George Stigler (1971), one of the founding members of the Mont Pelerin society. From a neoliberal perspective, nothing has done more to undermine the neutral operation of capitalism's institutions than progressive elites' conceited claims to expertise and the way in which this has facilitated those who seek bailouts and handouts.

Paradoxes of neoliberal time

The neoliberal subject is expected to achieve security not through avoiding risk but by embracing it – to be resilient, not simply safe. At work here is a logic of preemption, a paradoxical orientation that blurs the distinction between prevention and activation, defensive and offensive moves, security and risk. Preemptive reason can be understood as an operationalization of the dispositif that Hayek insisted was the only possible way to produce order through contingency: it is characterized by a willingness to move beyond a naïve doctrine of prevention and to proactively engage the future.

The concept of preemption has been explored by critical security scholars (Goede, 2008; Massumi, 2007), but here I would like to suggest it also provides a useful lens for looking at questions of political economy. The Bush administration demanded vigilance and preparedness in the name of security, while simultaneously declaring that the war on terror would have no end. Similarly, neoliberalism forever demands a commitment to the speculative logic of risk in the name of a future security that it simultaneously announces will never materialize. In this way it amplifies the paradoxes of the modern security dispositif: even as it presents itself as eliminating threats and obstacles to economic security, its modus operandi is predicated on the possibility of activating and engaging new sources of risk and contingency (Ewald, 2002, p. 294).

Along such lines, we can observe that neoliberal policies have often been oriented not to the prevention of crisis but rather to its preemption – in both senses of the word, i.e. both *activating* instability and *forestalling* its potentially most serious consequences. The shift in monetary policy initiated by Paul Volcker in 1979 – a seminal moment in the restructuring of the institutional landscape of the American political economy (Panitch & Gindin, 2013) – should be seen in that light. Volcker discerned a possibility that the American financial system was heading for a terminal crisis, and he acted on this awareness preemptively, by triggering a potentially productive crisis – one that he hoped would set in motion wider process of adjustment and set the US economy on a new pattern of growth.

What was not in itself surprising was the dramatic expansion of financial activity that followed the policy turn; it was precisely for that reason that the Federal Reserve had held back from contractionary policies in the past. The Volcker speculation consisted precisely in the wager that the instability caused by the Fed's persistence with those policies would set in motion wider processes of adjustment. The extent to which the success of the monetarist turn was contingent on wider adjustments was illustrated by Volcker's (2000) own admission that the Reagan administration's confrontation with organized labour had been crucial to the conquest of inflation. The resulting precarity and contingency for the bulk of the American population offered a wealth of investment opportunities and have served as important sources of renewed capitalist growth (Lazzarato, 2009; Martin, 2002).

Even as neoliberal restructuring brought down inflation and alleviated external pressure on the dollar, these developments were accompanied by significant financial volatility and the 1980s saw a series of bailouts of systemically important ('too big to fail') institutions, which fostered expectations regarding the way the American state would handle such events in the future (Stern & Feldman, 2004). This new institutional configuration facilitated a reorientation of financial governance: the new approach that emerged recognized that crises were likely to continue to occur periodically and that the use of bailouts could not be ruled out and that the aim should be to manage their application and minimize their undesirable side effects. Panitch and Gindin (2013, p. 266) capture this development in terms of a shift of concern from 'failure prevention' to 'failure containment'. Among Federal Reserve insiders this became known as the 'mop up after' strategy (Blinder & Reis, 2005).

It is crucial here to recognize that the neoliberal concern to provoke the future is accompanied by a reactionary moment that manifests itself fully when uncertainty threatens to tip over into failure (cf. Ewald, 2002, p. 285). At such times, acute uncertainty tends to create its own kind of certainty – not an ability to act on accurate knowledge of the future, but a definite certainty as to what needs to be done in the absence of such knowledge. At such times, society has no option but to fortify the historically generated nodal points of financial interconnectedness – that is, to bail out the banks. The logic of preemption now manifests itself in yet a different sense, as a foreclosure on the future. This reactionary moment too has a prominent presence in Hayek's work, which insists on the need to respect norms handed down from the past, even if we are unable to rationally justify such adherence (e.g. his dismissal of the very concept of social justice in Hayek, 1976, pp. 62–85). In this way, the different meanings of the concept of preemption provide a useful guide to the paradoxical logic of neoliberal temporality.

The logic that governs such processes is not a Polanyian one. The moral indignation triggered by bailouts has tended to work in paradoxical ways. The crises of neoliberalism do not represent moments of political openness, when a sudden absence of structural determinations could facilitate the emergence of a countermovement. Neoliberal reason faces uncertainty not as an external condition but as something that it works to incorporate into its mode of operation. Progressive talk of a double movement is preempted by an imaginary of neutrality that connects much more readily with the neoliberal experience of injury and betrayal (Konings, 2015). At no time does the normative image of the market as a flat, decentralized structure acting as a constraint on accumulations of power enjoy more traction than at times when it has been betrayed in the most spectacular way. There is of course an ideological dimension at work here, a politically relevant tension between the logic and image of capital. But precisely because the discrepancy is so dramatic that it is obvious, criticizing it as a sort of cognitive mistake or diversion is largely beside the point. Populists are only too aware that their ideals have been betrayed – that is exactly what they are responding to.

Austerity discourses sit at the heart of the generative tensions of neoliberal reason: they represent a paradoxical combination of reactionary and forward-looking sentiments, enjoining us to repay the debts inherited from the past in order to secure the future. The austerity turn has been widely interpreted in terms of the ability of financial elites to block the democratic impulses of the Polanyian countermovement (Blyth, 2013; Gamble, 2014), but such interpretations are unable to make much sense of the degree of popular support that it has enjoyed (Kiersey, 2018). It has been capable of eliciting popular support because of the way it manifests itself as the aim to restore a republican market that functions as a bulwark against unearned privilege and concentrations of power. Austerity is not primarily associated with dire necessity and the dreary idea that there is simply no alternative: it appears as a means to undo capture and drive out special interests. The popular traction that this has given austerity discourses was on full display when it became a rallying cry for the Tea Party movement. Its central aim is to restore an earlier, less decadent America founded on republican values, where the undeserving are not pampered with bailouts financed by taxes on hardworking citizens and where economic security is achieved not through welfare and handouts but through self-reliance and risk engagement.

Conclusion

The motivating force, ethical appeal and emotional purchase of the neoliberal image of the market have all too often eluded progressive critics. To the extent that they have recognized the affective aspects of neoliberal politics, they have tended to focus on its alliances with neoconservative philosophies and to view these as instrumental and external. According to such accounts, neoconservatives have legitimated laissez-faire economics and private enrichment through appeals to conservative religious values, and large sections of the American public have been curiously unable to see through this obvious hypocrisy – giving rise to the kind of despair at the people's irrationality that is expressed in the title of Thomas Frank's book *What's the matter with Kansas?* (2005) Such approaches conceive of the legitimating spirit of neoliberalism as an external ideological moment, portraying populists' loyalty to neoliberal discourses as a kind of cognitive impairment or moral failure.

This style of explanation has been stretched to new limits with the rise of Trump, a phenomenon has become truly incomprehensible, operating in ways that are beyond the perceptual register of the progressive worldview. Throughout the two-year election process itself, many dismissed his strong showings in early polls and confidently asserted that he would drop out of the primary race soon enough. As Trump's candidacy proved more resilient than expected, such predictions gave way to grudging acknowledgements that Trump enjoyed more appeal than initially expected but were quickly replaced with predictions that he would never be able to capture the nomination. After Trump did win the nomination by a wide margin, the second half of 2016 was dominated by claims that Trump had done so much to alienate key constituencies that his election had become a mathematical impossibility. For much of the campaign, the *New York Times* webpage showed an electoral barometer indicating a very high likelihood that Clinton would win the election. Manifesting the culture of data analysis and claims to technical expertise that progressive media outlets like to associate themselves with, it always seemed like a digital-era talisman meant to stave off impending doom. On election day, the dial flipped over to a decisive Trump victory in just a few hours, as Trump took the lead in several key states, revealing unsuspected resentment beneath measured political opinion.

All this reflected above all the inability to see Trump's victory as a real historical possibility. Progressives have doubled down on the logic of exceptionalism, taking their own sense of utter disbelief as reflecting the cognitive limitations and moral deficiencies of those supporting the Trump enterprise. Notions that we have entered a post-truth era that is qualitatively different from the traditional workings of ideology, or that there is something uniquely sadistic or punitive about Trump's politics, serve more as discussion material for the commentariat than as meaningful contributions to political theory. As explanations of recent developments, they are outdone by Steve Bannon's conviction that Trump is a modern-day Andrew Jackson, working to restore the republican promise of the American polity with a single-minded commitment to the ruthless subordination and eradication of those standing in the way of its realization. Progressives' focus on Trump's lack of basic policy expertise and personal incivility only served to reinforce the impression that he would and could take on the webs of Washington collusion that protected political and corporate elites alike and prevented any significant action on putting special interests back in their place.

The inability to discern this ethical core at the heart of neoliberal political projects leads to the dilemmas that are so familiar to progressives. To take two examples, historian Mark Lilla (2016) singled out the Democratic preoccupation with diversity and 'identity politics' as the main cause behind Trump's victory. Hillary Clinton, he argued, made the 'strategic mistake' of 'calling out explicitly to African-American, Latino, L.G.B.T. and women voters at every stop.' This rubbed the white working classes the wrong way, and they voted for Trump in droves. Lilla would be one of those progressive commentators that long-time *Critical Inquiry* editor W.J.T. Mitchell (2016) has in mind when he writes 'Can I just say that I am sick and tired of hearing liberals and leftists beating their breasts about how they failed to empathize sufficiently with the white working class in this country?' And he added:

> [P]lease, all you liberals, leftists, hipsters, intellectuals, progressives, school teachers, and people who read something besides Twitter feeds, and watch something besides Fox News, stop apologizing for losing this election. … Before you assemble in a circular firing squad to put the blame on yourselves, take a moment to assign the blame where it belongs: on the idiots who voted for this man.

Lilla and Mitchell voice what are fairly common sentiments on the left, and the logic of progressive politics leads to this standoff as a very real strategic dilemma. At work here is a certain kind of political blackmail, which asks us either to legitimate the exclusions and oppressions of neoliberalism in hopes of blunting their sharpest edges; or to turn a blind eye to the ethical force of the neoliberal image of market that drives this exclusionary politics, leaving us to view its supporters as simple idiots, unthinking hostages of false consciousness.

The limitations of exceptionalist explanations are particularly evident in the credulity-straining ways in which the Bush administration, previously accused of all manner of authoritarian and even fascist tendencies, have been reframed as representing a brand of moderate conservatism, at some distance from the racism, nativism and misogyny embraced by Trump (Perlstein, 2017). To be sure, the concern with fascism is hardly inappropriate – the problem is precisely that such readings make the situation seem exceptional, as a deviation from a more normal course of historical development that is unamenable to explanation and intervention. On the one hand, this entails a tendency to dramatize the immediacy of the danger and to overstate the ease with executive powers can abrogate the powers of democratic institutions. On the other hand, it diverts attention from the ugliness that neoliberal democracy is capable of producing even when its key institutions are still fully intact and functional.

Disclosure statement

No potential conflict of interest was reported by the author.

References

Agamben, G. (2005). *State of exception*. Chicago, IL: University of Chicago Press.

Blinder, A. S., & Reis, R. (2005). Understanding the Greenspan standard. In *The Greenspan Era: Lessons for the future* (pp. 11–96). Kansas City, MO: Federal Reserve Bank of Kansas City.

Block, F., & Somers, M. R. (2014). *The power of market fundamentalism: Karl Polanyi's critique*. Cambridge, MA: Harvard University Press.

Blumenberg, H. (1966/1983). *The legitimacy of the modern Age*. Cambridge, MA: MIT Press.

Blyth, M. (2013). *Austerity: The history of a dangerous idea*. Oxford: Oxford University Press.

Brown, W. (2015). *Undoing the demos: Neoliberalism's stealth revolution*. New York, NY: Zone Books.

Bruff, I. (2014). The rise of authoritarian neoliberalism. *Rethinking Marxism, 26*(1), 113–129.

Cahill, D., & Konings, M. (2017). *Neoliberalism*. Cambridge: Polity.

Cooper, M. (2008). *Life as surplus: Biotechnology and capitalism in the neoliberal era*. Seattle, WA: University of Washington Press.

Cooper, M. (2011). Complexity theory after the financial crisis. *Journal of Cultural Economy, 4*(4), 371–385.

Dardot, P., & Laval, C. (2013). *The new way of the world: On neoliberal society*. London/New York: Verso.

Dean, M., & Villadsen, K. (2016). *State phobia and civil society: The political legacy of Michel Foucault*. Stanford, CA: Stanford University Press.

Ewald, F. (2002). The return of Descartes's malicious demon: An outline of a philosophy of precaution. In T. Baker & J. Simon (Eds.), *Embracing risk: The changing culture of insurance and responsibility* (pp. 273–301). Chicago, IL: University of Chicago Press.

Foucault, M. (1978/2007). *Security, territory, population*. New York, NY: Palgrave Macmillan.

Foucault, M. (1979/2008). *The birth of biopolitics*. New York, NY: Palgrave.

Frank, T. (2005). *What's the matter with Kansas? How conservatives won the heart of America*. New York, NY: Holt.

Fraser, N. (2013). A triple movement? Parsing the politics of crisis after Polanyi. *New Left Review, 81*(May-June), 119–132.

Gamble, A. (2014). *Crisis without end? The unravelling of western prosperity*. New York, NY: Palgrave Macmillan.

Gane, N. (2014). The emergence of neoliberalism: Thinking through and beyond Michel Foucault's lectures on biopolitics. *Theory, Culture & Society, 31*(4), 3–27.

Goede, M. d. (2008). The politics of preemption and the war on terror in Europe. *European Journal of International Relations, 14*(1), 161–185.

Golumbia, D. (2016). *The politics of Bitcoin: Software as right-wing extremism*. Minneapolis, MN: University of Minnesota Press.

Harvey, D. (2005). *A brief history of neoliberalism*. Oxford: Oxford University Press.

Hayek, F. (1949). *Individualism and economic order*. London: Routledge & Kegan Paul.

Hayek, F. (1976). *Law, legislation and liberty, volume 2: The mirage of social justice*. Chicago, IL: University of Chicago Press.

Hayek, F. (1988). *The fatal conceit. The errors of socialism*. London: Routledge.

Hume, D. (1752/1985). Of money. In E. F. Miller (Ed.), *Essays: Moral, political, and literary* (pp. 281–294). Indianapolis, IN: Liberty Fund.

Kalyvas, A., & Katznelson, I. (2008). *Liberal beginnings: Making a republic for the moderns*. Cambridge: Cambridge University Press.

Klein, N. (2008). *The shock doctrine: The rise of disaster capitalism*. New York, NY: Picador.

Kiersey, N. (2011). Everyday neoliberalism and the subjectivity of crisis: Post-political control in an era of financial turmoil. *Journal of Critical Globalisation Studies, 4*, 23–44.

Kiersey, N. (2018). Austerity as tragedy? From neoliberal governmentality to the critique of late capitalist control. In D. Cahill, M. Cooper, M. Konings, & D. Primrose (Eds.), *The SAGE handbook of neoliberalism* (pp. 496–510). London: Sage.

Konings, M. (2015). *The emotional logic of capitalism: What progressives have missed*. Stanford, CA: Stanford University Press.

Konings, M. (2018). *Capital and time: For a New critique of neoliberal reason*. Stanford, CA: Stanford University Press.

Lazzarato, M. (2009). Neoliberalism in action: Inequality, insecurity and the reconstitution of the social. *Theory, Culture & Society, 26*(6), 109–133.

Le Goff, J. (1988). *Your money or your life*. New York, NY: Zone Books.

Lilla, M. (2016, November 18). The end of identity liberalism. *New York Times*.

Martin, R. (2002). *Financialization of daily life*. Philadelphia, PA: Temple University Press.

Massumi, B. (2007). Potential politics and the primacy of preemption. *Theory and Event, 10*(2).

Mirowski, P. (2013). *Never let a serious crisis go to waste: How neoliberalism survived the financial meltdown*. London: Verso.

Mitchell, W. J. T. (2016). Further night thoughts on the trump election. Retrieved from https://critinq. wordpress.com/2016/11/16/further-night-thoughts-on-the-trump-election/

Panitch, L., & Gindin, S. (2013). *The making of global capitalism: The political economy of American empire*. London/New York: Verso.

Perlstein, Rick. (2017, April 11). I thought I understood the American right. Trump proved me wrong. *New York Times*.

Plehwe, Dieter. (2009). Introduction. In Philip Mirowski & Dieter Plehwe (Eds.), *The road from Mont Pèlerin* (pp. 1–42). Cambridge: Harvard University Press.

Petsoulas, C. (2001). *Hayek's liberalism and its origins: His idea of spontaneous order and the Scottish enlightenment*. Abingdon: Routledge.

Schmitt, C. (1922/1985). *Political theology: Four chapters on the concept of sovereignty*. Chicago, IL: University of Chicago Press.

Sheehan, J., & Wahrman, D. (2015). *Invisible hands. Self-organization and the eighteenth century*. Chicago, IL: University of Chicago Press.

Skocpol, T., & Williamson, V. (2012). *The Tea party and the remaking of American conservatism*. Oxford: Oxford University Press.

Stern, G. H., & Feldman, R. J. (2004). *Too Big to fail: The hazards of bank bailouts*. Washington, D.C.: Brookings Institution Press.

Stigler, G. (1971). The theory of economic regulation. *The Bell Journal of Economics and Management Science, 2*(1), 3–21.

Streeck, W. (2012). How to study contemporary capitalism? *European Journal of Sociology, 53*(1), 1–28.

Vatter, M. (2014). Foucault and Hayek: Republican law and liberal civil society. In V. Lemm & M. Vatter (Eds.), *The government of life. Foucault, Biopolitics, and neoliberalism* (pp. 163–184). New York, NY: Fordham University Press.

Vogl, J. (2015). *The Specter of capital.* Stanford, CA: Stanford University Press.

Volcker, P. (2000). Interview. Commanding Heights, PBS, September 26. Retrieved from http://Www.Pbs.Org

Neoliberalism as a real utopia? Karl Polanyi and the theoretical practice of F. A. Hayek

João Rodrigues

ABSTRACT
This article interprets Hayek's theoretical practice with the help of Polanyi's framework. Hayek aimed at renewing liberalism after the interwar period, thus helping transforming it into neoliberalism, a real utopia instrumentally concerned with the political and moral economies underpinning markets. The distance between neoliberal theory and practice is less pronounced than it is sometimes assumed. The strength of neoliberalism partially stems from a capacity to articulate an effort to think about real-world mechanisms with an effort to demolish, reconfigure or transform existing structures. Despite his failure to anticipate neoliberalism, Polanyi gives ample intellectual resources to critically interpret the tasks that neoliberals would collectively have to face at the theoretical level, in an epoch of ideological marginality, before their triumphal political deployment at the global level.

Neoliberalism has been critically analysed by political economists with the help of the framework that Polanyi (1944/2001) developed to understand the long-term impacts of nineteenth-century liberalism, uncovering, in particular, the seemingly paradoxical relations between state power and market expansion. Mirowski (2009, p. 441) belongs to this tradition when he considers that the following quote by Polanyi (1944/2001, pp. 146–147) 'deftly captured the dynamic' that is at stake in neoliberalism:

> The road to the free market was open and kept open by an enormous increase in continuous centrally organized and controlled interventionism (…) Administrators had to be constantly on the watch to ensure the free working of the system. Thus even those who wished most ardently to free the state from all unnecessary duties, and whose all philosophy demanded the restriction of state activities, could not but entrust the self-same state with the new powers, organs, and instruments required for the establishment of laissez-faire.

Neoliberalism, as every actually existing socioeconomic system, is, and must be, always embedded, not only politically, in terms of class power, but also institutionally (Cahill, 2014). This critical understanding of contemporary reality is often contrasted with what, following Dugger (1989), one might label the ideological 'enabling myths' propagated by neoliberal ideologues. These myths range from the defense of the apolitical and amoral nature of free markets, premised, respectively, upon the separation of the economy and the polity and upon an ideal of neutrality among different conceptions of the good life allowed by market activity, to the related and quasi-naturalistic idea that the self-regulating market implies a disembedded order arising spontaneously out of the retreat of the state, thereby signalling its attunement to dominant human motives in a context of unavoidable scarcity.

In this context, one of the main intellectual strategies of many critical students of neoliberalism is best exemplified by Harvey's (2005, p. 19) denunciation of its 'theoretical utopianism', reduced to 'a system of justification and legitimation', i.e. to an ideology that is meant to mostly hide the mechanisms at work in actually existing processes of neoliberalization. Other critical geographers, for example, have shown that the latter consist of 'a tendential, discontinuous, uneven, conflictual and contradictory reconstitution of state-economy relations', within a 'politically guided intensification of market rule' (Brenner, Peck, & Theodore, 2010, p. 184). This entails a methodological precept: 'descend from the mountain top, moving beyond the interpretation of Hayekian encyclicals, and deep into the weeds of everyday market governance' (Peck, 2010, p. xiv).

While capturing crucial dimensions of what is at stake in the history of neoliberalism and providing a salutary reminder not to reduce neoliberalism to 'the high-church pronouncements of Hayek and his followers' (Peck, 2010, p. xiii), an excessive attention to the contrast between its variegated institutional realities and the relatively uniform political myths propagated by neoliberal ideologues has at least one potential cost. By eventually losing sight of the theoretical practice of neoliberalism before its triumph, in general, and of certain facets of F. A. Hayek's work, in particular, it overestimates the gap between neoliberal vision and the actual processes of neoliberalization. It is here claimed that the gap is narrower than is generally recognized and that it was implicitly anticipated by Hayek himself as an unavoidable feature of the eventual jump of any utopian blueprint to realist political action. As Peck (2008, p. 7) himself put it in his historical excavation of the original pronouncements, neoliberalism is, among other intellectual features, from the beginning 'framed by the distinctively post-laissez-faire question' of the much needed positive state interventions to reconfigure society in a certain direction. In an intellectual division of labour among critical scholars, some then need to stay on the mountain top and reinterpret attentively the encyclicals so that the original questions and answers given are not forgotten, even because their intellectual and institutional legacies are still with us.[1]

It will be here argued that probing Hayek's thought with Polanyian lenses before neoliberalism's political triumphs allow us to underline the plasticity and robustness of a set of ideas in movement, containing constructivist elements from their theoretical beginnings. There is indeed an early recognition of, and reflection upon, the political deliberation that is required to institute a certain economy, with a certain relation to democracy. These are substantivist elements, centred around the role played by institutions, and in Hayek's thought they are transparently, and one might say realistically, present from the very start in what was also explicitly an utopian project, in the sense of a project aimed at transforming reality in a certain preconceived direction.[2] Furthermore, the Polanyian lenses also allow us to see a neoliberal version of the double movement that is part of 'Hayekian dialectics' (Sciabarra, 1995), i.e. the contradictory interplay between antagonistic forces, where deliberation and spontaneity are intermingled in particular ways.

Despite the fact that there was never an explicit intellectual debate between Polanyi and Hayek and that in their works there are but a few and brief references to each other, it will be argued that part of the intellectual, and thereby political, strength of neoliberalism is rooted in the capacity of one of its intellectual leaders to think anew about some of the failures of liberalism and to take on board from the very beginning, as it were, some of Polanyi's ideas.[3] Reading Hayek with the help of Polanyi's framework, as done here, offers other potential rewards. First, it shows how Hayek's political economy, i.e. his analysis of the relation between state power and markets, can be thought of as if incorporating a neoliberal version of Polanyi's notion of the necessarily embedded economy.

Second, it helps uncover Hayek's moral economy, i.e. his analysis of the relation between institutions and human motivations, showing that it incorporates a neoliberal version of the 'reality of society'. According to Block and Sommers (2014, p. 228), Polanyi's conception comprises 'an ontological statement about the social nature of human agency and the interdependence of our collective existence'; and so does Hayek's, I argue. Third, this reading of Hayek helps identify new convergences and further clarify divergences between two influential thinkers.

Hayek's real utopia

In an important addition to the burgeoning literature on Karl Polanyi, two of his interpreters have presented an account of how, in his work, the 'tables are turned' against the hegemonic 'market fundamentalism' through the reasoned denunciation that it is actually based on a utopian idea: the subordination of society to the operation of a self-regulating market (Block & Sommers, 2014, p. 99). Polanyi (1944/2001) defines economic liberalism as the ideology behind the ultimately 'fictitious' commodification of labour, nature and money, which are not, in their essence, true commodities.[4] The market society envisaged is utopian in the sense that it was never an historical reality and it never will be. Polanyi is indeed very clear about the main thesis of *The Great Transformation* being 'that the idea of a self-adjusting market implied a stark utopia' since 'such an institution could not exist for any length of time without annihilating the human and natural substance of society' (Polanyi, 1944/2001, p. 3).

Given his influence, Hayek's (1949) transparent plea for a 'liberal utopia', five years after Polanyi's *magnum opus*, is used by Block and Sommers (2014, p. 99) as the main illustration 'of the prescience of Polanyi's rhetorical move'. Nevertheless, Hayek's (1949) embrace of utopianism was a qualified one and his plea for a 'liberal utopia' has to be understood within the context of the two usages of the term throughout his work.[5] Hayek tried to distinguish between what he saw as viable liberal utopias, which he praised, and unviable socialist utopias, which he criticized. He thereby retains the concept of utopia as something worth pursuing, as is visible in the following passage (Hayek, 1973/2003, p. 65):

> Utopia, like ideology, is a bad word today; and it is true that most utopias aim at radically redesigning society and suffer from internal contradictions which make their realization impossible. But an ideal picture of society which may not be wholly achievable, or a guiding conception of the overall order to be aimed at, is nevertheless not only an indispensable precondition for any rational policy, but also the chief contribution that science can make to the solution of the problems of practical policy.

Despite his skepticism about the usages of knowledge to effect great transformations (Gamble, 2006), Hayek retains the view that 'science' can realistically grasp the mechanisms of the 'overall order' and use this supposedly objective knowledge to differentiate between impossible and counterproductive 'radical designs' and those that are viable and desirable. This is a very demanding project from an intellectual and political point of view. It was captured, in its positive dimension, by Hayek (1944/2006, p. 18) through a powerful metaphor about the nature of knowledge as power:

> The attitude of the liberal to society is like that of a gardener who tends a plant and in order to create the conditions most favorable to its growth must know as much as possible about its structure and the way it functions.

Hayek then developed what he saw as a kind of real utopia, a way of contributing to a collective and organized project of renovating classical liberalism.[6] For this, he tried to develop a realist

THE UTOPIAN SPRINGS OF MARKET ECONOMY

understanding of the diversity of human institutions and their essential properties, an epistemological and ontological inclination he shared with Polanyi and which grounds the effort at their 'partial reconciliation' at the meta-theoretical level (Migone, 2011; see also O'Neill, 2001). A feasible market society, the utopia to be achieved, realistically required specific and demanding political and moral conditions, an institutional and motivational diversity, which science could help defining.

Neoliberal political economy

In his critical history of nineteenth century liberalism, Karl Polanyi uncovered the contrast between liberal discourses and their political practices aimed at effecting profound institutional transformations. This has inspired many recent critical readings of neoliberalism. But at same time, and much unnoticed in the secondary literature, he also considered that some of the strands of liberal discourse already acknowledged explicitly the spirit of a constructivist political economy: 'if ever there was a conscious use of the executive in the service of a deliberate government-controlled policy, it was on the part of the Benthamites in the heroic period of laissez-faire' (Polanyi, 1944/2001, p. 147). Polanyi concludes that there is one consistent position for economic liberalism and recognized that this position had its followers: 'only such policies and measures are in order which help to ensure the self-regulation of the market by creating conditions which make the market the only organizing power in the economic sphere' (p. 72). These policies presuppose a theoretical effort concerned with a form of embeddedness whereby polity or morality would be transformed into mere instruments devoted to the construction and ideological justification of a particular version of the market: it is as if 'social relations are embedded in the economic system', i.e. they are only justified if they contribute to the expansion of a particular version of that system (p. 60).

Polanyi has failed to anticipate the intellectual rise and political development of neoliberalism as a postwar phenomenon (Dardot & Laval, 2009). But it is also true that in his recognition of consistency within strands of economic liberalism there is an inadvertent, but keen, anticipation of some of the tasks in the domain of political economy that neoliberals would collectively face at the theoretical level. And this in an epoch of ideological marginality, before their triumphal political deployment: how to reinvent the 'Benthamite' tradition of interventionism in favour of markets in a new political and intellectual context.

Hayek's neoliberal political economy is explicitly marked by an effort to pursue the task formulated by Bentham: 'to distinguish between the agenda and non-agenda of government' (Hayek, 1948a, p. 17). Hayek had already made clear that 'the question whether the state should or should not "act" or "interfere" poses an altogether false alternative' and the term laissez-faire was to be abandoned because it 'is a highly ambiguous and misleading description of the principles on which a liberal policy is based' (Hayek, 1944/2006, p. 84). In this vein, his initial answer was to mobilize the idea of 'planning for freedom' or 'planning for competition' (Hayek, 1939a/1997, 1944/2006), meaning the deliberate assurance of the institutional arrangements of an evolving market order. Hayek, like all relevant neoliberals, was then being consistent in the sense formulated by Polanyi.

For Hayek (1939b/1948) planning for competition involved political engineering with transnational ambitions, a blueprint for a system of 'interstate federalism'. Ideally, it would be able to create a pro-market bias in economic policy, given the combination of socioeconomic and national heterogeneity and what could be labelled a supranational multi-level governance system whereby a single market and a single currency would be governed by a federal body somehow protected from the pressures of democratic politics mostly located at the now subordinated and constrained national level.[7] The latter level would then be partially hollowed out, given the absence of relevant instruments of economic policy, while it would be exposed, through the freedom of movement, of workers, but mostly of capital, to selective pressures towards liberalization. This would be realized through a process of arbitrage on behalf of capital and through a corresponding process of competition between social formations: virtuous races to the bottom as it were. Meanwhile, without the cement of a national identity, a transnational agreement would be limited in its capacity to recreate the communitarian ethos that would limit and embed markets in a collectivist project (Hayek, 1939b/1948).[8] Inspired by a Polanyian reading of political economy stressing the political power of original ideas, Streeck (2014) has recently pointed out that Hayek was an early exponent of the causal link between deliberate denationalization and the creation of a trend towards economic liberalization.[9]

Neoliberalism, a term that appears in the late thirties, can from the start be thought of as a theoretical practice that aims at advancing institutional arrangements that favour a commodification bias in public policies. This predisposition is particularly effective when a post-democratic structure of constraint is in place at the supranational level compelling national polities to follow a path that leads to market solutions to an increasing number of problems. In a sense Hayek (1939b/1948) is an early theorization of a more robust type of multi-scalar structure, after the exhaustion of the Gold Standard or the imperialism of free trade that was so trenchantly criticized by Polanyi (1944/2001) in the inter-war period. Indeed, what Hayek feared – the disintegration of the capitalist world economy – Polanyi saw as an opportunity for the processes of extension of democracy to the economy.

Meanwhile, Hayek never wavered in his constructivist conviction that 'government is necessarily the product of intellectual design' (Hayek, 1979/2003, p. 152). Forty years after the blueprint for 'interstate federalism', he would propose a more detailed multi-scalar constitutional blueprint for a 'limited democracy', blocking social-democratic outcomes in the areas of progressive taxation or other extensions of democracy to the economic realm, explicitly doubting 'whether a functioning market has ever newly arisen under an unlimited democracy' and thus concluding that 'it seems likely that unlimited democracy will destroy it where it has grown up' (Hayek, 1979/2003, p. 77).

Hayek (1960/2006) had already established the rule of law as a way to generate principled lines between the agenda and non-agenda of government within a renewed liberalism (Shearmur, 2006). This strict understanding of the legal architecture needed for such a demanding endeavor was of such a nature as to be explicitly compatible with a rather undefined principle of 'expediency' allowing many other activities of the so-called service state, his alternative to the welfare state. The state was conceived by him as a 'piece of utilitarian machinery' (Hayek, 1944/2006, p. 80). Whenever Hayek poses the question of the state in his version of capitalism, he is then never consistently far from a circumscribed utilitarianism, i.e. from the Benthamite problematic of the instrumental agenda of government better able to institute markets.

When Hayek (1979/2003, p. 65) approvingly quotes Ludwig von Mises (1949) – 'the pure market economy assumes that government, the social apparatus of compulsion and coercion, is intent on preserving the operations of the market system' – it is clear that preserving those instrumental operations was a much more demanding task than Mises classical laissez-faire vision of the minimal state was willing to account for (Rodrigues, 2013a). And this is particularly so in the areas corresponding more or less closely to Polanyi's 'fictitious commodities', where the visible hand of the state is unavoidable and the dilemmas it poses have to be clarified, going beyond classical liberalism and its supposedly simple and automatic institutional underpinnings. Money, for example, poses an acute problem once it is recognized that a return to the gold standard, and to the harsh discipline it imposed upon societies, is unthinkable (Hayek, 1937). Hayek then oscillated between the above-mentioned demanding political project of monetary unification above the nation-state (Hayek, 1939b/1948), or purely decentralized and private monetary solutions below the state, as if, in the latter alternative, money could still be thought of as a commodity (Hayek, 1978/1990).[10]

Beyond monetary dilemmas, it is also clear that the market economy had to be less pure, institutionally more variegated, for a variety of regulatory reasons. Indeed, Hayek recognizes that modern societies tend to multiply the areas where markets fail without public assistance, a veritable 'Pandora box' to use the apt expression of a libertarian critic (Block, 1996). These include unsatisfied basic needs that may undermine the political legitimacy of the market society, and that may justify, for precautionary reasons, a minimum income guaranteed by governments outside the market (Hayek, 1944/2006). That guarantee would even become more necessary given the diagnosed need of fighting trade-unions and at least partially recommodifying labour to ensure the functioning of market adjustments, since otherwise 'the unions will prevent competition from acting as an effective regulator of the allocation of all resources' (Hayek, 1960/2006, p. 238). Governments would also have to ensure some forms of so-called generic knowledge so as to diminish the asymmetries of information among contracting parties or to help achieving more enlightened private decisions with intergenerational impacts, as in the exploitation of natural resources.[11] In this context, Hayek (1960/2006) recognizes that externalities and other pervasive social interdependencies have to be managed, particularly in urban areas where property rights are more complex and intertwined.

As Hayek (1960/2006, p. 194) acknowledged in a revealing synthesis of his political economy:

> [I]t is the character rather than the volume of government activity that is important. A functioning market presupposes certain activities on the part of the state; there are some other such activities by which its functioning will be assisted; and it can tolerate many more, provided that they are of a kind which are compatible with a functioning market.

The concrete institutional expressions of this abstract concept – a 'functioning market' – would have to be defined within neoliberalism as a theoretical practice devoted to the political travails of assuring the institutional underpinnings of a market society. The already mentioned service state is a case in point: there are many goods and services, which should be made widely available, that private initiative through markets cannot efficiently offer, at least at an early stage, without the help from the state, (Hayek, 1960/2006). According to Hayek (1960/2006) the state should do this mostly through public financing instead of public provisioning or, much worse, through the monopolization of the goods and services in question.[12] The goal should be ultimately the promotion of market competition and political decentralization could help in this: 'Competition between local authorities or between larger units within an area where there is freedom of movement provides in a large measure that opportunity for experimentation with alternative methods which will secure most of the advantages of free growth' (Hayek, 1960/2006, p. 230). This is of course coherent with the mechanisms already identified in Hayek's (1939b/1948) article on interstate federalism, conceived as a process of selective centralization to promote an ideal of competitive decentralization. Hayek's neoliberal political economy is multi-scalar in nature from the start.

The subordination of the non-market spheres to the diverse and complex requirements of the market sphere could not be entirely specified in advance. Once it is recognized the problem of the political legitimacy of markets and their institutional and legal malleability and the incapacity of economic actors spontaneously to acknowledge the social costs and benefits of their economic activities, given the existence of externalities and public goods, then the scope of state activities automatically increases. This shows that Hayek ends up being closer to Polanyi's characterization of the paradoxical link between states and markets in capitalism: the development of markets might demand an expansion of the state. This eventual expansion has to be controlled and guided. It is its 'character' of the state, the nature of this political instrument, which is at stake.

Neoliberal moral economy

Karl Polanyi's moral economy can be read as an effort to show simultaneously what the institutional conditions are that make certain individual motives prevalent and by what mechanisms a society solely based on selfishness is a utopian endeavor that is destined to fail (Rodrigues, 2004). Polanyi considered the plasticity of human motivations when he argued that 'human beings will labour for a variety of reasons as long as things are arranged accordingly' (Polanyi, 1947, p. 113), while simultaneously characterizing institutions as 'embodiments of human meaning and purpose', affecting those motivations that are prevalent (Polanyi, 1944/2001, p. 262).

Hayek's moral economy also goes beyond the assumptions of liberal neutrality in political philosophy or the assumptions of *homo economicus* of neoclassical economics (Rodrigues, 2013b).[13] This means that Hayek's moral economy contains a double recognition: that 'man is as much a rule-following as a purpose-seeking one' (Hayek, 1973/2003, p. 11), and that social theory 'starts from men whose whole nature and character is determined by their existence in society' (Hayek, 1948a, p. 6). This is sufficient to distance Hayek' work from an atomistic view of socioeconomic reality and to make him further converge to Polanyi's institutionalist position, including also the way in which the 'agency structure dilemma' is tackled (Migone, 2011). Despite their differences, in terms of the concrete causal mechanisms posited, 'they both believe that agent and structure have an interactive relation that is not deterministic in either sense' (Migone, 2011, p. 366).

Hayek focuses on the complex patterns of relations between human agency and institutions and argues that the identification of these patterns – 'the kinds of circumstances which affect human action' (Hayek, 1967, p. 232) – is part of the proper aim of the social sciences (Rodrigues, 2013b). Hayek then developed an embedded view of the individual dependent upon rules (Davis, 2003). Hayek's (1948a, p. 12) rejection of the 'bogey of the "economic man"' operates both at the level of rationality and to a less recognized extent at the level of individuals' motivations.

Indeed, Hayek's neoliberal case for individual freedom through markets is based upon the idea of limited rationality; it 'rests chiefly on the recognition of the inevitable ignorance of us all' (Hayek, 1960/2006, p. 29), thereby downplaying to a certain extent the importance of human motivations (Rodrigues, 2013b). Markets are needed precisely because they generate prices that are considered to be unrivalled conveyors of information and incentives, allowing individuals to act also according to the tacit knowledge they possess about their own particular circumstances. This generates a learning process and a concomitant transformation of the way these market participants see the world. It is in this context that one can understand Hayek's (1948b, p. 106) claims that market 'competition is essentially a process of formation of opinion', also nurturing, thanks to the 'civilizing forces of commerce', 'eminently social virtues which smooth social contacts' (Hayek, 1944/2006, p. 153).[14] The selfish response to pecuniary incentives is a motivation considered to be adequate to the market sphere, but even there it is not enough, since it has to be tamed by an instrumental moral code, the so-called 'commercial morals' (Hayek, 1944/2006). In contrast to Polanyi, morality is valued in this sphere as long as it leads individuals to assume full responsibility for their results and to accept the rules, formal and informal, of the market society. Indeed, for Polanyi (1944/2001), markets can become immoral mechanisms, generating individual irresponsibility, particularly on behalf of those with power. Markets can hide from view the social costs that are generated by particular capitalist activities and then transferred to certain subaltern social groups.

Hayek's political economy recognizes the potential existence of failures of the market, even as epistemic devices, in dealing with the social costs of economic activities (Rodrigues, 2012). This is one of the reasons why markets have to rely on non-market institutions. If this is so, it is crucial, according to Hayek, for these non-market institutions, particularly at the state level, to be entrusted to an elite, a selected group of individuals who must be intrinsically motivated and committed to a particular view of the common good, understood as the promotion as far as possible of markets or of market-conforming solutions to their limited failures. In a sense, Hayek's moral economy has to distance itself from the idea that self-interest should be made universal: self-interest is not an adequate motivation for scholars committed to the production of expert knowledge or for judges and politicians who have to exhibit 'probity, wisdom and judgment' (Hayek, 1979/2003, p. 112) in their irreplaceable activities. The political and moral economies cohere, as Amable (2011, p. 18) perceptively argues, since 'in the neoliberal ideology, ethical requirements for elite members may act as substitutes for people's legitimacy'. This applies to Hayek who even hints that these requirements, which are also epistemic, for elites might be in accordance with, might even be nurtured by, the non-market character of the institutions in support of markets, hinting at particular connections between institutional pluralism and the diversity of motivations and knowledge which are absent from many neoliberal accounts.

Neoliberal political and moral economies: constructed and spontaneous?

Polanyi (1944/2001) considered that the plural countermovement of social protection against markets, therefore tending towards decommodification, was waging an imminently realist struggle, mostly using the nation-state as its regulatory instrument, countering the social costs generated by certain forms of commodification. While Hayek (1944/2006) considered this countermovement to be induced by a history of insufficient exposition of many groups to market forces, together with the propaganda of socialist intellectuals, Polanyi (1944/2001) viewed it as a spontaneous reaction against liberal planning and its social costs. But both agreed that this trend was an important feature of the capitalism of their time, despite their almost symmetrically antagonistic diagnoses and prescriptions.

Hayek's highly constructivist moral and political economy becomes even more visible if one is aware of his diagnosis about the resilience of the so-called ingrained political and moral atavisms behind anti-market initiatives (Hayek, 1988). Socialism was considered to be the most recent expression of a historically robust, but reversible, trend. It is here that Hayek tries to turn the tables against authors like Karl Polanyi: socialism is not only utopian, in the negative sense that this word can also have in his intellectual arsenal, but also conservative and ultimately reactionary; an expression of the longing for the 'tribal group', of which nationalism is for him a perverse but resilient expression behind all collectivisms (Hayek, 1976/2003, p. 134).

The perceived strength of collectivism can help understand why Hayek (1949) saw himself as part of a countermovement which had to be induced against all odds, which had to be utopian. But this utopianism required, as it was shown above, a theoretical practice deemed realist. Such practice was instrumentally concerned with the uncovering of the mechanisms better able to guarantee the political and moral embeddedness of markets within recognizably elitist institutions with a low degree of democratic participation and scrutiny.

It is in this combination of realism and utopianism that the most important antinomies of Hayek's thought, in particular, and of neoliberalism, in general, can be pointed out. If, on the one hand, the role of human reason is never in doubt in deliberately forging arguments and (re)forming institutional arrangements so as to guarantee the conditions for the 'liberal utopia'; on the other hand, the incomplete nature of human knowledge and the spontaneous order of market society is also present in the justification of that same market utopia.[15]

In Hayek's own thought this latter dimension points to a somewhat different vision of the market society: a self-generating and self-regulating mechanism, which is separated from the polity and from morality, given its apolitical and amoral nature. The description of a market society as both apolitical and amoral is a facet of Hayek's thought that manifests itself in the 'twin ideas' of spontaneous order and cultural evolution that are part of his meta-historical narrative. According to this, market society, or what he also labels 'catallaxy', is the result of 'human action, but not the execution of human design' to use Adam Ferguson's formulation that Hayek often quotes (Hayek, 1960/2006, p. 51). Hayek thus seems to assume a process of cultural evolution in which the most successful groups are precisely those that have 'stumbled' on certain institutional arrangements and rules underpinning markets, and were able to preserve and improve them at the margin, benefiting from the crucial aid these market rules provide for individuals to behave as rational as possible within a morally-neutral means-ends framework.

What to make of this uneasy coexistence in Hayek's thought of the spontaneous and the constructed? The former can be thought of as an ideological device directed at his adversaries, part of what Mirowski labels 'Hayek's playbook', exposing the gap between an utopian ideological discourse destined for the 'masses', including efforts at naturalizing the social order, and realist practical reasoning, which inspires the elitist intellectual and political investments that would have to be made for a market-conforming moral code and market order to be instituted. With the help of Polanyi's work, both Mirowski (2009) and Block and Sommers (2014) expose this feature of Hayek's thought. But there is another interpretation available, according to which the spontaneous and constructivist views can be reconciled by rightly declaring the provision process to be unavoidably an instituted one, 'the evolving result of deliberative and non-deliberative (spontaneous) elements' (Samuels, 2002, p. 87). This is not surprising as most authors who have thought about the evolution of social order have reached the same conclusion (Samuels, 2002).[16] In the spirit of Polanyi's institutionalism, Finn (2006, p. 123) articulates these two dimensions through a clarification of their respective places, warning that 'we ought not to confuse the spontaneity within markets with the erroneous view that markets themselves are institutions that have developed spontaneously'.

With the help of Polanyi's framework, it is then easy to find in Hayek's thought, between the decades of the 1930s and 1970s, a clear identification of the multi-scalar order that one needs to construct in order to 'induce' a spontaneous order, i.e. to create the conditions more favourable to their formation (Hayek, 1973/2003, p. 41), while guaranteeing that market forces, properly framed, produce, unintentionally in the perspective of their agents, as it were, certain overall patterns, thus further entrenching neoliberalism. The promotion of international integration, at the supranational level, on the one hand, and decentralization, at the national level, on the other, were both complementary and instrumental (Hayek, 1960/2006). They would guarantee a desired institutional competition, arbitrated by free capital movements, reinforcing a selective discipline upon states, complementing constitutional rules. That spontaneity has to be constructed, with the help of a properly motivated and enlightened elite, while the construction of a social order has to rely partially on the spontaneous forces of society, is thus a conclusion that can be reached by probing Hayek's thought with Polanyian lenses.

Concluding remarks

There are significant overlaps and zones of possible engagement between Polanyi and Hayek. The route followed here to underline this fact was one of reinterpreting Hayek's theoretical practice with the help of Polanyi's framework. Hayek aimed at renewing liberalism after the interwar fall, thus transforming it into neoliberalism, a real utopia instrumentally concerned with the political and moral embeddedness of markets. The distance between neoliberal theory and practice is less pronounced than it is sometimes assumed, given the institutionalist nature of the first. The strength of neoliberalism partially stems from a capacity to articulate an effort to think about real-world mechanisms with an effort to demolish, reconfigure or transform existing structures. Its combination of realism and utopia originated, among others, from an institutional goal whose implications Polanyi can help to grasp: an internationally integrated economy, to be achieved along new institutional lines, was one of the ways to limit democracy at the national level. In Hayek's hands neoliberalism is a form of institutionalist political and moral economy that ends up recognising in its more transparent moments that the economy is always an instituted process, to use Polanyi's famous formulation. At stake are the scales and normative goals of such a process.

Despite his failure to anticipate neoliberalism, Polanyi gave us tools to grasp critically its theory and some of the contours of its institutionalization, not to say some of its social costs. He was also aware of the final usefulness of utopianism in the liberal rhetorical arsenal, including the fact that 'it enabled its defenders to argue that the incomplete application of its principles was the reason for every and any difficulty laid to its charge' (Polanyi, 1944/2001, p. 149). Whenever the social costs of neoliberalism become clear this idea is never far away today. This is yet another instance of the manifold advantages of reading neoliberalism with Polanyian lenses. And this is even before denouncing its perversities and before thinking about alternatives to its ongoing hegemony.

Notes

1. Conceiving neoliberalism as a discourse, enlarging this notion to accommodate 'a materiality that is both constituted by and constitutive of discourse', as proposed by Springer (2012, p. 143), can also help to attenuate the aforementioned gap.
2. This does not mean that one is necessarily committed to an idealist position, to the causal primacy of ideas, but that one is attentive to the way neoliberals were consciously aware of the need for 'ideational embeddedness', to use Block and Sommers (2014) apt expression, as part of their original arsenal. This implies for example that people 'have to learn how to behave in particular market situations' (Block & Sommers, 2014, p. 96). Hayek was convinced of the need to 'influence people's conduct by education and example, rational persuasion, approval or disapproval' (Hayek, 1960/2006, p. 60). Persuasion is only part of a mix that must also include coercion, pecuniary incentives and a certain moral climate so that market-conforming motivations and actions can become hegemonic (Rodrigues, 2013b).
3. Hayek mentions Polanyi twice in his work. The first mention is made in an English edited volume of a collection of essays by German-speaking critics of socialism (Hayek, 1935). There he simply listed Polanyi's articles in the twenties as among the most important socialist contributions of the Austrian phase of the socialist calculation debate. More than fifty years later, Hayek (1988) would again mention Polanyi to critique his interpretation that the prosperity of ancient Athens might have anything to do with the particular ways through which public authorities framed and controlled the activities of market exchange. Despite the considerable time lapse and the different context of the discussions, there are elements of continuity, which say much about their major concerns: the relation between government and markets and the role and nature of prices. Polanyi, in turn, also mentions Hayek twice: in a critique of what he perceived to be the 'economistic prejudice' of the slippery-slope argument of economic interventionism leading to political authoritarianism in Hayek's *Road to Serfdom* (Polanyi, 1947) and in the critique of Hayek's English translation of the first edition of Menger's *magnum opus* (Polanyi, 1977).

4. By this Polanyi means the extension of the market mechanism to goods and relations which were not produced, or do not exist, to be bought and sold:

> [A]ccording to the empirical definition of a commodity they were not commodities. Labor is another name for a human activity which goes with life itself, which in its turn is not produced for sale but for entirely different reasons, nor can that activity be detached from the rest of life, be stored or mobilized; land is only another name for nature, which is not produced by man; actual money, finally, is merely a token of purchasing power, which, as a rule, is not produced at all, but comes into being through the mechanism of banking or state finance. (Polanyi, 1944/2001, p. 75)

The market cannot function properly here, or at least not without severe limitations, something which the 'liberal creed' is said to be incapable of recognizing. Indeed, the liberal idea of subordinating all spheres of social life and all institutions to the needs of the market mechanism is based on a 'commodity fiction', a 'postulate that cannot be upheld', but which can be influential to the point that all political efforts can be oriented by it so as to effectively shape the economy in perverse directions (Polanyi, 1944/2001, p. 76).

5. By contrast, in Polanyi's work the word utopia is always used with a negative connotation, as akin to a dystopia.
6. The expression 'real utopia' is taken from Erik Olin Wright's collective project, systematized in Wright (2010), trying to renovate the socialist imaginary in a context of a protracted crisis for that political project, envisioning an anti-capitalist and socialist strategy capable of articulating normative commitments to utopian post-capitalist ideals with an attention, deemed realistic, to empirical issues of institutional design and their feasibility. These are to be arbitrated by scientific knowledge available about institutions and their impacts. One can reinterpret Hayek's project (1949) as searching for the same kind of articulation from an opposing camp more than fifty years early: a way of renovating an anti-socialist and liberal strategy, which was perceived at that time to be intellectually and politically against the main ideological trends of the epoch.
7. Hayek's federal blueprint (1939b/1948) has recently been valued as important anticipation of several mechanisms at work in the European Union, explaining the resilience of neoliberalism there. This has been done by both neoliberal and Marxist historians: see, respectively, Gillingham (2003) and Anderson (2009).
8. See Miller (1995) for a critique of Hayek's anti-nationality views and for a defense of the importance of the principle of nationality for a decent society, which actually recognizes the validity of Hayek's diagnosis of national fellow-feeling as a precondition for collectivist projects.
9. Hayek was obviously not alone in this endeavor. In this, he was following Robbins (1937) explicit institutionalist plan to recreate a world economy through a supranational polity that limited the reach of democracy.
10. These alternatives were already framed in his early struggle against 'monetary nationalism' and the international instability and inflationary trend it supposedly generates (Hayek, 1937).
11. For textual evidence and critical analysis in all these areas, see Rodrigues (2012).
12. Hayek (1960/2006), for example, supported Friedman's (1955) plan to institute a state-financed voucher system, combining a certain public financing of education with its private provision through market competition between schools.
13. This is an instance where Mirowski's (2008) remark should be particularly noted: not all neoclassical economists are neoliberals and not all neoliberals are neoclassical.
14. One of the mechanisms through which endogenous preferences are manifested in Hayek's thought, and more generally in neoliberal thought, is through the idea that markets tend to foster social virtues, an idea with an ancient historical pedigree (Hirschman, 1977, 1982). Polanyi, of course, shares with Hayek the view that preferences are indeed endogenous, but the emphasis is put on the corrosion argument, to use Hirschman's (1982) taxonomy: the expansion of markets by promoting myopic selfishness tends to erode the moral foundations of a decent society (Rodrigues, 2004).
15. For an analysis of Hayek's thought with this antinomy in mind, see, among others, Gray (1998), mobilizing Polanyi for this task.
16. This, of course, includes Polanyi. The interesting distinction then appears in the usages and emphases given to the spontaneous and constructed elements, an aspect I shall not pursue here. Worth mention, though, that it is on these issues where Hayek and Polanyi thoughts become almost mirror images of each other.

Acknowledgements

I am grateful to the comments made by the participants in the international workshop 'Questioning the Utopian Springs of the Market Economy', held at the University of Sydney/Australia (15–16 August 2014). I also thank Damien Cahill, Adam David Morton, Martijn Konings, Ana C. Santos and two anonymous referees for the support and suggestions. All errors and omissions are of my own making.

Disclosure statement

No potential conflict of interest was reported by the author.

References

Amable, B. (2011). Morals and politics in the ideology of neo-liberalism. *Socio-Economic Review*, 9(1), 3–30. doi:10.1093/ser/mwq015

Anderson, P. (2009). *The new old world*. London: Verso.

Block, F., & Sommers, M. R. (2014). *The power of market fundamentalism: Karl Polanyi's critique*. Cambridge, MA: Harvard University Press.

Block, W. (1996). Hayek's road to serfdom. *Journal of Libertarian Studies*, 12(2), 339–336.

Brenner, N., Peck, J., & Theodore, N. (2010). Variegated neoliberalization: Geographies, modalities, pathways. *Global Networks*, 10(2), 182–222.

Cahill, D. (2014). *The end of laissez-faire? On the durability of embedded neoliberalism*. Cheltenham: Edward Elgar.

Dardot, P., & Laval, C. (2009). *La nouvelle raison du monde. Essai sur la société néolibérale*. Paris: La Découverte.

Davis, J. B. (2003). *The theory of the individual in economics: Identity and value*. London: Routledge.

Dugger, W. (1989). Instituted process and enabling myth: The two faces of the market. *Journal of Economic Issues*, 23(2), 607–615.

Finn, D. R. (2006). *The moral ecology of markets*. Cambridge: Cambridge University Press.

Friedman, M. (1955). The role of government in education. In R. A. Solo (Ed.), *Economics and the public interest* (pp. 123–144). New Brunswick: Rutgers University Press.

Gamble, A. (2006). Hayek on knowledge, economics, and society. In E. Feser (Ed.), *The Cambridge companion to Hayek* (pp. 111–131). Cambridge: Cambridge University Press.

Gillingham, J. (2003). *European integration, 1950-2003: Superstate or new market economy?* Cambridge: Cambridge University Press.

Gray, J. (1998). *Hayek on liberty*. London: Routledge.

Harvey, D. (2005). *A brief history of neoliberalism*. Oxford: Oxford University Press.

Hayek, F. (1935). The nature and history of the problem. In F. Hayek (Ed.), *Collectivist economic planning* (pp. 1–40). London: Routledge and Kegan Paul.

Hayek, F. (1937). *Monetary nationalism and international stability*. London: Longmans.

Hayek, F. (1939a/1997). Freedom and the economic system. In B. Caldwell (Ed.), *The collected works of F. A. Hayek – Volume X* (pp. 189–212). London: Routledge.

Hayek, F. (1939b/1948). The economic conditions of interstate federalism. In F. Hayek (Ed.), *Individualism and economic order* (pp. 255–272). Chicago: University of Chicago Press.

Hayek, F. (1944/2006). *The road to serfdom*. London: Routledge.

Hayek, F. (1948a). Individualism: True and false. In F. Hayek (Ed.), *Individualism and economic order* (pp. 1–32). Chicago: University of Chicago Press.

Hayek, F. (1948b). The meaning of competition. In F. Hayek (Ed.), *Individualism and economic order* (pp. 92–106). Chicago: University of Chicago Press.

Hayek, F. (1949). The intellectuals and socialism. *University of Chicago Law Review, 16*(3), 417–433.

Hayek, F. (1960/2006). *The constitution of liberty.* London: Routledge.

Hayek, F. (1967). *Studies in philosophy, politics, and economics.* London: Routledge.

Hayek, F. (1973/2003). *Law, legislation and liberty – rules and order.* London: Routldege.

Hayek, F. (1976/2003). *Law, legislation and liberty – The mirage of social justice.* London: Routldege.

Hayek, F. (1978/1990). *Denationalisation of money: The argument refined.* London: The Institute of Economic Affairs.

Hayek, F. (1979/2003). *Law, legislation and liberty – The political order of a free people.* London: Routldege.

Hayek, F. (1988). *The fatal conceit: The errors of socialism.* Chicago: University of Chicago Press.

Hirschman, A. (1977). *The passions and the interests: Political arguments for capitalism before its triumph.* Princeton, NJ: Princeton University Press.

Hirschman, A. (1982). Rival interpretation of market society: Civilizing, destructive or feeble? *Journal of Economic Literature, 20,* 1463–1484.

Migone, A. (2011). Embedded markets: A dialogue between F. A. Hayek and Karl Polanyi. *The Review of Austrian Economics, 24,* 355–381. doi:10.1007/s11138-011-0148-2

Miller, D. (1995). *On nationality.* Oxford: Oxford University Press.

Mirowski, P. (2008). Review of David Harvey, 'A brief history of neoliberalism'. *Economics and Philosophy, 24,* 111–117.

Mirowski, P. (2009). Postface: Defining neoliberalism. In P. Mirowski & D. Plehwe (Eds.), *The road from Mont Pelerin – The making of the neoliberal thought collective* (pp. 417–455). Cambridge, MA: Harvard University Press.

Mises, L. (1949). *Human action.* London: William Hodge.

O'Neill, J. (2001). Essences and markets. In U. Mäki (Ed.), *The economic world view: Studies in the ontology of economics* (pp. 157–183). Cambridge: Cambridge University Press.

Peck, J. (2008). Remaking laissez-faire. *Progress in Human Geography, 32*(1), 3–43. doi:10.1177/0309132507084816

Peck, J. (2010). *Constructions of neoliberal reason.* Oxford: Oxford University Press.

Polanyi, K. (1944/2001). *The great transformation.* Boston: Beacon Press.

Polanyi, K. (1947). Our obsolete market mentality – civilization must find a new thought pattern. *Commentary, 3,* 109–117.

Polanyi, K. (1977). *The livelihood of man.* New York: Academic Press.

Robbins, L. (1937). *Economic planning and international order.* London: MacMillan.

Rodrigues, J. (2004). Endogenous preferences and embeddedness: A reappraisal of Karl Polanyi. *Journal of Economic Issues, 38*(1), 189–200.

Rodrigues, J. (2012). Where to draw the line between the state and markets? Institutionalist elements in Hayek's neoliberal political economy. *Journal of Economic Issues, 46*(4), 1007–1034. doi:10.275/JEI0021-3624460409

Rodrigues, J. (2013a). The political and moral economies of neoliberalism: Mises and Hayek. *Cambridge Journal of Economics, 37,* 1001–1017. doi:10.1093/cje/bes091

Rodrigues, J. (2013b). Between rules and incentives: Uncovering Hayek's moral economy. *American Journal of Economics and Sociology, 72*(3), 565–592. doi:10.1111/ajes.12018

Samuels, W. (2002). Hayek from the perspective of an institutionalist historian of economic thought: An interpretative essay. In W. Samuels (Ed.), *Economics, governance and law - essays on theory and policy* (pp. 81–94). Cheltenham: Edward Elgar.

Sciabarra, C. M. (1995). *Marx, Hayek, and utopia.* Albany: State University of New York Press.

Shearmur, J. (2006). Hayek's politics. In E. Feser (Ed.), *The Cambridge companion to Hayek* (pp. 148–170). Cambridge: Cambridge University Press.

Springer, S. (2012). Neoliberalism as discourse: Between Foucauldian political economy and Marxian post-structuralism. *Critical Discourse Studies, 9*(2), 133–147. doi:10.1080/17405904.2012.656375

Streeck, W. (2014). *Buying time: The delayed crisis of democratic capitalism.* London: Verso.

Wright, E. O. (2010). *Envisioning real utopias.* London: Verso.

Hayek and the *Methodenstreit* at the LSE

Jeremy Shearmur

ABSTRACT

Friedrich Hayek's Inaugural Address at the London School of Economics (LSE), 'The Trend of Economic Thinking' (1 March 1933), has been recognized as of particular importance for the understanding of his work. In it, Hayek argues that economics has a key role of showing what we cannot achieve: of showing that some attractive ideals are utopian. In developing this theme, Hayek referred to Mises' arguments about the problems of economic calculation under socialism; but the idea – which I suggest might be seen as a theory about the structural constraints imposed by a flourishing market economy – becomes a more general motif in Hayek's work. In the lecture, Hayek's ideas are developed through engagement with the younger German Historical School of economics, which is criticized for espousing methodological ideas that would call the idea of such constraints into question. In this article, I suggest that there were also local targets at the LSE. I discuss the way in which William Beveridge, the Director of the LSE, and Lancelot Hogben, who held a Chair in Social Biology there, were engaged in an extended empiricist critique of the methodological ideas of the LSE economists and of theoretical economists more generally in ways close to the younger German historical school.

Hayek's Inaugural Address at the London School of Economics (LSE), 'The Trend of Economic Thinking' (Hayek, 1991), is of particular importance for his work. It introduces what was to become a key motif which runs through the rest of his writings.[1] This is important not only for those interested in his work who wish to understand Hayek better, but also for those who wish to take issue with his views. For the argument of his 'The Trend of Economic Thinking' also sums up what in Hayek's view is an important problem for those who wish to *reject* the kind of market-centered economic system that he came to favour.

Its key point might be summarized in the following way. Hayek argued that theoretical economics in general, and Mises' work on the problems of economic calculation under socialism in particular, should teach us an important lesson. It is that various social ideals which we might find morally attractive, are in fact utopian in the sense of not being things that could be put into practise. To use un-Hayekian language, one might say that he was arguing that things from which we were benefitting under the existing economic and social system, and which, if we knew what we were doing, we would wish to retain, might *require* structural features to be in place which produce consequences which we are liable to find morally problematic.

On the one side, he argued that in a large, non-face-to-face economy, there was simply no alternative to having private property and the price system if it was to operate at all. On the other, he came to identify other institutions which we needed to retain if a market economy was to function well. This Hayek argued to be important, in part because of the material benefits that people in general might hope to enjoy within such a society; in part because of the kind of freedom that it made available to them. Hayek's argument in his 'Inaugural Address' was poignant, just because it is clear that he, himself, had been, and in some ways continued to be, attracted to ideals which he came to think were incompatible with the functioning of these market-based institutions.[2] His argument in the Inaugural Address was concerned with economic issues. In particular, his concern there was with the idea that some methodological ideas which had become popular, if they were taken seriously, would lead to our losing sight of the tensions with which he was concerned. Subsequently one might see Hayek in his later work, as seeking to identify further features of our existing societies which we might be tempted to reform away, notably some characteristics of the legal and constitutional order of Western societies, that were also required for such societies to flourish.

Hayek's challenge to those who disagreed with him (and thus implicitly to Karl Polanyi, although Hayek did not engage with him directly) was, in effect, to say: it is not enough to argue that what is involved in a market-based social order is morally problematic. You need also to produce your own alternative account of the structure of the society that you favour, such that it could be expected to work so as to produce the features of our existing society which you are expecting still to be in place, and which would also allow the society that you favour to have the moral characteristics that you are looking for. It should be stressed that Hayek was all too aware of the ways in which a market-based society could be seen as morally problematic. He was also critical of those American conservatives who thought that, in some sense, the rewards which people might obtain in a market-based society could be expected to track personal merit.[3] While he was also interested in investigating whether and if so in what ways, ideals to which he and others might be attracted, could be realized within such a market-based society. All this, it seems to me, can be seen as developed in embryo in Hayek's 'Inaugural Address'.

My concern in the present article, however, is with a rather different problem. Why was it, if this was Hayek's particular concern, that a major theme of the Address was a critique of the ideas of the German Younger Historical School of economists?

Hayek's 'the trend of economic thinking'

When Friedrich Hayek delivered his Address, on 1st March 1933, I suspect that at least some of his audience might have been a little puzzled. For while the paper summed up his overall approach to social issues in a manner that would not have been clear from his more specialized writings, some of his listeners might have wondered why he was engaged, in much of it, in a denunciation of German-speaking writers on methodology from the previous generation. The original *Methodenstreit*, which involved Carl Menger and his followers, including Ludwig von Mises with whom Hayek had worked, and German proponents of different kinds of 'historical' approaches to economics, played an important role in Hayek's intellectual background (see Shearmur, 1986). I will here argue that there was a more specific but analogous context in which it might be useful to place Hayek's Inaugural Address. This consisted of ongoing exchanges about the methodology of the social sciences which were taking place between Sir William Beveridge and Lancelot Hogben, on the one side, and Lionel Robbins and Hayek on the other, at the LSE. Beveridge and Hogben were not consciously setting out to defend the views of the younger Historical School. But they wrote, and with passion, on ideas which were closely akin to theirs,[4] and used these ideas as the basis of hard-hitting denunciations of methodological approaches associated with economists at the LSE, and, indeed, of work in theoretical economics more generally. In speaking as he did, Hayek was concerned to explain and defend views which he felt were at the time under attack in the very institution within which he was working.

Hayek grew up at the tail-end of the *Methodenstreit* in the German-speaking world. In its last stages, it pitched the more abstract, theoretical analysis of Carl Menger and his successors and, in Hayek's view, the tradition of theoretical economics (Hayek, 1933; see also Shearmur, 1996), against the more inductivist and historically-based approach of Schmoller and his followers. For Hayek, more than just methodology was at stake. For he took the issues to be important for people's understanding of society, and their approach to social policy, too. Hayek made this clear in 'The Trend of Economic Thinking', in which he argued that the approach of the younger Historical School put at risk the kinds of anti-utopian lessons in social theory which had been provided by the whole tradition of theoretical economics, and more specifically by Mises' work on economic calculation.

Hayek's ideas on methodology were influenced by Ludwig von Mises. Hayek had not been a student or an assistant of Mises.[5] However, when Hayek returned to Vienna in 1924 (after spending some time in the United States), he joined Mises' *Privatseminar* in which there were extensive discussions of the methodology of social science. Hayek was also strongly influenced by Mises' critique of socialism (see Shearmur, 1996). Hayek had some misgivings about Mises' specific arguments in this field, but he believed that Mises' conclusions were correct, and Hayek was led to offer further arguments, himself, about the problems of economic calculation under socialism. The debate about this was an obvious illustration of the significance of a purely theoretical approach towards economics; something that, he argued in his Inaugural Address, was called into question by the approach that was favoured by the younger Historical School.

Hayek favoured a distinctive approach to the methodology of economics. Methodology had been the subject of much discussion among members of the Austrian School. Hayek equated their approach with Lionel Robbins' account, in his *Essay on the Nature and Significance of Economic Science* (Robbins, 1932).[6] Howson (2004) has argued that Robbins' essay is better understood as a product of a British approach to these issues, and that references to Austrian writers were an afterthought.[7] Be this as it may, Hayek, in a contribution to an encyclopaedia on 'The Austrian School' which was uncompleted on his death (see note 6), identified Robbins as setting out the ideas that the Austrians had favoured, and with which the younger Historical School were in disagreement. In Hayek's view, it was by the following of the sort of method that he favoured, and of which Robbins had offered an account, which gave rise to results as significant as those of Mises: knowledge of real practical importance which might be put at risk, if the approach of the younger Historical School was adopted.

But why should anyone be concerned about the younger Historical School in the early 1930s in London? In particular, why should Hayek spend time in his Inaugural Address at the LSE, taking issue with a viewpoint of which one imagines that few of his audience had much knowledge. There are, I suspect, two reasons for this.

The first (see Bruce Caldwell's introduction to Hayek, 2010), is that when Hayek was in the United States during the 1920s, he was able to attend the lectures of Wesley Mitchell at Columbia. Hayek was impressed by the vigour of Mitchell and those around him. But at the same time, he was (at least in retrospect[8]) disturbed by what he heard. For, or so it seemed to him, what they were offering was remarkably close to the approach of the younger Historical School. Mitchell championed an atheoretical empiricism as the correct approach to the study of trade cycles. He also favoured behaviourism, something that Hayek came to see as a threat to his favoured approach to the methodology of economics (see his 1942–4, reprinted in Hayek, 1952). This, however, was not the end of the story. For this kind of approach not only started to become *intellectually* influential. (Hayek, possibly mistakenly, took Carnap and Neurath also to be advocating such views).[9] In addition, those who were running one of the key sources for the funding of social research, the Laura Spellman Rockefeller Memorial Foundation (the 'Memorial'), came to favour this same approach (notably, from 1922 onwards; see on all this Shearmur, 2013). Hayek was well aware of them: he had applied to them for funding for the Institute for Trade Cycle Research in Vienna, of which he was the director. It is striking, however, just how hostile the Memorial's academic advisors were to the idea that any kind of theory should be brought to the study of trade cycles.[10] Accordingly, Hayek felt that what he was encountering was not just a movement that was influential in the previous generation, but something that still had influence, not least through access to a considerable source of finance, in his own time.

Second, while Hayek was at the LSE, the Director was Sir William Beveridge. He was an enthusiastic champion of the idea that economics should adopt an empiricist approach. Beveridge had been deeply impressed by some writings by T. H. Huxley on methodology, and was keen to champion them whenever he had the chance. His first effort at this was (Beveridge, 1921). He returned to the fray in the final public lecture that he delivered at the LSE, in which he submitted to scathing criticism what seemed to him economists' striking disregard for the empirical evaluation of their theoretical claims (Beveridge, 1937). Beveridge was also a critic of another side of Hayek's work. For when he delivered the Herbert Spencer Lecture in Oxford (Beveridge, 1936, pp. 1–13), he took as his topic Hayek's then-recent collection, *Collectivist Economic Planning* (Hayek, 1935), in which Hayek had reprinted in translation Mises' initial criticism of socialism, together with a range of other papers which raised issues concerning socialism and economic calculation.

Hayek had a very low opinion of Beveridge. Hayek saw him as a fluent writer, but as an intellectual lightweight, who was, in effect, a pen for hire (Hayek, 1989, pp. 83–88). Beveridge was particularly successful at obtaining large sums of money from the Memorial for the support of a range of academic activities at the LSE, and also for its library. One of the things for which he obtained funding was the study of 'social biology', which led to the appointment of Lancelot Hogben to a research-only position at the LSE in 1930 (although he also did some teaching, offering a course in popular science to undergraduates). Hogben was an interesting but an awkward man (and seems to have impressed Hayek, although Hayek disagreed with him). The unit that he headed up was not received particularly well at the LSE, or, in the end, by the Memorial, who withdrew their funding. The Department was closed in 1937 (Shearmur, 2013).

Hogben published a volume, *Political Arithmetic*, in 1938, which put the department's achievements in population studies on display. Hogben's Preface, however, contains an attack on 'Austrian' economics, in which Robbins' *Nature and Significance* (Robbins, 1932) is singled out for attention. Hogben had previously, in his Conway Memorial Lecture *Retreat from Reason*, delivered in Red Lion Square, a short walk from the LSE, also criticized Robbins (Hogben, 1936, 1937a). There would seem to me enough in common between the approaches, and the lines of criticism, offered by Beveridge and by Hogben, to consider them close intellectual allies.

On the other side stood Hayek and Robbins. The issues about which the four people were in disagreement were methodological. However, as I have already indicated, there was an interconnection with political issues. D. H. Robertson, reviewing Robbins' *Great Depression* (Robbins, 1934) in *Economica* (Robertson, 1935), suggested that it exhibited what he referred to as an LSE fixed price menu. In this, interconnections were depicted as existing between a particular view of the socialist calculation argument, a particular view of the Great Depression, and the policy responses (or lack of responses) appropriate to it. It was this very view which Hayek saw as under threat from the kind of view that was favoured by the younger Historical School, and by American and British writers who took similar approaches.

Beveridge and the methodology of social science; Robbins' and Hayek's responses, and the aftermath

On 4th October 1920, Beveridge, as Director of the LSE, delivered a public lecture, 'Economics as a Liberal Education', which was subsequently published in the first volume of *Economica* (Beveridge, 1921). In the course of offering an overview of the kinds of things that were studied at the LSE and their relation to a liberal education, Beveridge gave an account of his view of the appropriate methods to be pursued in the social sciences. Here, he took his lead from an essay 'The Educational Value of the Natural History Sciences', that T. H. Huxley had originally delivered in 1854. (Huxley, 1854) offered a view of the method of science which he drew from John Stuart Mill's *System of Logic*. Beveridge's approving account is as follows (Beveridge, 1921, p. 4):

> The methods of science, Huxley, following Mill, describes under four heads: 1. Observation of facts, and experiment, which is only a special form of observation. 2. Comparison and classification of the facts observed, leading by induction to general propositions. 3. Deduction from general propositions to facts again, so as to foretell these latter in advance of observation. 4. Verification of deductions by fresh observations.

Beveridge continues: 'These, [Huxley] argues, in opposition to views advanced by Comte and other writers, are the common methods of all sciences. Each method is used to some extent in every study worthy of being called a science at all.'

After some general discussion, Beveridge turns to economics, and offers the following reflections (Beveridge, 1921, pp. 6–7):

> Economics, as one of the youngest sciences, has still to make its way in the world. It is the business of economists to justify their study by its methods and results; to show that they have a subject matter to which the methods of science can be applied successfully. That these methods are in fact applicable and necessary is, I think, clear. We have only to consider a few typical problems. There is, for instance, the phenomenon of cyclical fluctuation of commercial and industrial activity, with its attendant consequences, in all the main industrial states of the modern world. It is our business to observe the phenomenon, to collect, classify and compare all the facts, to work up from those to general propositions concerning it, and infer its cause, or causes, to make deductions if possible in advance of observation, and to get these deductions verified by the course of events.

Beveridge then made various observations about, for example, such issues as rationing, but from time to time returned to make general comments about the methodology of economics, typically with reference to Huxley (Beveridge, 1921, p. 8):

> The biological sciences, as Huxley points out, are more in the inductive stage than the mathematical and physico-chemical ones. The economic sciences must for the present be more inductive still. There was a time when the natural sciences had to be freed from the purely deductive method. The chief discredit of political economy in the past has been due to premature deduction on too narrow a basis of fact and of induction.

It is striking, however, that Beveridge offers no *arguments* for his views – neither in relation to the English tradition of reflection on the methodology of economics in general, nor in respect of John Stuart Mill's ideas about methodology, in particular.

It is, in consequence, interesting to note that Lionel Robbins, when he delivered his Inaugural Address at the LSE, offers what I think may clearly be interpreted as a response (Robbins, 1930). On Page 20 he takes issue with those who want to use 'historical and statistical inductions', Robbins referring to them as 'institutionalists'. Robbins suggests that good economics in the past has combined deductive and inductive approaches, and that statistical work needs to be guided by theory, arguing that: 'The passive observation of facts, unguided by theoretical hypothesis, must of necessity be sterile.' He does not rule out that we may 'see a vast extension of quantitative investigations' (p. 21), and on page 24 he indicates that he is happy to 'embrace technicality with open arms if technicality will help us'. But from his overall tone, he is clearly sceptical.

Hayek's own Inaugural – 'The Trend of Economic Thinking' – is largely devoted to the criticism of the younger Historical School, and to what Hayek saw as the problems that flowed from their anti-theoretical approach. I will not discuss his argument there beyond what I have said in the introduction, as I have done so elsewhere (Shearmur, 1996).

This, however, was not the end of this particular discussion. For on 24th June 1937, Beveridge delivered an address at the LSE, 'The Place of the Social Sciences in Human Knowledge' (Beveridge, 1937). Beveridge starts by looking back to his earlier discussion, and recapitulates on the ideas from Huxley which he had there discussed. Next, after noting that at the time at which he gave that address Lionel Robbins was a first-year student, he refers to Robbins' *Nature and Significance* (Robbins, 1932). Beveridge says that Robbins' definition of economics is something for which 'I shall always be grateful', but expresses misgivings about Robbins' discussion of 'ends' (Beveridge, 1937, p. 462).

It turns out, however, that this is not the centre of Beveridge's concern. For he then writes (Beveridge, 1937, p. 463) that 'We cannot claim recognition as scientists, unless our methods are scientific' and launches into an attack on Keynes' *General Theory*, complaining that 'Mr Keynes neither starts from facts nor returns to them' (Beveridge, 1937, p. 464). He says, further:

> Mr Keynes starts, not from any fact, but from the definition of a concept, of what he (Mr Keynes) means when he says 'involuntary unemployment'. He proceeds to a fresh series of concepts and of their definitions. In a large proportion of those definitions, words are used in senses different from those of most other economists and of Mr Keynes himself six years ago. Mr Keynes does not return to facts for verification. There is no page throughout his work on which a generalization is set against marshalled facts for testing. [Beveridge continues by saying that the testing itself does not have to be done by the proponent of a theory, but] ... It is the duty of the propounder of every new theory, if he has not himself the equipment for observation, to indicate where verification of his theory is to be sought in facts – what may be expected to happen or to have happened if his theory is true, what will not happen if it is false.

Beveridge further says that Keynes is not alone (Beveridge, 1937, p. 465):

> That [i.e. the requirement for empirical evidence] is the demand that would be made of the propounder of a new theory in every natural science. [but adding that none of the reviewers of *The General Theory* in the] *Economic Journal, Economica* [or] ... the *Quarterly Journal of Economics* ... makes the point that the truth or falsehood of Mr Keynes' theory cannot be established except by appeal to facts ... The distinguishing mark of economic science, as illustrated by this debate, is that it is a science in which verification of generalizations by reference to facts is neglected as irrelevant.

Beveridge is consistent in his championing of an empiricist approach to the methodology of economics. Clearly, he is at odds, in this respect, with both Hayek and Robbins. But as is made clear by his use of Keynes' and his reviewers, his quarrel went well beyond the economists at the LSE, to take in the mainstream of the profession. If one puts Beveridge's inductivism to one side, his complaint is one which has been voiced in various ways by others (from Hutchison to Blaug). But in context it is striking that Beveridge did not stop to consider the defences of economists' ways of proceeding that were readily available (e.g. Robbins, 1932, which he had read).

Enter Hogben, stage left

Beveridge's methodological views were not particularly sophisticated. In addition, Beveridge himself did not link them to political issues. Things were very different in the work of Lancelot Hogben.

Hogben was appointed to a Research Chair in Social Biology at the LSE, using money that Beveridge raised from the Laura Spellman Rockefeller Foundation. Hogben was a brilliant man. He was exceptionally widely read – including in the history of science. But a unity was in some ways given to his thought by his socialism (Werskey, 1978). He was impressed by what might be called the agrarian/romantic strand in British socialism, sharing William Blake's dislike of dark satanic mills, and sympathizing with the ideas of William Morris. What, however, is distinctive about Hogben, is that in his view developments in science had made possible a different kind of developed society from that feted by both liberalism and many socialists. In Hogben's view they shared the ideal of urbanization and the consumption of consumer goods. For Hogben, a good society would be one in which possibilities opened up by science would be utilized to allow people to live in more rural-like surroundings, but in which their needs were met. Hogben disagreed with the idea that people's needs are best indicated by what they choose as consumers. In his view, rather, what their needs are, is something that should be the subject of expert investigation (but subject to the scrutiny of informed citizens). He mentions that he as a biologist can determine that people need a certain amount of ascorbic acid in their food. But they typically do not know this, and have (unaided) no means of knowing whether or not it is present in their food. For Hogben, we live in an age of potential plenty: not in the sense of being able to furnish what we might all want, but in respect of what it might be determined that we all need. Expert knowledge was to play a key role. But he argued that ordinary people needed to have the kind of understanding of science and of mathematics which would make what was being proposed comprehensible and open to discussion, and through this means, to subject technical experts to their control. His work in popular science: *Mathematics for the Million* (Hogben, 1937b), *Science For the Citizen* (1938b), and (in collaboration) on language and on history, was a step towards giving people the kind of understanding that in his view was needed for them to play their role as citizens in the Age of Plenty.[11]

Hogben develops his views in ways that contrast with those of many people at the time. He is a socialist and a biologist – but he is at the same time not in agreement with, and sometimes highly critical of, the Marxism of Bernal, Haldane, and Needham (compare Werskey, 1978; Desmarais, N.D.) He was also critical of vitalism, and non-materialistic interpretations of science. He was strongly anti-fascist, but also critical of liberalism – and more specifically, of the kind of views with which Hayek and Robbins were identified. He was explicitly critical of the emphasis within their work on consumer choice and its significance, and he favoured behaviourism in psychology. But it is, particularly, the methodology of economics as found in the work of Robbins and the 'Austrians',[12] of which he is critical, in work to which we will shortly turn.[13]

It is a pity that Hayek did not engage in any detail with Hogben.[14] For such an engagement would have been not only intrinsically interesting, but would I think have made some of Hayek's own critical writings rather more effective. Hayek's 'Abuse of Reason' project – a planned four-volume study, of which only his *Road to Serfdom* appeared as a book, and which plays a key role in his turn from economics[15] – contrasts in an interesting way with Hogben's *Retreat from Reason*. Hayek was, in a sense, wishing to speak particularly to the scientists of his own day who were attracted by the ideal of planning, on which see (Hayek, 1941). But they were, typically biologists and often Marxists – while

Hayek in the main historical part of his project that was published (Hayek, 1952), was concerned, instead, with the historical influence of physicists and engineers on the Saint-Simonians. While this work is interesting, it hardly constituted an engagement with his contemporaries.

What had Hogben got against 'Austrian economics' in general, and against Robbins in particular? He offers a case that is in the same spirit as Beveridge's, but which is not developed simply by reading Huxley's synopsis of lessons from Mill's *Logic*. Rather, Hogben offers an account of the scientific revolution as an exemplar of empiricism, and, quoting from Hooke and Bacon, develops a case by analogy against Robbins. For example, he quotes Bacon's *Novum Organum*:[16]

> It cannot be that axioms established by argumentation can suffice for the discovery of new works, since the subtlety of nature is greater many times over than the subtlety of argument.

He then goes on to quote Robbins at some length, concluding with his statement: 'In the last analysis … our proposing rests upon deductions which are implicit in our initial definition of the subject-matter of Economic Science' (Hogben, 1937a, p. 6; quoting Robbins, 1932, pp. 72–73).

There is, though, more going on in Hogben. His own approach is not just empiricist, for he also champions a view of knowledge in which a scientific law is seen as embodying 'a recipe for doing something' (Hogben, 1937a, p. 7). This, in turn, is related to Hogben's wider concerns. For in his view, 'there has never been a greater discrepancy between the poverty which exists and the plenty which lies within our reach'. In this situation, there is a desperate need for an understanding of 'the social forces which are deciding the fate of Western civilization'. But 'the expensively uneducated classes from which Capital and Labour alike attract their intellectual leaders and administrators are increasingly at the mercy of technical experts, whose own training involves no recognition of their social responsibilities' (Hogben, 1937a, p. 2). What is needed is complex. In part, it involves the provision of education to all in both science and mathematics, in a manner which brings out their practical relevance and interest. In part, he thinks that reason is in retreat because of the influence of what he calls the 'new humanism' – of which he has had experience in his five years at the LSE. This he thinks has produced knowledge which is of little use – and against which he takes the anti-rationalism of fascist youth to be in part a reaction.

In Hogben's view, Robbins' methodological approach was flawed, and the output of 'Austrian' economics sterile and scholastic. For Hogben, however, there was better work to be found – for example the quantitative work about issues to do with human population, work in the 'British Empirical tradition of naturalistic enquiry' (Hogben, 1939a, p. 70), undertaken by his colleagues in the Department of Social Biology.

In Hogben's introduction to *Political Arithmetic* (Hogben, 1938a, 1939b), he argued for the significance of the work of his department, for the importance of knowledge which could be put to use, and for the continuity of their approach with the concerns of early British empiricists associated with the Royal Society. This is contrasted with the approach exemplified by Robbins, which is condemned – using parallels that Petty drew with those of whom he was critical – as scholastic. Hogben criticizes theory removed from practical application. He is also scathing about the idea that economics should be pursued without connection to issues of psychology. In addition, he takes exception to a claim, which he attributes to Hayek, that principles must be settled before realistic enquiry can be undertaken with impunity,[17] and to some of the argument in John Hicks' *Theory of Wages*. Hicks wrote: 'If now the employer's concession curve cuts the resistance curve on the horizontal part … '.[18] Hogben complained that, while curves in physics or biology record the results of 'real measurements', this is not the case for claims like that being made by Hicks, who also does not provide any indication of how they are to be tested (1937a, pp. 86–87).

Conclusion

For Hayek, key issues were posed by the *Methodenstreit*, and the challenge from the younger Historical School to theoretical economics and the social lessons that it offered – ones which he illustrated by the argument that socialism faced problems about economic calculation. To the influence of the Younger Historical School, and its latter-day allies, was added the might of the Memorial. This was a particularly significant source of research money in the 1920s and early 1930s, not least at the LSE. The Memorial was firmly in the hands of people who favoured an anti-theoretical, empiricist approach to the study of economic phenomena – an approach which Hayek had experienced when he was in the US.

Beveridge, who took his views about methodology unreflectively from Huxley, found himself on the same wavelength as people at the Memorial, and was able to extract huge amounts of money from them for the LSE (Shearmur, 2013). At the same time, what was involved was not just a local quarrel, but related to a wider issue in economics concerning testability and differences in sensibilities between those who saw themselves as empiricists, and those who favoured a more Robbinsian approach (Caldwell, 1991).

One of the fruits of the Memorial's money was Hogben's social biology programme. Hogben also espoused a strongly empiricist view of knowledge, and championed it against the LSE economists. He also favoured socialism, planning and behaviourism: the very things against which Hayek was arguing. But, alas, there was not extended discursive engagement between Hogben and Hayek. This led to losses on both sides. For Hogben, I think, would have had a lot to learn from Hayek's work on knowledge and the problems of economic calculation under socialism. At the same time, while the empiricism of Beveridge and of Hogben is crude and at times inductivist, there are surely issues to be raised about the empirical testing of theoretical constructions – not least because the starting-points of these are clearly under-determined by our common-sense knowledge (Shearmur, 1991a). In addition, while Hogben's colleagues were scathing about Hogben's use of toads and rabbits in his biological work, not only was his scientific work distinguished, but his department clearly produced important work in the social sciences. For example, David Glass, who started in Hogben's department, subsequently had a stellar career in demography. At the very least, empirical work in the social sciences of this kind is important, and also poses interesting problems about how it (and also more empirical work in economics), is supposed to inter-relate to work in economics of a more purely theoretical kind, such as that which was championed by Hayek (see also Shearmur, 1991b).

All told, while there was a *Methodenstreit* in (and around) the LSE, there was equally a sense in which those involved did not fully engage with one another. I believe that it would have been good for everybody – and for the development of our knowledge – if they had done so, and that the points at issue between them are well worth re-examination. On the issue of methods more narrowly conceived, it seems to me that Hayek was right about the danger of dismissing theoretical work, and that, as the discussion of socialist calculation indicated, important issues may be raised on a completely theoretical basis. At the same time, what the inter-relationship should be between empirical and theoretical work in economics is still something on which debate continues.[19]

In this article, I have not only explained the existence of a local context to Hayek's Inaugural Address, but I have illustrated the way in which discussion of these issues continued at the LSE through the 1930s. It seems to me a shame, however, that there was not direct engagement between Hogben and Hayek, not least because, if there had been, it might have served to bring out a key point raised in Hayek's inaugural which was of relevance not just for Hogben's political views, but also for those of Karl Polanyi and those who have been influenced by his work. This relates to Hayek's claim that there exist structural features to our existing society which have consequences which we may find morally problematic, but which we need to keep in place if key features of our present society, or indeed anything that shares with it the kinds of extended 'cooperation' between strangers which is its key feature, are to exist. Hayek may or may not be right in what he is claiming. But if he is, it is of the greatest importance, and those who disagree with him need to show how they propose to overcome the problems which he has raised.

Notes

1. See, for an early appreciation of this Caldwell (1988) and also Caldwell (2004). It was also something the importance of which was stressed in Shearmur (1987) and Shearmur (1996).
2. For some evidence as to his persisting attachment to them, see Shearmur (1996). It is also worth noting the way in which, to the consternation of those with whom he became politically allied (compare Rand, 1995), he showed some continuing attachment to measures which required a moderate amount of governmental intervention, and also to a modest notion of a welfare state.
3. See for example his critical discussion of Irving Kristol in Hayek (1973-9), chapter 9.
4. It is striking that Beveridge also pursued research in economic history which was much in the spirit of the younger Historical School.
5. He put this particular forcibly in a letter to Percy L. Greaves of 17th June 1976 Hayek Archive 22–18, Hoover Institution Archive, Stanford University.
6. Cf. Hayek's comment in material written for an entry on the Austrian School in the *New Palgrave* and included as an Addendum to 'The Austrian School of Economics' in (Hayek, 1992); see p. 53: 'Robbins's own most influential work, *The Nature and Significance of Economic Science*, made what had been the methodological approach to microeconomic theory established by the Austrian school the generally recognized standard.'
7. See (Howson, 2004). This documents the domestic origins of Robbins' ideas, and argues that references to the Austrians were added at a late stage: 'the Austrian references in the first edition were late additions, made partly under the influence of Hayek and mainly in order to mention the most recent literature' (p. 414).
8. This comment is made in the light of the character of the correspondence between Hayek and Mitchell, largely about Wieser, which was much more friendly than one might have expected in the light of Hayek's later views. See Hayek Archive 38–28.
9. Hayek was engaged in correspondence about this with Neurath in 1945. See Hayek Archive, Box 40–7. My reason for hesitation about this, is because Hayek was I think mistaken in attributing physicalism in a realist sense to Carnap, while Neurath's views on this issue seem to me ultimately obscure.
10. An example of this is provided by an assessment (which as a whole was favourable!) by Charles J. Bullock whom the Memorial consulted when considering the funding of the Vienna Institute for the Study of Trade Cycle Research, of which Hayek was the first director. See (Craver, 1986, pp. 212–213).
11. Two useful works for getting a feel for Hogben's approach are his (1936) and his 'The Creed of a Scientific Humanist', in (Hogben, 1940b; see also 1940a).
12. He refers frequently to 'Austrian economics', but his specific criticisms seem to focus particularly on Robbins, although, as we shall see, he is also critical of Hicks.
13. I will, again for reasons of space, not discuss Hogben's more positive views about the possible contributions of social biology, in which context see for example (Hogben, 1931)
14. There is a reference to Hogben in 'Scientism and the Study of Society', part 2, page 40, in which Hayek notes correctly that Hogben is among those who talk about available energy in relation to the meeting of human needs. But Hayek does not go on to explore what, in Hogben, is behind all this (i.e. his critique of consumer choice). He also refers briefly but critically to Hogben in essays now included in (Hayek, 1997).
15. See Caldwell's editorial introduction to Hayek's *Studies in the Abuse of Reason* (Hayek, 2010).
16. Hogben does not himself provide a reference, but Isabel Stearns, who provided annotations to (Hogben, 1937a), identifies it as Aphorism 24. The quotation is from (Hogben, 1937a, p. 6).

17. The quotation is from (Hogben, 1940b, p. 84); Hogben provides a reference simply to '*Economica*, 1937', which must be to (Hayek, 1937), although it is not obvious what specifically Hogben had in mind.
18. Hogben does not provide a reference, but the passage is to be found at (Hicks, 1966, p. 153).
19. Compare, for example, current discussions around the subject of 'experimental economics' and its relation to work in economic theory.

Disclosure statement

No potential conflict of interest was reported by the author.

References

Beveridge, W. (1921). Economics as a liberal education. *Economica, 1,* 2–19.
Beveridge, W. (1936). *Planning under socialism and other addresses.* London: Longmans, Green & Co.
Beveridge, W. (1937). The place of the social sciences in human knowledge. *Politica, 2,* 459–479.
Caldwell, B. (1988). Hayek's transformation. *History of Political Economy, 20,* 513–541.
Caldwell, B. (1991). Clarifying Popper. *Journal of Economic Literature, 29,* 1–33.
Caldwell, B. (2004). *Hayek's challenge: An intellectual biography of F.A. Hayek.* Chicago, IL: University of Chicago Press.
Craver, E. (1986). Patronage and the directions of research in economics: The rockefeller foundation in Europe, 1924–1938. *Minerva, 24,* 205–222.
Desmarais, R. J. (N.D.). Tots and Quots (act. 1931–1946). *Oxford dictionary of national biography.* Oxford: Oxford University Press. http://www.oxforddnb.com.virtual.anu.edu.au/view/theme/95704
Hayek, F. A. (1933). The trend of economic thinking. *Economica, 13,* 121–137. doi:10.2307/2548761
Hayek, F. A. (1935). *Collectivist economic planning.* London: Routledge.
Hayek, F. A. (1937). Economics and knowledge. *Economica, 4,* 33–54.
Hayek, F. A. (1941). Planning, science and freedom. *Nature, 143,* 550–554.
Hayek, F. A. (1942-4). Scientism and the study of society, part I. *Economica, 9,* 267–291; Part II. *Economica* 10: 34–63; Part III, *Economica* 11: 27–39
Hayek, F. A. (1952). *The counter-revolution of science.* Glencoe, IL: Free Press.
Hayek, F. A. (1973-9). *Law, legislation and liberty.* London: Routledge and Chicago, University of Chicago Press.
Hayek, F. A. (1989). *Hayek on Hayek.* (Stephen Kresge and Leif Wenar, Eds.). London: Routledge.
Hayek, F. A. (1991). *The trend of economic thinking.* (W. W. Bartley and Stephen Kresge, Eds.). London: Routledge.
Hayek, F. A. (1992). *The fortunes of liberalism.* (Peter G. Klein, Ed.). Chicago: University of Chicago Press.
Hayek, F.A. (1997). *Socialism and war.* (Bruce Caldwell, Ed.). Chicago: University of Chicago Press.
Hayek, F.A. (2010). *Studies in the abuse of reason.* (Bruce Caldwell, Ed.). Chicago: University of Chicago Press.
Hicks, J. R. (1966). *Theory of wages* (2nd ed.). London: Macmillan.
Hogben, L. (1931). The foundation of social biology. *Economica, 31,* 4–24.

Hogben, L. (1936). *Retreat from reason*. London: Watts & Co.

Hogben, L. (1937a). *Retreat from reason with notes by Isabel E. Stearns*. New York: Random House.

Hogben, L. (1937b). *Mathematics for the million*. London: Allen & Unwin.

Hogben, L. (1938a). *Political arithmetic*. London: Allen & Unwin.

Hogben, L. (1938b). *Science for the citizen*. London: Allen & Unwin.

Hogben, L. (1939a). *Dangerous thoughts*. London: Allen & Unwin.

Hogben, L. (1939b). Sir William Petty and Political Arithmetic. In Hogben 1939a.

Hogben, L. (1940a). *Author in transit*. New York: Norton.

Hogben, L. (1940b). *Dangerous thoughts*. New York: Norton.

Howson, S. (2004). The origins of Lionel Robbins's *essay on the nature and significance of economic science. History of Political Economy, 36*, 413–443.

Huxley, T. H. (1854). On the educational value of the natural history sciences. In T. H. Huxley (Ed.), *Science and education*. London: Macmillan, 1899. https://ebooks.adelaide.edu.au/h/huxley/thomas_henry/science-and-education/chapter2.html

Rand, Ayn. (1995). *Ayn Rand's marginalia: Her critical comments on the writings of over 20 authors*. (Robert Mayhew, Ed.). New Milford, CT: Second Renaissance Books.

Robbins, L. (1930). The present position of economic science. *Economica, 10*, 14–24.

Robbins, L. (1932). *An essay on the nature and significance of economic science*. London: Macmillan.

Robbins, L. (1934). *The great depression*. London: Macmillan.

Robertson, D. H. (1935). Review of Lionel Robbins. *The great depression. Economica, 2*, 103–106.

Shearmur, J. (1986). The Austrian connection: F. A. Hayek and the thought of Carl Menger. In B. Smith, & W. Grassl (Eds.), *Austrian economics: Historical and philosophical background* (pp. 210–224). London & Sydney: Croom Helm.

Shearmur, J. (1987). *The Political Thought of F. A. von Hayek* (Ph.D. Thesis). London School of Economics, University of London, London.

Shearmur, J. (1991a). Common sense and the foundations of economic theory: Duhem Versus Robbins. *Philosophy of the Social Sciences, 21*, 64–71.

Shearmur, J. (1991b). Popper, Lakatos and theoretical progress in economics. In M. Blaug, & N. de Marchi (Eds.), *Appraising modern economics. Studies in the methodology of scientific research programmes* (pp. 35–52). Cheltenham: Edward Elgar Publishing.

Shearmur, J. (1996). *Hayek and after*. London: Routledge.

Shearmur, J. (2013). Beveridge and the brief life of 'social biology' at the LSE. *Agenda: A Journal of Policy Analysis and Reform, 20*, 79–94.

Werskey, G. (1978). *The visible college*. New York: Holt, Rinehart.

Reading Polanyi in Erbil: understanding socio-political factors in the development of Iraqi Kurdistan

Robert Smith

ABSTRACT

The Kurdistan Regional Government emerges out of the chaos of post-Saddam Iraq as a rare positive, providing both political stability and economic growth. However, the outward display masks a more complex domestic settlement where the trappings of the free market coexist with political parties who are significant economic actors. How can this model of development in Iraqi Kurdistan be explained? Turning to the writings of political economist Karl Polanyi, does his thinking on relations between society and economy offer a way to unpack the development? And what does this analysis tell us of prospects for Iraqi Kurdistan?

The 'success' of Iraqi Kurdistan has been a recurrent theme in the retelling of its recent past. Prior to the invasion of Iraq in 2003 Kurdistan was presented by advocates of 'regime change' as the prosperous and peaceful future for post-Saddam Iraq (Ferguson, 2008, pp. 8–9). After regime change, as the rest of Iraq descended into lawlessness and violent civil war, Kurdistan appeared as a location blessed with security and political stability. Since 1991, the Kurdistan Regional Government (KRG) had taken opportunities presented to it and a burst of economic activity has transformed the region's capital, Erbil, from a compact city clustered around an ancient citadel to an urban sprawl boasting an international airport, shopping malls, gated communities, and luxury hotels. The KRG supported a campaign to market the region as a tourist destination under the heading of 'The Other Iraq' (Kamen, 2006). As civil war eased, the KRG became a centre for investment and business, particularly in the oil and gas sector, where in 2012 it was declared the 'exploration capital of the world' (Kent, 2012). When Islamic State emerged as an existential threat to the future of both the KRG and Iraq, it was once again the security forces of Kurdistan that stepped up to face down the foe. Then-Presidential candidate Donald Trump declared that he was 'a big fan of the Kurdish forces' (New York Times, 2016). However, this success may be coming to an end. In late 2017, the KRG was entering a period of crisis that threatened to reverse the gains of the previous twenty-five years. An independence referendum that resulted in a significant 'yes' vote ultimately gave rise to the Iraqi federal government reasserting its right to decide the future of the Iraqi state and its Kurdistan territory. The expulsion of Kurdish peshmerga from Kirkuk in October 2017 sealed a humiliating defeat for the KRG and threatened the future of the regional government (Hiltermann, 2017).

How did the KRG move from success to crisis? Contrasted with the rest of the country, Khalil noted a narrative of Kurdistan exceptionalism: in 'the mixed report card on Iraqi progress, one consistent theme is that Iraqi Kurdistan has been a quiet success story ... a snowy oasis, free from the sectarian strife that has marred the rest of the country' (Khalil, 2009). As Leezenberg noted, on first viewing, Kurdistan appeared to be, 'the neoliberal success story of post-Saddam Iraq' (Leezenberg, 2005, p. 631). These perceptions of success informed writings on how KRG had utilized its own nationalist history in the development of a resilient notion of statehood (Richards & Smith, 2015): However, as others have also noted, when looked at closely, the narrative of a successful Kurdistan is more complicated (Jabary & Hira, 2013). It would take a selective view of events not to notice some of the limitations of the politics, governance and economics in the territory. The much-trumpeted democracy of Kurdistan ran alongside the longstanding dominance of two political parties, the Kurdistan Democratic Party (KDP) and the Patriotic Union of Kurdistan (PUK), who ruled their respective sections of the region as personal fiefdoms. Freedom of speech coexisted with the violent suppression of protest and the arresting of journalists. In the economic sphere dynamism coexisted with allegations of 'nepotism and corruption' (Ahmed, 2012, p. 110). Kurdistan is complex and this raises the question of how to understand its development.

A more nuanced perspective of Kurdistan's development must highlight that the successes, and some of the failures, of the region, were also closely linked to the dominant role played by the two principal political parties of the region. Deeper still, the analysis must consider the role of the two families that led these parties. To understand the political economy of Kurdistan, it is necessary to comprehend its political settlement and the social relations that enabled them: the economic and the political cannot be separated. To unpick the puzzle of the success of Kurdistan, while also considering its future development, theoretical guidance is required.

To help with unpacking this, the writings of Karl Polanyi act as a useful tool. Kari Polanyi Levitt summarizes her father's work as 'addressing the relationship of the market to the whole of society, including institutions of political governance' (Polanyi Levitt, 2017, p. 390). Of interest in Polanyi's work is his emphasis on the relations between society and economy reflected in his historical analysis of 'archaic' economies. Do these works provide a new way of understanding the contemporary settlement in Iraqi Kurdistan? The dominant narrative of Iraqi Kurdistan is that it represents a success story and an exemplar of a modern dynamic market economy. However, closer inspection through the prism of Polanyi highlights the historical development of state and economy, providing a more nuanced grounding that is needed not only to explain Kurdistan today, but also to provide clues to its future trajectory.

The purpose here is not to engage in an in-depth examination of Polanyi's work, but to use the insights of Polanyi to contribute to the analysis of the economic and political development of KRG. This article first considers characterizations of the state in the Middle East before going on to look at the development of Kurdistan within the modern history of Iraq. Polanyi's work on the political economy of Mesopotamia will be deployed as a way of understanding the role of the dominant political parties in modern-day Kurdistan.

Ancient and modern: politics and society in the Middle East

Before analysing the contemporary settlement of Kurdistan it is necessary to establish some groundwork for how Polanyi and others have characterized politics and society in the Middle East. Looking for evidence of economic activity outside of the market, Polanyi had researched ancient Mesopotamia and the development of the economy in pre-modern times. A model that was advanced during this research with Assyriologist Leo Oppenheim emphasized the importance of 'palaces and temples' as centres of influence (Oppenheim, 1957, p. 31) Local economies were 'dominated by large palace and temple complexes, which owned the greater part of the arable land and virtually monopolised anything that can be called "industrial production" as well as foreign trade' (Dale, 2010, p. 149 quoting Finley). Polanyi observed that trade in this setting 'was not a two-sided act resulting in a negotiated contract but a sequence of one-sided declarations of will.' These interactions taking place 'within the frame of a governmental organisation and a network of official and semi-official institutions.' (Polanyi, 1957, pp. 22–23) Dale notes that the analysis put forward by Polanyi on ancient Mesopotamia was 'less successful than his other forays into comparative economic history' Dale, 2010, pp. 150–152). However, for Polanyi, the importance of the palaces in the ancient economic structures was that they stood apart from the subsistence level of economics that characterized the dominant economic sector, agriculture.

What the palaces allowed for was the creation of surpluses that could be pushed into the 'public' sector. As Dale notes, this upends the models of development that see 'small private scale' trade expand to a 'larger, and ultimately public, scale.' The reverse happens whereby the palaces create surpluses allowing for investment, capital accumulation, and ultimately entrepreneurial innovation (Dale, 2010, pp. 159–160). Hudson states this results in the capturing of the commanding heights of the economy by individuals in the palaces: 'Rulers and their bureaucracies ... behaved simultaneously in public and private ways. Their "public" position could readily be transmuted into private advantage, the temple and palace officials exploiting their powers for personal material gain' (Dale, 2010, p. 160 quoting Hudson). During these periods of palace rule, 'significant privatization dynamics were in play, centred on the palace bureaucracy.' Eventually, these periods of development controlled from the centre would pass as the economic activity created the environment in which 'public business activity regained its customary upper hand' (Dale, 2010, pp. 151–152 quoting Oppenheim).

Echoes of Polanyi's research into pre-modern Mesopotamia can be found in contemporary accounts of the state in the Arab world. Ayubi argues that how a state organized itself and what values it espoused reflected the economics, society, and culture of the region. One of the factors that made the state in the Middle East different for Ayubi was the basis of its economy, which was described as 'the tributary mode of production' (Ayubi, 1995, p. 58). Initially the economy was dominated by agriculture, tribute was extracted from tribes by central authorities. The role of the state in this process was one of 'distribution and circulation' of the tributes (Ayubi, 1995, p. 58). Through this practice, classes become 'excessively dependent on the state,' and the success or survival of a class was dependent on their relationship with the state. This process and the resulting relationships inform the organization of the state. Therefore, according to Ayubi, ' ... politics in such a society is not characterised by the orderly process of aggregating demands but by acts of capturing the state and acts of resisting the state' (Ayubi, 1995, p. 25). Given the centrality of the state to the political process and individual prosperity that is linked with it, those who achieve power work hard to hold on to it, becoming consumed by strategies for maintaining it, with the individual or group who challenges the status quo viewed as 'a threat.' The result is that states are strong in terms of coercion but often weak in terms of popular support and legitimacy (Ayubi, 1995, p. 23). Ayubi argues that as the Arab state expanded in size and scope, the space for these non-state opponents diminished. Colonial rule simply inherited and then refined these techniques (Ayubi, 1995, p. 24).

Both theoretical accounts of the state, ancient and modern, emphasize the dominance of central authority. With the 'palaces and temples', change is gradual as the economic forces unleashed slowly replace the existing order. With Ayubi's model, opposition to the dominant order is suppressed and change relies on a confrontation over reform. In Iraq, confrontation to the existing order came with the revolution in 1958. However, the revolution proved more effective at changing the leadership of the centralized state rather than altering its structure. The growing economic importance of the oil sector allowed the state to expand in 'size and scope' but the centralization of power remained. As Davis notes when describing the Baath Party seizure of power in 1968 the '[Iraqi] political system failed to develop enduring political institutions ... [w]ithout political institutionalisation, politics reverted back to subnational groups based on tribal, ethnic or regional identities' (Davis, 2005, p. 153). There was no incentive for rulers to move away from this model of statehood and it remained in place, growing 'more exclusionary and more tightly consolidated' (Ayubi, 1995, p. 426). Therefore, it can be stated that the historical development of the Iraqi state had resulted in the intertwining of social, economic and political structures: a system that favoured limited circles of power based on tribalism, ethnicity, and regionalism. Power resides in these relations.

Polanyi aids in deciphering the economic and the political:

> ... the anthropologist, the sociologist or the historian in his study of the place occupied by the economy in human society was faced with a great variety of institutions other than markets, in which the sphere of man's livelihood was embedded. (Polanyi, 1953/1959, p. 218)

In the case of Iraqi Kurdistan, the variety of institutions are less about the state and more about the role of political parties. The domination by political parties in Iraqi Kurdistan resulted in the ascendancy of two families, where the sphere of economic development and political control can be located. To understand the development of Kurdistan, these relations must be considered.

Becoming Kurdistan: political tribes and tribal politics

As Polanyi states, analysis requires historical perspective. The modern history of Iraq begins with the attempt to map out a national identity for the new territory. The irony of this was that as Iraq sought to establish its own identity a coherent nationality was already being articulated in the Kurdish-dominated north of the country. The British government, ruling the territory under the mandate system, was already reporting in the mid-1920s that Kurdish engagement with the political processes of the mandate was driven by a 'desire to get British support for a Kurdistan free from Turkish influence than any solidarity with the Iraqi government: many Kurds still hankered after a wholly independent Kurdistan' (Sluglett, 2007, p. 63). As the new state of Iraq took shape the British incorporated both coercion and economic incentive to gain sufficient control over the territory to fulfil the mandate. Inspired by the model of rule used in India, the British sought out and, in some cases revived, tribal groupings to provide cost-efficient governance. The tribal leaders fulfilled the dual role of landlords and law enforcement. They were the 'socio-political backbone' of mandate-era Iraq (Ayubi, 1995, p. 95). This created opportunities for local tribal leaders to either cooperate or oppose colonial rule. In Kurdistan, local tribal leaders worked to maintain their autonomy of action from the British and from central powers (Tripp, 2002, pp. 34–36). In the 1930s, Mullah Mustafa Barzani, of the Barzani tribe, emerged as the leader of Kurdish resistance to rule from Baghdad. Driven by the desire to maintain the autonomy of his tribe, but also influenced by an emergent Kurdish nationalism, he would maintain this position until his death in 1979 (Sluglett, 2007, p. 152).

Most interesting to note from this period of state formation in Kurdistan was the struggle between nationalism and tribalism in the disputes with Baghdad and the British. The tribal groups, linked as they often were to the ownership of land, could be conservative groupings resistant to radical reforms. But in Kurdistan, their desire for autonomy made them actors for change. When Barzani led a revolt against the wartime control of the British in 1943 it marked a turning point in the politics of Kurdistan. Stansfield notes that this revolt was the point when, if 'Barzani did not choose nationalism, the nationalists chose him … [f]rom 1943 onwards, it is increasingly apparent that the nationalists are less inclined to be used as pawns in tribal politics, and attempt to exploit tribalism for their own agenda' (Stansfield, 2003, p. 63). The nationalist political narrative was formalized in the creation of the KDP in 1946, with Mullah Mustafa Barzani named as its President-in-exile.

The KDP would dominate the politics of Kurdistan nationalism for the next thirty years. During this period there were significant advances for the Kurdish cause within Iraq. The revolution of 1958 produced a constitutional settlement that recognized that Iraq was both an Arab and a Kurdish state. Barzani could return from exile to lead the KDP from Iraqi Kurdistan, but there was no immediate transfer of power from Baghdad to Erbil in this new era. As under previous rulers, the Iraqi Kurds became an irritant for the government of Baghdad as a series of conflicts unfolded. During this period, whichever group found itself in power in Iraq recognized that it would struggle to bring a military solution to the Kurdish question. Equally true for the Kurds was the fact that they alone did not command sufficient power to force a solution on Baghdad (Sluglett & Farouk-Sluglett, 2003, p. 81).

The early 1970s was a difficult but significant period in the development of the modern KRG. In 1970, Baghdad had agreed to allow for autonomy in the territory where a majority Kurdish community existed. This began the process of establishing the reach of the contemporary KRG. However, when progress towards this goal stalled, Barzani once again took up arms. The military defeat that KDP forces suffered in 1975 was calamitous. In its aftermath, a split occurred within the nationalist movement. In June 1975, the PUK was established to pursue a more overtly revolutionary path towards Kurdish autonomy. The new party was led by Jalal Talabani and inspired by the actions of 'Third World' liberation movements. The PUK set itself out as a left-wing party that contested the traditional conservatism of the KDP and its tribal leadership. The PUK rejected 'the right of an individual family, the Barzanis, to head the Kurdish national movement' (Stansfield, 2003, p. 86). The division that the PUK highlighted was not only political but was also cultural, a divide between the urban and rural, the modern and the traditional. Stansfield notes that this 'enhanced segmentation' of the area would remain as 'a major obstacle to the unification of the region' and of its governance (Stansfield, 2003, p. 86). However, despite the PUK rejecting rule by family, their own organization would, in turn, become dominated by the Talabani family and in the future Kurdistan would emerge from the competition between these two familial groupings. Following the death of Mullah Mustafa Barzani in 1979, his son, Masoud, assumed the leadership of the KDP, a role he still holds.

The position of power that the KDP came to hold within Iraqi Kurdistan, which later they would again turn into economic advantage, is built on their positioning in the long struggle for autonomy. In this struggle, Mullah Mustafa Barzani became the 'father of the nation' bestowing legitimacy on the KDP. While this singular narrative is challenged by the formation of the PUK, it is never entirely removed. The KDP is legitimized by its historic struggle.

The state in Kurdistan: divided governance

The 1970s was a period of rapid economic modernization within Iraq. The nationalization of the oil sector had arrived prior to two major spikes in the price of oil. Iraq had been able to invest in public goods because of its oil wealth through most of its modern history, but the growth in the 1970s was quantitatively different. The new wealth allowed the state to implement large-scale development projects. Provision for education and health care improved; electrification projects reached out to villages; transport infrastructure was expanded; telecommunications was upgraded; there was state-led industrialization; and large-scale housing projects were built. Amongst developing nations, Iraq was 'a relatively strong state, an elaborate bureaucracy and a government that because of its expanding oil income was relatively autonomous from society' (Leezenberg, 2005, p. 63).

The increase in national oil revenue had a mixed impact on the economic outlook for Kurdistan. The new money coming into the national economy allowed for the expansion of the state. Kurdistan was not immune from these changes and there was a dramatic growth in either direct or one-stage removed government employment. However, the investment that came with oil production was limited to the sites of production. In the north of the country, this was mostly concentrated in Kirkuk. Iraqi government industrial projects that sought to diversify away from oil production were mostly located outside of the Kurdistan region. Official figures in 1987 stated that only 4.9 per cent of Iraq's heavy industry was in Kurdistan. In 1990 the region only contained nine 'major factories' with these concentrating on the production of cement and cigarettes (Leezenberg, 2002, p. 290). The most productive sector of the economy in Kurdistan had been agriculture. In 1980, it was still producing nearly half of the wheat in Iraq (Stansfield, 2003, p. 42), but agriculture by this point was in decline. Its previous dominance was affected by the growth in urban employment which drew agricultural workers away from the land and the new prosperity which enabled Iraq to import foodstuffs. Oil wealth had resulted in an economic settlement in Kurdistan that was 'overwhelmingly agrarian in terms of employment, but dependent financially upon the distribution of oil revenue' (Stansfield, 2003, p. 44).

Thus, the Kurdistan region was already struggling with structural imbalance. These economic problems worsened when Saddam Hussein assumed the presidency of Iraq. A decade of conflict followed. War with Iran halted the oil revenue that had expanded the Iraqi state through the 1970s and the genocidal Anfal campaign, beginning in 1988, dispersed and destroyed the rural communities that maintained the agrarian economy within Iraqi Kurdistan. This dislocation within Kurdistan meant the centres that survived were now more dependent on the state to maintain economic activity. Almost immediately after the Anfal campaign ceased, Iraq was once again plunged into economic turmoil as UN sanctions were imposed following the annexation of Kuwait in August 1990.

The economic and physical destruction that the Gulf War visited on Iraq after 1990 provided the starting point for the development of the present-day KRG. When the Kurdish 'safe haven' was established through a combination of internal agitation and external intervention the economic prospects were terrible. As noted, the agricultural sector had been badly disrupted by the Anfal campaign. In addition to this, the Kurdistan region was now cut off from central government funding as it lived through the period of dual sanctions: referring to both international sanctions imposed on Iraq by the UN and internal sanctions imposed on Kurdistan by Saddam's government in Baghdad. Government employment in Kurdistan, that had accounted for much of the economic activity, gave way to a period when the state had a limited role in the economy, allowing for a private informal sector to emerge (Stansfield, 2003, p. 57).

The most notable political development at this time was that the groups attempting to re-establish government in Northern Iraq chose to hold elections to decide on the composition of the new assembly for Kurdistan. This was an innovation for Iraq and for much of the Middle East. Elections were held in May 1992 and voting was dominated by the two nationalist parties, the KDP and the PUK. The elections were rudimentary but seen as fair. The result ended in a rough fifty-fifty split between the KDP and PUK. Where the introduction of elections had produced a degree of transparency, what followed would set the template for future politics. Without a clear victor, government posts were shared out between the two parties. The leaders of the two parties, Masoud Barzani and Jalal Tala-bani, did not take up positions in government. The two were the most powerful political actors in Iraqi Kurdistan and the most visible representatives of the region internationally. Yet neither held government posts. Power in the new Kurdistan would remain within the hands of the political parties rather than any new institutions that would be established. Government posts divided between the two parties became centres of power and patronage. When the haggling was completed, government posts reflected the geographical spread of support for the two parties: the KDP in control of the western half of the region and the PUK in charge of its eastern sector.

Cut off from the rest of Iraq and having no official international status, the economy subsisted on smuggling, with petroleum products being the most profitable sector. The KDP was left in control of the more lucrative crossing between Kurdistan and Turkey, while the PUK controlled the border with Iran. Some of the income from the smuggling operation went to the Kurdistan Central Bank, but in addition to this, the two parties also took their share of the duties being charged (Lee-zenberg, 2002, p. 307). Both parties sought to maximize their revenues from the smuggling routes and disputes over who controlled which routes were part of the basis for a civil war between the two, that began in 1994 and continued at different levels of intensity through much of the rest of the decade (Graham-Brown, 1999, p. 225). At various times Baghdad and Tehran interfered and it took the efforts of the United States to bring settlement between the KDP and PUK. The conflict eased when Kurdistan was effectively divided into 'two one-party statelets under the control of the KDP and the PUK, respectively' (Leezenberg, 2005, p. 632).

This settlement only strengthened the role of the parties in the economic process, undermining the possibility of stronger institutions emerging from the centre of the new state. This tendency was reinforced by the main international economic input in this new settlement, humanitarian aid. Con-forming to the norms of the times, humanitarian agencies sought out NGOs rather than state bodies to deliver aid. The practice pushed more funds into groups linked with either the KDP or the PUK. More funds flowed in after the UN Oil-for-Food Programme was agreed in 1995, guaranteeing the Kurdish region a 13 per cent share of humanitarian aid coming into Iraq from limited oil sales. While it took time for the practice to match the promised funds, when the additional aid eventually reached Kurdistan it proved beneficial to the local economy (Aziz, 2015, p. 12). What was beneficial for the economy, was inevitably beneficial for the political parties. This enabled the political parties to act as state-like bodies, collecting tax, distributing aid, and maintaining security. The safe havens period created a 'bubble' for the establishment and embedding of what has become today's Kurdistan economy.

By the end of the 1990s, finance was entering the Kurdistan region and circulating through formal and informal structures. Revenue from the informal economy flowed towards the political parties and towards the 'individuals high up in the party hierarchies' (Leezenberg, 2002, p. 308). The period between 1991 and 2003 had at times been economically precarious for the Kurdistan region, but as the period came to an end this was no longer the case. In 2004, the population of the Kurdistan region enjoyed a per capita income that was approximately 25 per cent higher than anywhere else in Iraq (Aziz, 2015, p. 13).

The development of the Kurdistan region during the period after 1991 resulted in a complex settlement. During this time there was more entrepreneurialism in Kurdistan than was witnessed elsewhere in Iraq. However, much of this entrepreneurial activity was connected to and controlled by the parties of government. Therefore, we must acknowledge and bring into the analysis that the market is influenced by the society that hosts it: 'Man's [sic] economy is, as a rule, submerged in his social relations' (Polanyi, 1969, p. 65).

Polanyi is useful to consider the complex socio-political network that makes up the functioning of a modern economy. He reminds us that economic relations are the result of cultural legacy, shared history and societal relations, and thus understanding economic development demands also understanding social and political developments. Nowhere is this more evident than in his focus on the sway of catallactic logic—the science of exchanges—within a substantive meaning of the economy where trade and money are functions of the market forming a conceptual triad to argue that 'the human economy is an instituted process' (Polanyi, 1953/1959, p. 168). In Kurdistan, business is carried out between companies because of familial or political allegiance and these social and political structures thus become instrumental to the establishment and strengthening of economic structures. The market in Kurdistan, as we have seen, has been shaped by recent and distant history. The nationalist movement is dominated by tribal groups. Political competition is created by the break-up of the dominant grouping to create a political settlement that has two dynastic families. When these competing forces join to control the Kurdistan region, they inherit a broken system of governance that allows them to insert themselves into the state beyond the reach of government. They also insert themselves into economic activity.

As the next section will further explain, even when contemporary economic activity takes place, carried out by the new entrepreneurs of Kurdistan, it is 'embedded' in society. Or, as Polanyi more elegantly puts it: 'instead of economy being embedded in social relations, social relations are embedded in the economic system' (Polanyi, 1944/1957, p. 57).

After 2003: capitalism with Kurdish characteristics

The end of Saddam Hussein's regime in spring 2003 was a period of opportunity for the region after decades of oppressive rule from Baghdad. The KDP and PUK started to play a significant role in shaping the political settlement for post-Saddam Iraq. It was important for the Kurdistan leadership to protect the autonomy that they had gained after 1991. The removal of Saddam Hussein from power would not result in the KRG being reincorporated into the Iraqi state. When the constitution settlement was reached in 2005, it was for a federal Iraq where governorates could link up and rule with significant freedom in their defined territory. At present this right has only been exercised by the KRG.

In the brief period of American-led statebuilding within Iraq, Kurdistan remained largely untouched by any attempts at reshaping government or economic structures. If the United States did entertain serious plans to restructure Iraq, these were soon undermined by instability in the rest of the country. The attempts of the Coalition Provisional Authority (CPA) to introduce new business regulations and laws had limited impact when applied to commerce in Iraq and it is difficult to discern any significant impact in the Kurdistan region. In the chaotic aftermath of regime change, Kurdistan was soon looked on as an area of calm. There were no significant security problems within the region and unlike the rest of the state, the governance structures that had existed before March 2003 remained in place. The occupying forces could send the Kurdistan region its monthly budget, confident that the money would be spent and services would be provided to the population. The period of CPA oversight built on the investments of the UN Oil-for-Food period and, thus, Kurdistan emerged as a new centre of prosperity in modern Iraq.

The period immediately after regime change was therefore important politically and economically. The political leadership solidified the gains made during the 'safe haven' decade and the Kurdistan region benefited from the increased funding that came from the lifting of UN sanctions and the newfound ability to encourage international investment. Elections held in Iraqi Kurdistan in 2005 rewarded the two established parties. In 2006, the KRG began drawing up new investment laws that would be more generous than those found elsewhere in Iraq. Iraqi Kurdistan marketed itself as a gateway to investment in the rest of Iraq labelling the regional capital, Erbil, as 'the new Dubai' (Hamid, 2012).

But much as this political stability and economic growth built on the achievements of the period of autonomy in the 1990s, they also inherited some of the weaknesses of that period. Soon after the introduction of the new investment laws aimed at foreign companies it was noted that business in the Kurdistan region still depended 'heavily on party affiliations and connections' (Khalil, 2009, p. 34). In 2015, the anti-corruption NGO Transparency International noted that while levels of corruption in Iraqi Kurdistan where lower than in Iraq, they remained higher in comparison with other states in the region. The dominance of the political parties in Kurdistan created, 'risks of nepotism and clientelism based on political party affiliation, tribal kinship and/or family connections' (Pring, 2015). The business laws of 2006 resulted in significant investment in the region and, between 2006 and 2013, infrastructure projects brought more than $30 billion to Kurdistan. However, much of the money has, 'reportedly been awarded to those close to the dominant political parties' (Sahin, 2015, p. 102).

There were many examples of the role that the political parties played in everyday commerce but possibly the most obvious came in the telecommunications market where the KDP and PUK ran rival mobile phone networks. Kurdish businessman Faruk Mustafa Rasool began his Asiacell telecommunications company in the 1990s when he smuggled the components for a mobile phone network into the Kurdistan Region. An early investor in Rasool was the PUK, which saw that a successful communications firm would allow Sulaymaniyah to contact the rest of the world. The extent of the PUK investment is a source of conjecture with figures ranging from 3 to 20 per cent (Wall Street Journal, 2007). The rival phone network in the KDP sector, Korek Telecom, disputed Asiacell's claim to be the pioneer of mobile services in the region. However, as with their Sulaymaniyah rival, close party ties where apparent. The chair of the company is Sirwan Barzani, 'the nephew of Masoud Barzani, the KRG president and KDP leader' (Hamid, 2012).

While both can claim to have led the way in bringing mobile communications to Iraq, a vital service in a nation recovering from conflict and with a disrupted infrastructure, they failed to enable Iraqi Kurds to communicate directly between their two largest cities, with Asiacell blocked in Erbil and Korek locked out of Sulaymaniyah. Plotting the emergence of the Kurdistan state, Lawrence noted that, while this dispute was 'probably not the dirtiest … in Kurdistan, just the most obvious,' before adding, the prominence of the Barzani name highlighted the involvement of the KDP in questionable business practice. The PUK was just as responsible for problematic dealings, 'but with more than one family name in the party, it looked less obvious' (Lawrence, 2008, p. 305).

With the political parties acting as strategic investors in the economy, it was not surprising that they should be linked with Iraq's most significant resource: oil. As has been noted, during the time of the safe haven, Iraqi Kurdistan survived through smuggling oil products. The most lucrative route, via Turkey, was controlled by the KDP. In 2002, the leadership of the PUK moved beyond smuggling into the realm of oil production, encouraging Turkish businessman Mehmet Sepil to take on the Taq Taq oil field located to the west of Sulaymaniyah, the main city within the eastern PUK controlled sector. The choice of Sepil was notable because he was not from an established oil company but instead the head of a construction firm. This selection of an industry outsider to begin the extraction of oil in Kurdistan may well have been a reflection of the questionable legal status of such a project. An established international oil company would have been wary of striking a deal with what, at the time, was a non-state body. Sepil, however, went ahead established a new company, Genel Enerji, and agreed to a Product Sharing Contract (PSC) with the PUK (Hurriyet Daily News, 2012).

The PUK had been the first party to move into oil production, but it was not the last. From 2006, the KDP began to play a significant role in the further exploitation of the resource as the KRG sought to encourage oil exploration in the territory. Appointed in May 2006, the Natural Resources Minister for the KRG, Ashti Hawrami, was aligned with the KDP (Mills, 2016, p. 8). Hawrami successfully used PSCs to encourage international oil companies to invest in the potential of Kurdistan, dividing the territory up into a series of exploration blocks. Mills notes that this economic success was linked to politics. 'The KDP's control over the oil portfolio has been extremely important in increasing its powers versus the rival PUK. It makes them the key interlocutors with Turkey and gives them access to additional sources of funding and patronage.' Despite the success of the KRG in attracting oil companies into the region, there was little transparency about their dealings, Hawrami was subjected 'to allegations of corruption and mismanagement' (Mills, 2016, p. 31).

In 2006, the US Department of State in Kirkuk documented how the different components of the KRG interacted. Highlighting 'corruption' as the greatest threat to the future of the region, the State Department noted that corruption began at the top and from the 'two ruling parties' and 'family-clan' ties (US Department of State, 2006). The political parties dominated the KRG making 'judiciary and legislature' subordinate to their rule (US Department of State, 2006). Corruption came from 'the godfathers', individuals with close ties to party leadership and party security forces. This meant that business rarely crossed party boundaries, companies would do business in either Erbil, with the KDP, or Sulaymaniyah, with the PUK. Without a 'godfather' it is difficult to do business. In Sulaymaniyah, without help, a business would 'not even receive the tender advertising the project' (US Department of State, 2006). The result was an economy dominated by 'vertically integrated cross-sectoral conglomerates' which were linked to 'godfathers' in the dominant parties. The State Department identified an array of such conglomerates: Diyar Group, Eagle Group, Falcon Group, KAR Group, Nasri Group, Sandi Group, Silver Star Group and Ster Group. Signage for these conglomerates could be observed around Erbil from hotel sites to business parks to private security companies. This was not by chance. The corruption was such that for the companies to succeed they needed to control all aspects of business from the import of materials and shipment to construction to protection. The burst of construction that was changing the skylines of Kurdistan was the result of conglomerates overseen by 'non-competing "godfathers" in the local ruling party' (US Department of State, 2006).

The modern palaces of Kurdistan

The Iraqi Kurdistan that emerges in the early twenty-first presented a puzzle. Outwardly, it is a prosperous enclave benefitting from a sustained period of peace and stability. At election times it displayed and still displays a vibrant political culture. However, despite this outward display of vibrancy and plurality there appeared to be little possibility of change. Political parties may lose popularity, as the PUK did, but they never lost power.

Deciphering Kurdistan through Polanyi offers new openings for analysis. Starting with the observation that 'normally, the economic order is merely a function of the social order' (Polanyi, 1944/1957, p. 71) The modern territory of Kurdistan can trace its history to the uprising against Saddam Hussein in 1991. This presented a unique set of circumstances in which to construct governance and economic structures. But the KRG did not begin in 1991, it was the culmination of a long historical process. The political actors that took control following the uprising owed their legitimacy and position to the history of Kurdish nationalism that stretched back to the early twentieth century. This history had built networks of influence and security forces that were loyal to them. It had established social orders that had withstood the wars of Saddam Hussein and the genocidal Anfal campaign. This social order was replicated in the economic development that would follow the creation of the safe haven for the Iraqi Kurds.

Polanyi, therefore, provides a basic starting point for analysis. But there are some limitations. The hope that Polanyi holds out that a 'double movement' will occur and society will protect itself from the perils inherent in a free market (Polanyi, 1944/1957, p. 76) is difficult to envisage within the economic setting of Kurdistan. Here, the insights of Ayubi are worth repeating. The structures of the state in the Arab world bring power to the centre. Those who attain power devise strategies to maintain it, alternate voices can only challenge the state through confrontation rather than through the 'orderly process of aggregating demands.' As Ayubi highlights in this process of state formation, 'classes [are] excessively dependent on the state' (Ayubi, 1995, p. 25). Success and advancement in Kurdistan is an outcome that is influenced by proximity to the leadership of the two dominant political groupings.

While the 'double movement' thesis may struggle with the reality of Kurdistan, Polanyi's research of the pre-modern economy of Mesopotamia provides a new way of thinking about the development of the economy in the territory after Saddam. The KRG emerges from a rare confluence of circumstances in 1991. The region was effectively isolated from international trade and national interaction through a regime of double sanctions. The economy survived through smuggling and humanitarian aid. Both streams of income were controlled by the dominant political parties. The territory established new governance structures, but power and wealth resided outside of these in parallel institutions linked to the political parties. A civil war between the KDP and PUK, in 1994, formalized the geographical division of the territory and enhanced the power of the parties over their separate enclaves.

It was during this period that the actions of the two parties began to show some similarities to the 'temples and palaces complexes' analysed by Polanyi. The palaces commanded a significant role in the pre-modern economy. They established the terms of trade which enabled competitive exchange and interactions that were guided by 'custom and treaty'. More interestingly, for the development of Kurdistan, the pre-modern palaces existed outside of the subsistence sector the economy. The palaces produced economic surplus. The surplus was reinvested in the economy either for the public good or private gain. Echoes of this could be found in the emerging economy of Iraqi Kurdistan where the political parties were closely linked to new business. The relative isolation of the Kurdistan territory from the global economy was an additional advantage. The political parties maintained significant control over access to the territory and its economy, putting them in an advantageous position to broker deals and to gain benefit.

When regime change brought an end to rule by Saddam Hussein, the structures established in times of scarcity benefitted as the global political economy explored investment opportunities in 'the other Iraq'. Returning to the palaces and temples complexes described by Polanyi and Oppenheim, Hudson argues that they represented a form of privatization of public wealth. The palaces created the environment for the entrepreneurs, but these private actors owed their opportunities either to their position within the ruling elites or to their close ties to them. The palaces brought progress, but the cost of this is an economy that revolves around societal relations. The risk in this mode of development is 'corruption [that] underpinned a privatisation process that was initiated and propelled by ruling families, warlords and other powerful individuals at the apex of the social pyramid' (Dale, 2010, p. 160 quoting Hudson).

It is difficult not to detect echoes in the contemporary palaces of Kurdistan. The structures established in Iraqi Kurdistan during the period of relative isolation have been engorged by foreign investment and 'these shifts have helped develop the region'. But this development has also 'led to extreme social inequalities [and] rampant corruption at the highest levels' (Hassan, 2015). Polanyi forces us to consider the relationships between society, economics and politics. Kurdistan, with its complex interweaving of the personal and political and the public and the private, provides a compelling case study.

Acknowledgements

I thank the editors of this volume and the peer reviewers for their constructive advice and feedback throughout the process of completing this article. I thank the staff of the Department of Social and Political Science at Brunel University and the School of Politics, Philosophy, International Relations and Environment at Keele University who listened to earlier versions of this article and provided invaluable feedback. I would like to thank Rebecca Richards, for all her help and assistance in completing this article. Finally, I would like to thank Maurice Glasman for being the original inspiration for this article when we sat and talked about Polanyi over a drink in a bar in Erbil in spring 2013.

Disclosure statement

No potential conflict of interest was reported by the author.

References

Ahmed, M. M. A. (2012). *Iraqi Kurds and nation-building*. New York: Palgrave Macmillan.
Ayubi, N. N. (1995). *Over-stating the Arab state: Politics and society in the Middle East*. London: IB Tauris.
Aziz, M. A. (2015). *The Kurds of Iraq: Nationalism and identity in Iraqi Kurdistan*. London: IB Tauris.
Dale, G. (2010). *Karl Polanyi: The limits of the market*. Cambridge: Polity Press.
Davis, E. (2005). *Memories of state: Politics, history, and collective identity in modern Iraq*. Berkeley: University of California Press.
Ferguson, C. H. (2008). *No end in sight: Iraq's descent into chaos*. New York: Public Affairs Books.
Graham-Brown, S. (1999). *Sanctioning saddam: The politics of intervention in Iraq*. London: IB Tauris.
Hamid, T. (2012, September 5). Corruption and cronyism hinder Kurdistan. *The Financial Times*. Retrieved from http://www.ft.com
Hassan, K. (2015, August 18). *Kurdistan's politicised society confronts a sultanistic system*. Beirut: Carnegie Middle East Centre. Retrieved from http://carnegie-mec.org
Hiltermann, J. (2017, October 31). The Kurds are right back where they started. *The Atlantic*, Retrieved from http://www.theatlantic.com
Hurriyet Daily News. (2012, December 10). Investor sees Kurdish oil as Turkey's best chance since Ottomans. *Hurriyet Daily News*. Retrieved from http://www.hurriyetdailynews.com
Jabary, K., & Hira, A. (2013). The Kurdish mirage: A success story in doubt. *Middle East Policy, 20*(2), 99–112.
Kamen, A. (2006, July 26). The Iraq we haven't seen. *Washington Post*. Retrieved from http://washingtonpost.com
Kent, G. (2012, December 11). Exploring the Erbil-Baghdad Ankara Triangle. *Huffington Post*. Retrieved from http://www.huffingtonpost.co.uk

Khalil, L. (2009). *Stability in Iraqi Kurdistan: Reality or mirage?* (Working Paper No. 2). Washington: The Saban Center for Middle East Policy at the Brookings Institution.

Lawrence, Q. (2008). *Invisible nation: How the Kurds' quest for statehood is shaping Iraq and the Middle East.* New York: Walker Publishing Company.

Leezenberg, M. (2002). Refugee camp or free trade zone? The economy of Iraqi Kurdistan since 1991. In K. Mahdi (Ed.), *Iraq's economic predicament* (pp. 289–319). Reading: Ithaca Press.

Leezenberg, M. (2005). Iraqi Kurdistan: Contours of a post-civil war society. *Third World Quarterly, 26*(4-5), 631–647.

Mills, R. (2016). *Under the mountains: Kurdish oil and regional politics.* Oxford: The Oxford Institute for Energy Studies.

New York Times. (2016, July 21). Transcript: Donald Trump on NATO, Turkey's Coup Attempt and the World. *New York Times.* Retrieved from http://www.nytimes.com

Oppenheim, L. (1957). A bird's-eye view of mesopotamian economic history. In K. Polanyi, C. M. Arensberg, & H. W. Pearson (Eds.), *Trade and market in the early empires: Economies in history and theory* (pp. 27–37). Glencoe: The Free Press.

Polanyi, K. (1944/1957). *The great transformation: The political and economic origins of our time.* Boston: Beacon Press.

Polanyi, K. (1953/1959). Anthropology and economic theory. In M. H. Fried (Ed.), *Readings in anthropology, volume II: Readings in cultural anthropology* (pp. 161–184). New York: Thomas Y. Cromwell.

Polanyi, K. (1957). Marketless trading in Hammurabi's time. In K. Polanyi, C. M. Arensberg, & H. W. Pearson (Eds.), *Trade and market in the early empires: Economies in history and theory* (pp. 12–26). Glencoe: The Free Press.

Polanyi, K. (1969). *Primitive, archaic, and modern economies: Essays of Karl Polanyi.* Boston: Beacon Press.

Polanyi Levitt, K. (2017). Kari Polanyi Levitt on Karl Polanyi and the economy as a social construct. *Review of Social Economy, 75*(4), 389–399.

Pring, C. (2015). *Kurdistan region of Iraq: Overview of corruption and anti-corruption.* (No. 2015:7). Berlin: Transparency International.

Richards, R., & Smith, R. (2015). Playing in the sandbox: State-building in the space of non-recognition. *Third World Quarterly, 36*(9), 1717–1735.

Sahin, S. B. (2015). *International intervention and state-making: How exception became the norm.* London and New York: Routledge.

Sluglett, P. (2007). *Britain in Iraq: Contriving king and country.* New York: Columbia University Press.

Sluglett, P., & Farouk-Sluglett, M. (2003). *Iraq since 1958: From revolution to dictatorship.* London: IB Tauris.

Stansfield, G. (2003). *Iraqi Kurdistan: Political development and emergent democracy.* Abingdon: Routledge Curzon.

Tripp, C. (2002). *A history of Iraq.* Cambridge: Cambridge University Press.

US Department of State. (2006, February 16). *Corruption in the Kurdish North.* Wikileaks. Retrieved from http://www.wikileaks.org

Wall Street Journal. (2007, November 26). Asiacell and Korek, Kurdistan rivalries play out on cellphones. *Wall Street Journal.* Retrieved from http://www.wsj.com

Index

'Abuse of Reason' project 15
activism 99–105
agency 117, 140
always-embedded market economy 94–5, 96–7, 105
Asiacell 167
austerity 129
authoritarianism and populism 123
Ayers, A. 98
Ayubi, N. N. 161–2, 169

bail outs 128–9
Barzani, Masoud 165
Barzani, Mullah Mustafa 162–3
Barzani, Sirwan 167
Bauer, Otto 73
Bernstein, Eduard 48
Beveridge, W. 148–9, 150, 151–3
bias towards neoliberal policies 97
Block, F. 12–13, 94, 136, 142
Blumenberg, H. 122–3, 125
'bottom-up' analysis 27–31
bourgeois ideology 65
Branch, L. 40
Burgin, A. 103–4
Burke, E. 45

Caesarism 84–5
Cantillon, R. 42–3
capitalism: exceptionalism 127; neoliberalism and
    125; rationality/irrationality 65–6; singularity 63;
    transformation through fascism 72–3
'catallaxy' 142
centralized states 161–2
Cerny, P. G. 95–6, 111
class and class struggle: fascist social change 77–8, 85–6;
    'great trasformismo' 71; Polanyi on 60; neoliberalism
    and 97–8; 'survivals' of feudalism 75–6
classic liberalism 124–5
Clinton, Hillary 130
collectivism 1–2, 91
Collectivist Economic Planning 150
commodities: fictitious 15, 19–20, 59–60, 93, 138; as
    freedom 60–1; labour as 58; social relations and 63–4
'commodity effect' 61–3, 67
'commodity fiction' 59–60

competition 62
Concert of Europe 30–1
Connolly, W. 47
consciousness 65
conservatism 12
constructed order 17–19, 47–8
constructivism 141–2
consumer choice 153
corruption 167, 168, 169–70
Crispi, Francesco 85
'Critical Economy' 78–9
cultural evolution 142

Dale, Gareth. 1, 11, 93, 161
Deleuze, G. 110–11
democracy 18–19, 98–9, 138
DeMuth, C. 101
denationalization 138
determinate markets 78–81, 86
disembedding 25, 29, 59–60, 92–3, 95, 121–2, 125
'double movement' 26–7, 60, 74, 93–4, 116–17, 169
'double truth' doctrine 99

Eagleton, T. 40
economic calculation under socialism 147, 149, 150,
    155
'economism' 60–1
economy: Cantillon on 42–3; integral theory of 74–5;
    Iraqi Kurdistan 163–4, 165, 166–7; of Middle East
    161–2; spatial theory 111, 112
embeddedness: disembedding and re-embedding 121–
    2; economy and society in Kurdistan 166; Hayek and
    Polanyi on 92; historical variable or methodological
    principle 92–5; markets in society 12–14; spatial
    theory 110–11
empiricism 149–50, 152, 154–5
Engels, Friedrich 48
entrepreneurs 43, 165–6
equilibrium 42–3
Erbil, Iraq 159, 163, 167–8
Essay on the Nature and Significance of Economic Science
    (Robbins) 152
European Union 96
Evans, P. B. 111
'Evolution of the Market Pattern' (Polanyi) 113

exceptionalism 121–2, 127, 129–31, 130–1
exchange 60–1

failure 125–6
fascism: as 'new' liberalism 84–5; origins 70–1; as passive revolution 77–8; social change 76–7
Ferguson, A. 12, 45, 47
feudalism 73, 75–6, 86
fictitious commodities 15, 19–20, 59–60, 93
financial bubbles 41–2, 43
financial crises 67, 121–2
financial deregulation 98
formalism 112
Foucault, M.: *The Birth of Biopolitics* 56–7, 58–9, 62–3; birth of political economy 57; end of 'commodity effect' 61–3; on governmentality 57–9; *laissez-faire* 56–7; Lukács on 65–6; on neoliberalism 124; neoliberalism as end of 'commodity effect' 61–3
Frank, T. 129
French Revolution 28–9, 83

Garibaldi, G. 82
Gemici, K. 75, 92
Genel Enerji 168
gentry 43
geographical dimensions in Polanyi's work 109–20
German Younger Historical School 148–50, 152, 155
Glass, David 155
globalization 26, 111, 117
Godelier, Maurice 74–5
governmentality 58–9, 61, 62; *see also* states
Gramsci, Antonio 71, 78–88, 109–10, 111
Great Depression 31–2
'great *trasformismo*' 81, 85–6
Guattari, F. 110–11
Guicciardini, F. 12
Gulf War 164

Hacker, J. 98
Halperin, Sandra 1, 71, 76
Hawrami, Ashti 168
Hayek, Friedrich: on capitalism 125; civilized order 46–8; on collectivism 91; commodity form of law 65; on embeddedness 12–14; Polanyi and 9, 11–21; *laissez-faire* 56; markets as constructed/spontaneous 17–19, 20; *Methodenstreit* at the LSE 147–56; moral economy 140–1; neoliberal political economy 137–9; on neoliberal reason 126; politics 11–12; real utopia 136–7, 141–2; role of nature 14–17, 19–20; Scottish Enlightenment thinkers and 43–4, 46; state power and markets 135–6
Hayek's works: *Collectivist Economic Planning* 150; *The Constitution of Liberty* 101, 103; *The Fatal Conceit* 13; 'The Intellectuals and Socialism' 100–1; *Law, Legislation and Liberty* 13–14, 101; *The Road to Serfdom* 1–3, 10, 18, 50, 55, 56, 60–1, 91, 100, 103–4, 153; 'The Trend of Economic Thinking' 147–56
heroes 8
Hess, M. 110–11
Hicks, J. 154

historical materialism 79–80, 82
Historical School of economics 148–50, 152, 155
historical variable, socially embedded economy as 92
Hogben, L. 148–9, 150, 153–4, 155
homo economicus 62–3, 65–6
humanitarian aid 165, 169
Hume, D. 44, 125–6
Huxley, T. H. 151

identity politics 130
ideology: bourgeois 65; embeddedness and 98
'incorporated comparison' 118
individualism 102
industrial expansion 29–31
institutional capture 122, 127
institutions: always-embedded market economy 94–5; fascism 77–8; of international order 30–1; Iraq 162, 165, 169; Polanyi and Hayek on 50; spatial theory 113
integral economy 78–9
integral state 78–9, 80–1
intellectual histories 8–11
intentional activity 113–14, 116–17
international structures 25, 30–1
international system 82, 85, 115–17
'interstate federalism' 138, 139
'invisible hand' 42–4, 125, 126
Iraqi Kurdistan: capitalism 166–8; the state and divided governance 163–6; state formation 162–3; success and beyond 159–60; twenty-first century 168–70

Jessop, B. 81
Jevons, W. S. 42
Jones, S. 101

Kant, I. 41
Kautsky, Karl 48
Keynes, J. M. 103, 152
Knight, F. 10
knowledge 65
Konings, M., chapters by 1–7, 121–33
Korek Telecom 167
Krätke, M. 79, 81
Kurdistan *see* Iraqi Kurdistan
Kurdistan Democratic Party (KDP) 160, 163, 164–8, 169
Kurdistan Regional Government (KRG): capitalism 166–8; the state and divided governance 163–6; state formation 162–3; success to crisis 159–60; twenty-first century 168–70

labour: commodification of 58; neoliberalism and 97–8
Lacher, H. 110
laissez-faire: FH on 17–18, 55, 102–3; Foucault on 63; Polanyi on 17–18, 55, 73–4, 92–3; planned 56–7
Laura Spellman Rockefeller Memorial Foundation 150, 153, 155
law: 'lawfulness without' 41; rule of 61, 62, 65, 67
Leibniz, Gottfried 41
Lemke, T. 62

liberalism: the determinate market and 78–81; fascism and 73, 84–5; Hayek and 12; market economy and 73–5
liberty 56, 60–1, 65
Lilla, M. 130
London School of Economics (LSE) 147–56
Lucretius 39
Lukács, G. 55–6, 63–6, 67, 80
Luxembourg, Rosa 48

Mandeville, B. 43–4
market economies: always-embedded 94–5; incompatible ideals 147–8; liberalism and 73–5; social content 74–5
market fundamentalism 11, 12
market society: space and 113–15; as utopia 136–7
markets: as constructed/spontaneous 17–19, 20; determinate 78–80; embeddedness in society 12–14; Hayek's functioning 139; freedom through 140–1; as monolithic 20–1; as natural/unnatural 14–17; neutrality of 125–6, 127, 129; rise and fall of nineteenth-century European system 27–31; self-organization 137; social protection against 141; voluntary interaction and 102
Marxism 60, 63, 73, 84–5, 109, 115
Mazzini, G. 82
McMichael, P. 118
Menger, C. 50, 149
Mesopotamia 160–2, 169
Methodenstreit 148–9, 155–6
methodology 82–4, 92, 148–52, 153, 155
Middle East politics and society 160–2
Mill, J. S. 151, 154
Mirowski, P. 1, 99, 134, 142
Mises 147
Mises, Ludwig von 9, 45, 73–4, 125, 138, 149
Mitchell, W. J. T. 130, 149–50
monetary policy 128
money 114, 125–6
Mont Pèlerin Society 10, 91, 99–100, 101
moral economy 27–30, 140–1
Müller-Armack, L. 13–14
Munck, R. 111

nationalism and tribalism 162–3
nature: role in markets 14–17, 19–20; space and economy 112–13, 115
Nazism 100
neoliberal thought collective 9, 14, 18–19, 99–105
neoliberalism: as end of 'commodity effect' 61–3; Hayek and 2–3, 9–10, 99–105; Polanyi and 2–3, 95–9; *laissez-faire* and 56–7; moral economy 140–1; paradoxes of 127–9; political economy 137–40; as a rationality 125–7; resilience or end of 121–4; situating conceptually 124–5; theoretical practice 134–5, 138, 141–2
neutrality 125–6, 127, 129
nineteenth-century market system: Polanyi on 26; rise of 27–30; states and international structures 30–1; unravelling of 31–2

non-market institutions 139–40, 141

oil industry 163–4, 167–8
Oppenheim, Leo 160–1, 169

Paine, T. 45
palaces and temples 160–2, 169–70
passive revolution 71, 77–8, 81–7
Patriotic Union of Kurdistan (PUK) 160, 164–9
Peck. J. 9, 111, 135
Perelman, M. 43
Pierson, P. 98
planning for competition 137–8
Plehwe, D. 125
Polanyi, Karl: birth of political economy 57; commodity fiction and double movement 59–60; on embeddedness 12–14; on essence of fascism 72–3; Hayek and 9, 11–21; Iraqi Kurdistan analysis 168–9; *laissez-faire* 56; lens on Middle East 160–2, 165–6; lens on neoliberalism 134, 135–6, 142–3; markets as constructed/spontaneous 17–19, 20; moral economy 140; on neoliberal political economy 137; politics 11–12; role of nature 14–17, 19–20; Schmitt's political theology and 122–3; on social forces 27; spatial theory 109–17; against 'spontaneous spontaneity' 48–51; two transformations 25–7
Polanyi Levitt, K. 70, 160
Polanyi's works: 'The Economy as Instituted Process' 94; 'The Economy as Instituted Process' 112; *The Great Transformation* 1–3, 9–10, 25–33, 49–51, 55, 56, 58, 71, 73–86, 91, 92–5, 110–12, 116–18, 136; 'Planning and Spontaneous Order' 46; 'Ports of Trade in Early Societies' 113
polarities between Polanyi and Hayek 11–19
policy 56, 101–2, 104–5
political economy: birth of 55, 57–9; neoliberal 137–40
politics: Iraq 162–3, 164–5, 166–7; of Polanyi and Hayek 11–12; in Middle East 160–2
Poor Laws 57–8
populism 123, 129–30
post-war period 91
power conflict 31–3
preemption 127–8
privatization: palaces and 161; pre-Thatcher 104; of public wealth 169
Product Sharing Contracts (PSCs) 168
production/consumption 28–9, 62–3
progressive approaches and exceptionalism 122–3
Proudhon, P.-J. 64–5
public interpretation of ideas 103–4

'Questioning the Utopian Springs of Market Economy' conference 1

Rasool, Faruk Mustafa 167
rationality 62, 63, 65–6, 125–7, 140
'red tide' 31–2
re-embedding 26, 33, 94, 95, 121–2
regime change 161–2, 166–7, 169
regulation of markets 28–9

reification 64
religion and spontaneity 39–41
'reverse English' argument 19
revolution 28–9, 71, 73, 77–8, 81–7
Risorgimento 82–4
Robbins, L. 148, 149, 150–2, 154
Robertson, D. 47
Rodrigues, J., chapter by 134–46
Rothbard, Murray 9
Rousseau, J.-J. 48–9
Rule of Law 61, 62, 65, 67

Saad-Filho, A. 98
sanctions 164, 167
scale and space 115–16
Schmitt, C. 122–3, 124, 127
Schumpeter, J. 42
'scientism' 15–16, 20
Scottish Enlightenment 43–4, 125–6
secularization 125
security 126, 127
self-determination 40–1
self-interest 44–5
self-organization 41–2, 47
self-regulating markets 26, 50, 59, 74, 93
Sepil, Mehmet 167–8
Serge, V. 85–6
Shearmur, J. 147
Sheehan, J. 41–2, 43
similarities between Polanyi and Hayek 19–21
Smith, Adam 44, 45, 46–7, 125, 126
Smith, N. 115
smuggling 165, 167, 169
social activity 115–17
social content 74–5
social forces 27
social ideals 147
social sciences methodology 148–52, 153, 155
socialism: Hayek on 100; Hogben on 153; Polanyi on 11–12; Mises' critiques 149, 150
Socialist Calculation Controversy 9
socially embedded economy 91, 92–5, 97–8
'socially protective counter-movement' 26, 93–4, 96
society: commodity form and 63–4; competition and 62; 'discovery' of 57–8; embeddedness in 12–14; Polanyi and Hayek on 12–14; in Middle East 160–2; progression of 45, 46–7; protectionist countermoves 26
Somers, M. R. 94, 136, 142
spatial theory 109–17
Speenhamland 'law' 57–8
Spencer, H. 45–6

spontaneity 38–40, 48–52
spontaneous order 18, 40, 43–5, 46–8, 117, 142
Stansfield, G. 163
states: formation and governance in Kurdistan 162–6; free markets and 93; freedom from coercion and 102–3; Gramsci on 80–4; international structures and 30–1; *laissez-faire* and 74; in Middle East 161–2; regulation of markets 27–30; role in market society 113–14; role in political economy 138–41; theories of formation 81–3
Stigler, G. 127
strikes 31–2
subjectivity 63–4, 67
'substantivism' 112–113
Sulaymaniyah, Iraq 167–8
surpluses 161
'survivals' of feudalism 75–6, 86

Talabani, Jalal 163, 165
Thatcher, Margaret 104
theoretical economics 148–50
think tanks 101
top-down analysis 25–6, 32–3
totalitarianism 11
Townsend, J. 15
trade: palaces and temples as settings for 161, 169–70
trade unions 32
tribalism and nationalism 162–3
Trump, Donald 129–31

urban environments 113–14
utopias 2–3, 50, 100–2, 136–7, 141–2, 147

van Apeldoorn, B. 96
veridiction 58–9
Vienna 9, 17, 70–1, 125
Volcker, P. 128
voluntary interaction 102
von Mises, Ludwig 5, 9, 45, 70, 73–4, 125, 138, 148, 149

Wahrman, D. 41–2, 43
war effort 32
Weber, M. 65
welfare capitalism 103
welfare systems 28
working classes 32

Younger Historical School of economics 148–50, 152, 155

Zhuang Zhou 39